The Poetry of Jayanta Mahapatra

The Poetry of Jayanta Mahapatra

A Critical Study

Rabindra K Swain

PRESTIGE

Published by
PRESTIGE BOOKS
3/28, East Patel Nagar
New Delhi 110 008

2000

ISBN: 81-7551-085-4

Composed by Vivek Mathur, Delhi 110 006 Ph. 3981867
Printed by Chaman Offset Press, New Delhi 110 002

CONTENTS

Preface

This book attempts at a study of the poetry of Jayanta Mahapatra in the perspective of his commitment to a personal vision embedded in the materials, practices and values of Oriya culture. While the idiom of Mahapatra's poetry is governed by an acute awareness of the cultural and socio-political ethos of his native place, his vision transcends all national boundaries to achieve a universal significance. This book aims at exploring the metaphors and symbols of culture in the poetry of Jayanta Mahapatra to substantiate the contention that the images of locale eventually build his visionary world characterized by pain and suffering, memory and loss, hope and the possibilities of redemption. It will also examine the poems of Jayanta Mahapatra in terms of the embodiment of Oriya consciousness and suggest that the authenticity of the poetry of Jayanta Mahapatra lies in his keen perception of the physical reality and his deftness in nativizing the English language to embody the soul of an Indian milieu. This work in effect examines the various levels of relationship between self and reality in the poetry of Jayanta Mahapatra and suggests that his poetic vision encompasses the possibility of integration of the self and reality.

This study is divided into eight chapters. The chapters have been planned in terms of the chronology of Mahapatra's publications from 1971 to 1997.

The first chapter entitled "The Man, the Place and the Poet" is an attempt to place Jayanta Mahapatra in the context of his personal history and cultural ethos. It traces the socio-cultural forces that have gone into the shaping of Mahapatra's poetic language and vision. It also attempts at a survey of critical writings on the poetry of Jayanta Mahapatra.

The second chapter, "The Form is the Thing," examines the

early poetry of Jayanta Mahapatra by a close reading of his first two collections, *Close the Sky, Ten by Ten* and *Svayamvara and Other Poems*. It is contended that though his early poetry reflects his keen concern for intimate human relationships, it also betrays Mahapatra's desperate search for an idiom of his own. The first two collections of Mahapatra's poetry may be taken as experimentations in language and form and as anticipating the essential lyricism of his later poetry. The images employed in these two collections mainly relate to house-building, love-making and the creative process.

The third chapter, "A Man Becomes the Place," proposes that there has been a significant shift in language, form and sensibility in his third, fourth and fifth collections. At this stage his poetry seems firmly rooted in the myths, legends and cultural practices of his native land. At the same time, there is a pervasive sense of introspection, a disposition to turn inward and view the people and milieu around him through a subjective consciousness. At this stage of Mahapatra's poetry the dominant image is rain.

The fourth chapter, "Novas of the Self," seeks to analyse poems in the collection, *The False Start* and suggests that this collection is an interregnum between *A Rain of Rites, A Father's Hours* and *Waiting* on the one hand and *Relationship* on the other. In *The False Start* the locale is transformed into metaphoric and symbolic dimensions that reveal an inward quest. In this book the central images are the cloud and the moon.

The fifth chapter, "The Tapestry of Stones," is a study of Jayanta Mahapatra's first long poem, the *Relationship*. This chapter proposes that the relationship of the self with reality as well as with the history and culture of his native land forms the matrix of *Relationship*. It explores the images of stone perceived through the ruins of Konarka. *Relationship* centres round the images that reflect the quintessence of Oriya history and culture.

The sixth chapter, "The Centre of the Web," takes into account *Life Signs* and *Burden of Waves and Fruit*. With these two volumes Mahapatra's poetry turns more personal and direct. There are frequent references to the familiar scenes of his place like hippies, lepers, destitute and desolate fields. While *Life Signs* limns more or less the physical landscape of the poet's locale, *Burden of Waves and Fruit* constantly refers to the inner landscape of body and mind. The significance of the poems in these two books lies in the poet's deep concern for the imminent threat to his physical being. This concern is articulated through images that suggest the elemental forces of life and nature.

The seventh chapter, "The Sleep-Habit of the Golden Deer," deals elaborately with Mahapatra's second long poem, *Temple*. This chapter tries to explore the metaphoric relationship between the protagonist of the poem, Chelammal, and the structure and spirit of the temple. It also makes a brief study of *Dispossessed Nests* in which Mahapatra steps out of the Orissan locale and reflects a pan-Indian concern. It is also suggested that with the shift of locale there has been a significant change in the tone of Mahapatra's poetry. It is through the image of sleep that Mahapatra perceives human suffering as a mode of redemption.

In the concluding chapter, "The Sentient Being," an assessment of Mahapatra's latest two books of poems, *A Whiteness of Bone* and *Shadow Space,* has been attempted in the context of his contemporaries. In this chapter, the poet's concern is once again with the challenges a poet faces in his day-to-day world. Even, he finds his exercise in poetry to be futile. He meets these challenges with an equanimity rarely to be found among his contemporaries. And finally at the end of this chapter a brief discussion is made about his foray into Oriya poetry.

I cannot close these prefatory remarks without expressing my gratitude to those who helped me in the preparation of this book. I wish to deeply thank the poet Jayanta Mahapatra for helping me at every step in this venture and his wife Runu Mahapatra for informally giving some insight into the working of the poet's mind. I am immensely grateful to Prof. J.N. Patnaik for his perceptive comments on this work. My special thanks to John Oliver Perry who also showed interest in this work, even offered suggestions at its initial stage. Finally I am grateful to the editors of the following books, journals and newspapers in which my writings on Jayanta

Mahapatra's poetry appeared: *The Poetry of Jayanta Mahapatra*, ed. Madhusudan Prasad, *Verse, World Literature Today, Indian Literature, Kavya Bharati, Indian Horizons, Literary Endeavour, The Book Review, New Quest, Debonair, The Independent, The Indian Post, The Patriot, Indian Express* and *The Times of India.*

RABINDRA K SWAIN

The Man, the Place and the Poet

> I am sorry I am unable to use your poems. There is an unmistakable poetic quality in almost all the poems, but something eludes me. I should like to understand what I want my readers to understand.
>
> (*Bombay Literary Review* 6)

This was one of the numerous rejections that came Jayanta Mahapatra's way at the beginning of his poetic career. It was around the year 1970. Jayanta Mahapatra had not yet perfected his medium but he had already made his foray into Indian English poetry by writing such well-crafted poems as "I Hear My Fingers Sadly Touching an Ivory Key:"

> Swans sink wordlessly to the carpet
> miles of polished floors
> reach out
> for the glass of voices
>
> There are gulls crying everywhere
> and glazed green grass
> in the park with the swans
> folding their cold throats

This poem, among many others which were rejected by editors in India, was later published in the *Chicago Review* (Autumn 1971).

The letter of rejection and the poem quoted above demonstrate the change Jayanta Mahapatra brought into Indian English poetry. The letter obviously suggested that there certainly was something radically different in his poetry, that there was a decisive shift from the trend set by such poets as P. Lal, Nissim Ezekiel, A.K. Ramanujan and R. Parthasarathy. This change, as Mahapatra himself reflects, was constituted of "a strong stand on language, " "new modes of expression, " "the need to invent (his) own legends" and above all "the ideas of the self" which served as the main reference point in his poetry. Reflecting on his beginnings as a poet, Mahapatra says:

> It was apparent to me that I was not writing the kind of poems in which meaning was stated clearly and explicitly, and that this poetry did not have a sharp focus was what the critic had in mind when he commented on my work. In other words, this poetry had no flat statements. What I was perhaps trying to do was to put together images and symbols so that the reader would draw the implicit connection for himself. (*Bombay Literary Review* 7-8)

In other words, Mahapatra's modernity was characterised by a revolt against the poetry of statement, against the notion of paraphrasability.

Born in 1928 in Cuttack, Jayanta Mahapatra was trained as a physicist. Dilly-dallying with photography and then with short fiction, he began writing poetry. Born and brought up in Orissa, he might have written in his mother tongue Oriya, though, of course, he did not for several good reasons. Explaining these reasons, he says:

> I am in love with English. And then, my schooling was in English—and I learnt my language from British schoolmasters—mainly from English novels: so blame H. Rider Haggard and Edgar Rice Burroughs and Ballantyne from whom I caught the first delight of words gravid with meaning. Further I feel I can express myself better in English than in Oriya. (Raghavan 59)

Mahapatra was twice removed from his immediate surroundings—first, he was born into a Christian family in a predominantly Hindu society and second, he wrote in an acquired medium, English, which was conventionally considered not adequate to encompass the cultural spirit of his native land. Yet the themes which dominate his poetry are related to such stark realities of India as hunger, myths, rituals, sexuality, spirituality, the self and eternity. His poetry, whether describing the locale, its environs and landscape or the relationship of his self to his land, attempts to reflect an awareness of this milieu. This study aims at analysing and evaluating the form and vision of his poetry in the perspective of the locale, in terms of the images drawn from the geographical, social and cultural sources of his native land of Orissa. The place with all its ethos and myths, its lives and beliefs, superstitions and transitions has been the governing factor of Mahapatra's perceptions and vision.

In many of his autobiographical statements articulated in his short prose pieces and interviews, Mahapatra has repeatedly and candidly said that when he started writing poetry, his knowledge of poetry did not go beyond a few poems of Wordsworth, Keats and Shelley prescribed in the school syllabus. At heart he is a romantic; only his intellect sharpened by the profession of teaching physics won't let him indulge in it. In his poetry one feels the presence of "the still, sad music of humanity" of Wordsworth, the sweeping lyrical grace of Shelley and the sensuousness of Keats. He has always remained close to the Romantic notion of the poet's inescapable presence in the poem. Though his poetry does not lack in the distanced and detached self of an Ezekiel, it nevertheless embodies in such a self a deep subjectivity that sets it apart from contemporary Indian poetry in English. As John Oliver Perry says, "Mahapatra has developed a profoundly sincere inner voice surprisingly unironic, unalienated, unmediated, of interest to very diverse but contemporaneous Indian and foreign audiences. Making such broadly successful poems of his inner life has, furthermore, changed his circumstances and modified his vision in ways that poetry, since romantic times, has been imagined to do, but rarely does in fact." (Perry 57) Commenting on this inner life in his poems, the poet himself reveals:

> I am aware, fully aware that my poems deal with the life

> within myself, where the mind tries to find a sort of coherence from the mass of things in the world outside it. (Samantaray 18)

In writing poems that seek to embody the world of the inside, operating in the context of his time and place, the poet had to forge private symbols and images, or had to deviate from the regular syntax, so that they would all taken together, carry the force of his poetry on the subjective plane. This effort to "mould English to private needs, " as he put it later to Konnakuzhy Ittira in an interview (Ittira 3) has prompted the critics to note that his poetry is "written not in quite standard English, but it is fascinating and moving." (Grosholz 330)

This element of subjectivity helped him to relate himself to his milieu and landscape in a delicate way never done before in Indian English poetry. The exploration of the inner self is intricately woven with his childhood experiences as much as with the Oriya fairy tales, myths and legends and the great Indian epics. Along with these sources close to his locale, he updated himself with a voracious reading of modern classics of the world as well as contemporary writing in scores of established periodicals like *The Sewanee Review, The Hudson Review, The Kenyon Review, The Times Literary Supplement, Critical Quarterly, Poetry* where he himself has published profusely. If this acquaintance with modern Anglo-American and European literature shaped the form and partially the content of his poetry, it is the Oriya sensibility as well as the lyrical quality of traditional Oriya poetry which provides charm and grace to his poetry. The tight-knit family life, the rites and rituals associated with the cyclic agricultural seasons, the rich tradition of arts and crafts and an easy, quiet pace of life are some of the major Orissan elements that recur in terms of imagery, metaphor and symbol. Trying to express the appeal of Mahapatra's poetry to western readers, Norman Simms says that despite typical poetic allusions to the very specific local customs of Orissa, in his poetry "one constantly catches the images and tonalities of a contemporary western sense of the myth of the eternal return" (Simms 35). Simms brings in the instance of Mircea Eliade to substantiate his argument:

> Like Eliade, Mahapatra engages the myths, legends and the sacred architecture of his immediate environment and confronts it with the analytic and personalised introspection of his missionary and scientific education. Each poem tends to become in this way a ritual of passage, inwards through the spirals of questioning, self-doubts and intellectual scepticism, to a tenuous sense of self, of individuality; and yet, like all rituals, it must be repeated again and again, almost compulsively, though unlike public ceremonials, there is no recurrent liturgy—for Mahapatra there are always new starts, fresh vantage points, rethought-of accesses to the problematic of his own status as in a mental world.

Mahapatra's concern with the local emerged gradually as he realised the need of an idiom that would transcend passions and sensuousness into an awareness of the self in search of an identity. He began writing poems as any other poet would. Frustrated with his love for a woman when his only child, a son, was ten years old, he wrote a number of love poems. In these poems unobtainable women featured. He himself admits:

> my poems were born of love, of love's selfishness and of a huge self-pity, like the poems of many whom I admire. And it was only of myself I thought as words took possession of my senses, measured me and linked me with the fabled kingdom of love. (*Youth Times10*)

His love poems were brought out in two small volumes, *Close the Sky, Ten by Ten and Svayamvara and Other Poems*, both published in 1971. The poems in these two early volumes dealing with the intimacy and passion of love were contrived and abstract in nature, though in them the seeds of his future poetry were already sown. Here were for his favourite images of sun and nun, beggar, helpless women and children.

The responses to these two volumes were mixed. Some of the reviewers were optimistic about the promise discernible in the use of images and in the powerful play of imagination. These reviews spoke of "an unquestionable vein of poetry" (N.E.3), "a deft, surre-alistic arrangement of words, " "care and elegance, " "lyrically enchanting" (*The Sunday Statesman*), "Music from a World Of-ten Stricken by Tragedy" (*The Fayetteville Observer*), "robust tenderness and gentleness" and "an intensely realised experience" (Patnaik 62). Many other reviews made a scathing attack on the inherent drawbacks in the form and content of Mahapatra's poetry. Writing love poems, he ran the risk of "fall(ing) into the rut of mean-ingless verbiage" (*The Sunday Statesman*). In order to present this worn-out theme strikingly, he had to experiment with uncon-ventional diction and syntax, and it is precisely on this score that he was mostly faulted: "The syntax of the lines is often dependent on poetic license and so is the phrasing while the punctuation is incon-sistent and the imagery hit-or-miss." "The adjectives are quite sim-ply unnecessary" and "words are added like 'weights' to balance the forms" (*The Times of India*). However, commenting on his first two books and conceding to Jussawalla's observation that he was a "Poem-maker, " Mahapatra says:

> My first two books of verse were mainly experimental; it was the language again I wanted to exploit, because I felt I would mould it like clay, and I suppose Adil Jussawalla was right in his own way when he said in a review that I was a "poem-maker". (Raghavan 60)

He was, at this stage, desperately trying to come to grips with the medium, with the tools with which he was to build his vision in future work. Thus the two early volumes of Mahapatra's poetry lacked depth and range though they were apparently elegant and lyrical.

In his next three volumes, *A Father's Hours* (1976), *A Rain of Rites (*1976) and *Waiting* (1979), Jayanta Mahapatra grows to be a poet of substance. The syntax and the lines become relaxed. There is now something natural about the form and structure. The concrete physical details are coupled with an inexplicable sense of wonder and mystery "against or within" which he almost works, as Dick Allen aptly observes (35). These books, especially *A Rain of Rites* received high critical acclaim in US periodicals. Vernon Young said: "The manner of apprehension in his wonderful, sensate poems inevitably brings to the tongue the word, 'sophistication'. His psychology is at once more historical, more anxious, more involuted than that of any Chinese poet, old or modern, known to me." (627). Frank Allen praised Mahapatra for encapsulating "the paradox of the Indias; both impeccable, both determined to dominate; the blank, shameless agrarian world with its polytheistic fatalism" (340). These two worlds of contrast between "asceticism and sensuality, control and release, human and mythical ways of looking at reality" are manifested in the images of "Two gods copulating on the warm tar" ("Sunburst"). In India, critics like K. Ayyappa Paniker put Jayanta Mahapatra at the fore of his contemporaries: "Mahapatra's treatment of sex and love is quite a contrast to the calculated cynicism of Ezekiel, the flaunting sick melody of Kamala Das or the sly indulgence of Shiv Kumar. In 'The Whorehouse in a Calcutta Street' we find a man who wanted to know more about women turn into a statue and the body disobeys (Does it ever disobey in Ezekiel, Kamala Das or Shiv Kumar?)" (68)

In contrast to the empty spaces in the heart of the early poems in *Close the Sky, Ten by Ten and Svayamvara and Other Poems*, the poems of the early seventies are concrete with local details. The characters that crowd his poetry are typical of the Indian milieu. They are priests, lepers, crows and unscrupulous businessmen. The titles of some of the poems point to his concern with the locale: "Main Temple Street, Puri, " "Indian Summer Poem, " "Bhubaneswar, " "Orissa, " "Learning to Flow Free in the Chariot Festival at Puri." In one such significant poem ("Somewhere, My Man"), Mahapatra declares his total identification with his place:

> A man does not mean anything.
> But the place.
> Sitting on the riverbank throwing pebbles

into the muddy current,
a man becomes the place. (*A Rain of Rites 42*)

The False Start, which came out in 1980, marked a retreat into the self with all the feelings of hurt and silence at the falseness of the world. In the walled interiority of his poetic form, he tries to find and forge a private world where he can attain metaphysical transcendence. Reviewing *The False Start,* C.B. Cox says that Mahapatra's poetry "reflects a form of quietism, a sense of inevitability which is peculiarly Indian."

James Finn Cotter feels that with the poems in this book the reader is "mesmerized, " that the poems offer no "easy solution" and further that they move "from abstract to sensible imagery" (478). The images like rain, cloud, moon, ash, voice and door are drawn from the very source of living in an intimate world and yet they are so smoothly internalized that the images transcend their physicality and point to spiritual and metaphysical perceptions. For instance, the door placed on the threshold of two eternally opposite worlds, gives an access to the poet to enter into either or both the worlds. In an essay entitled "The Door, " Mahapatra traced the origin of the image of "door" to his childhood days and associated it with an inner freedom. The door

> served both as a refuge from the terrors of the outside world which mutely went on to lock me in, offering me no escape. It became both a haven and a prison, and my mind positioned itself both inside and out. . . . There is always something very final, very secretive about doors. ("The Doors" 191)

This "very final, very secretive" element of the door deepens further the sense of mystery that is pervasive in his poetry:

Huge door
drifting
with feet of light,

My eyes
quietly open
before the night's (*The False Start* 69)

Relationship, published in the same year as *The False Start*, gave him the final stamp of recognition. *Relationship* is set in Orissa. "To Orissa, " Mahapatra said in his Sahitya Akademi Award address, "I acknowledge my debt and relationship." *Relationship* fuses the poet's immediate world and his personal memory through familial and corporeal images of torture, sullenness and solitude. He was hailed abroad as having unwrapped "the realm of mystery" (Corseri 20) and in India as having the first substantial long poem "interrogating the myths" (Rain 326) and "explor(ing) into the past, indicating that one of the most rewarding strategies for the Indian English poet is "only connect" (Naik 16).

If in *Relationship* Jayanta Mahapatra reaches the peak of his imaginative height, with *Life Signs* (1983) he comes down to the day-to-day physical world. The thematic concerns of *A Rain of Rites* is carried further in *Life Signs*. With *Life Signs* the poet becomes more simple and the poems become paraphrasable. The characters, events and objects that hold his attention are the contemporaneous ones, like the Western hippies wandering on "the dusty, malarial lanes of Cuttack" ("The Lost Children of America"), the women workers tarring the road in a hot summer afternoon ("Again, One Day, Walking by the River"), "Total Solar Eclipse, " etc. In a lecture at Mysore, Mahapatra says:

> Governed as one is , as I am , by the unconscious—which in more ways than one acts like a power-generator, like a God—I would be satisfied if I can reveal a consciousness in my writing in agreement with today's realities. (13)

He describes hunger in such poems as "A Country" and "Again, One Day, Walking by the River". One gets the picture of hunger and pangs of destitute women camping on the riverbanks in "Again, One day, Walking by the River."

> It is two in the afternoon, and the heat of yesterday
> still clings to the old walls like a harsh salt on the skin (39)

John Barnie comparing Mahapatra with Wordsworth suggests that "the differences between the two poets are profound, yet in one sense at least the comparison is just, for few poets in our century have evoked 'The still sad music of humanity' so movingly as Mahapatra." (*Kunapipi* 107)

Dispossessed Nests:1984 Poems was a slender volume, published in 1986. Though the book with its slackened structure, did not merit much attention, it was important in the sense that it formed a transitional stage in the chronological development of the poet. It marked the shift in location; from Orissa to the Punjab and Bhopal. In his bid to capture the pulse of his time he tried political verses dealing with the senseless bloodshed in the Punjab and the disaster of gas-leak in Bhopal. Although the work is ambitious, it did not have the intellectual rigour and formal discipline that would lend a volume its unity. But certainly it opened paths further into the new areas. With this book, he becomes transprovincial. *Temple* (1989), the second long poem, was set in the South of India.

Even though *Dispossessed Nests* came out in 1986 and *Burden of Waves and Fruit* in 1988, the poems for the latter were collected and scheduled for publication prior to the former. So it would be better to position *Dispossessed Nests* just before *Temple* in order to show the chronological growth of the poet and to place his poetry in proper perspective.

Burden of Waves and Fruit is a continuation of the motifs of *Life Signs*. It is distinct from his early works at least in one sense: most of the poems here deal with the theme of death. Either the signs of death are written large on the physical world—the massacre at Nellie, the ruined Shivaji Fort at Pannhala or the junk-yard of an automobile garage—or within the self and the body of the poet. This book is rather a creative attempt at relating physical decrepitude with moral disintegration and the breakdown of the spirit. However, henceforth, conspicuous presence of death makes itself felt in the various manifestations of the poet's imagination. The isolate, subtle touch of the inevitable biological end turns violent in *Dispos-*

sessed Nests.

Temple, published in 1989, sublimates death and elevates the spirit of life even in its most miserable state. To celebrate life and death on equal footing, Mahapatra takes woman as the medium of endless human sufferings and possible redemption. Mahapatra uses the concept of the female principle, the source of all energy, the Shakti, in terms of Putana, a mythical demonic woman, as the central metaphor. Chelammal is the protagonist of the poem *Temple*. She is projected from the beginning of the poem as a sensitive and suffering woman who ultimately commits suicide out of "poverty and loneliness." Mahapatra eventually infuses into her spirit the strong will of Putana who was prepared to die in the hands of Lord Krishna with the hope of deliverance from the cycle of birth and death. *Temple*, however, is not written in the traditional narrative mode. The absence of a linear narrative makes it complex and subject to multiple interpretations.

A Whiteness of Bone and *Shadow Space* are the latest books of English poems of Jayanta Mahapatra. The focus of these two books is again on the problems, both personal and social. His concern with his ageing brings him closer to his creative self. He continues to question the validity of his act of writing poetry for, as he finds, it has never done anything to change the society. In such moments of helplessness, he finds solace in exploring the hidden corners of one's mind, hinting at the unspeakable. In the poem, "A Day on Marburg on-the-Lahn," an elegy on the death of A.K. Ramanujan, he feels he has nothing to say but to celebrate that moment of happiness they both shared.

In the nineties, Mahapatra has so far published three volumes of Oriya poems, *Bali* (The Sacrifice), *Kahibi Gotia Katha* (I Will Tell You a Story) and *Baya Raja* (The Mad Emperor). In these Oriya poems, his favourite subjects are those small things happening around him, the life of the rickshaw-puller, the cycle mechanic, etc. But whatever thing he chooses for his Oriya poems, he approaches it in a more direct way than he usually did in his English poems.

Although Jayanta Mahapatra started writing poetry at the age of thirty eight, he quickly made up with his prolific writing. Thrice he brought out two books in one year. Nonetheless, he has moved with each successive book from strength to strength. Even though Nissim Ezekiel has been writing poetry since the early fifties and has appropriately been regarded as the doyen of post-Independence Indian English poetry, Mahapatra became the first Indian poet in English to be honoured with the Central Sahitya Akademi award in 1981. In a recent anthology, Vilas Sarang asserts that Mahapatra's poetry "seems to point towards the direction that Indian English poetry will take most fruitfully" (31). This critical acclaim that Sarang accords to the poetry of Jayanta Mahapatra is not surprising considering the fact that, despite the apparently unparaphrasable nature of his poetry, Jayanta Mahapatra continues to be read and discussed widely both in India and abroad and his influence on the younger poets writing today is distinctly perceptible.

The Form is the Thing: *Close the Sky, Ten by Ten* and *Svayamvara and Other Poems*

While other poets in different parts of India were trying to evolve an Indian poetry in English in their individual ways, in one quiet corner of Orissa, with no Indian English co-poet around him to discuss and develop a conscious body of poetry, Jayanta Mahapatra made his shy but decisive start with his very first book, *Close the* Sky, *Ten by Ten*. In the same year, in 1971, his second book *Svayamvara and Other Poems* also came out.

These two volumes, it must be conceded, consist of poems that not only appear today as somewhat naive in terms of perception and form but also reflect a certain degree of immaturity in the handling of themes and language that Mahapatra overcame with surprising alacrity in his third volume *A Rain of Rites* published only five years after these two first volumes came out. The poems in *Close the Sky, Ten by Ten* and *Svayamvara and Other Poems* hardly show Mahapatra's awareness of his place, its milieu and the people around him and in the perspective of his total work, they might seem irrelevant today. What apparently was important to Mahapatra in those early years of his infatuation with poetry was a zest for disentangling himself from the conventional modes of expression and syntax and a passion for startling images and sweeping lyricism. These poems showed the promises of his later poetry both in terms of shaping his attitude towards life and reality as well as evolving a style characterised by the novelty of perception and elegance of poetic execution.

The title of the first book *Close the Sky*, *Ten by Ten* is suggestive of the kind of poetry Jayanta Mahapatra was going to write, and has written. Not only is he isolating a world of his own from the public world but he is also sealing his world with the sky as the "essential" roof. The mention of the sky is significant in its being a fifth element, in addition to the western concept of the four elements that constitute the cosmos: earth, air, fire and water. The image of sky recurs in his poetry and reinforces his poetics. The house he intends to build is his vision which, he says, shall be "apocalyptic". The two early collections of Mahapatra, *Close the Sky, Ten by Ten* and *Svayamvara and Other Poems*, basically repeat his concern with form and language. In both these two books, the poet is obsessed with the imagery of building materials for the house of his choice: his visionary world. Mostly, the imagery of house, its different components and aspects, are seen to be dominating his early poetry. In this essential search of the poet for a house, one finds his vision unsteady and tone faltering. The meaning is also sacrificed for the sheer beauty and sound of words. One such poem is "Apartment":

> Sunlight comes down,
> marks time.
> The walls come apart,
> without cause.
> To be on terms,
> anonymous;
> building an ark
> of conscientiousness,
> all seasons all seas
> to the captive
> beginning.
>
> When was it
> that compassion's
> white face
> began cruelly grinding?

(*Svayamvara and Other Poems* 12)

One of the poems in *Close the Sky, Ten by Ten*, "The Farewell", begins with the declaration: "The form is the thing/always." There is nothing tentative about the statement: it is "always." Within the form lies "the suggestion/of the foundations/of solitude" pointing "long hands/into future despair." This despair which the poet brings in abruptly into the context of the poem is the very condition of the poet. It is more clearly articulated in the image of darkness:

this darkness
has to be lived,
before it's long enough
to be unlived. (*Close the Sky*, unpaginated)

In most of the poems the imagery clearly hints at his preoccupation with "form." Some of these poems are "Day Thought," "The Builders," "Love," "The Movement," "Curriculum," "Apartment," "Sometimes," etc. But the "form" he is after goes on eluding him like Lord Rama's illusion of the golden deer, as described in "The Circle." His attempt to attain his desired form is most conspicuous in "Sanctuary" from which the title of the book *Close the Sky, Ten by Ten* is derived:

now i close the sky
with a square ten by ten

the roof essential
hides the apocalyptic ideal

parting from
fabled parables

i stretch my body
into a trembling flatness

wishing to fall
through the space

of truly right mistakes

the space sings
where i live
at home
to hyperbolas of sky-tasted love

for the blessing of absence
is its essence

Here the poet draws the contours of the ideal world he would build for himself. He 'closes' his world with multiple layers of imagery, every irregular couplet forming a layer. Though his world shall be a closed one, his "home" shall have the "sky-tasted love." The paradox of enclosing the vast, infinite space within the closed space is sustained to the end of the poem. At the end, almost concluding what he has been trying to establish, that of a vision of a world of his own which will encompass both the imagined and the real, he brings in the paradoxical nature of our existence: "for the blessing of absence/is its essence." The real thrust of the poem lies in the third couplet: "parting from/fables." As the poem suggests, Jayanta Mahapatra's deviation from the styles of poetry as were practised in India till he started writing would be two-fold: his poetry would not be a plain narrative with linear development of sequences and the form of his poetry would be open like the "sky". Interestingly, Mahapatra follows this creed almost faithfully in all his later poetry.

The short poem "Faith" suffers from a blurred vision. Even with its allusion to Virgil as a clue to its theme, the meaning of the poem does not emerge clearly:

Standing still, i am suspect
against my earth. The star
to symbol, as this open night.

I humour them if i must stand:
no truth could be more alive
than this: that there

are fears for things,
naked when i only will. (*Close the Sky*)

The other poem bearing the same title "Faith" is similarly obscure:

We have not known.
How light leaves by the door.
The masses of memory
that grow, nailing them
to doors when we want
them to, are lunging eyes
in a glass wall.
We plod on.
And those eyes, closed,
imprison our reasons. (*Svayamvara* 29)

Though this poem deals with an apparently visual world, it ends with a heavy emphasis on an invisible world. But the movement from the one world to the other does not take place coherently. It lacks that subtle, tenuous thread which might provide a formal unity to the poem. Jayanta Mahapatra overcomes this weakness in his later poem of the same title "The Faith" in *Waiting*.

In these indistinguishable mornings
like pale-yellow hospital linen,
a legless cripple
clutters up the wide temple street,
the quiet early light crouched in his palms.

What sentence of old
moves him towards the furious wrinkled walls?
The Puri priest standing in indulgent sunshine
plays a small ridicule across the melting festival,
safe in place above a pile of hard-eyed ancestors.

Climbing down the stairs into the dark shrine
the sudden light overtakes me,

> my blood drowsy in the mosquito-hum of chanting,
> and a frail white flower of worship
> pays for my sins and watches. (*Waiting* 14)

The two early poems are important in the sense that they are apprentice works preparing us for Mahapatra's mature work in the later period. The poem quoted above exhibits clarity of thought and expression. This poem is a negotiation between the poet's faith and the priests' betrayal of it, whereas the early two poems fail to achieve a comprehensible meaning.

Thus, the open anti-conventional form Mahapatra cherished so fondly often obscures his vision. His emphasis in the first two collections is on experimentation with syntax and imagery, on evolving a style of his own to articulate a subjective perception of the world around him. His grappling with the medium to achieve a distinct form perhaps accounts for the startling and often puzzling brevity of the poems. The length of the poems in the first two books, with the exception of only a few like "Traditions," "Intimacy," "Henry the Robot," "A Theme of Love" and "If I Am Wrong" is from four to forty lines. The lines are minimal—often a word or two, enclosed by blank spaces. The stanzas are irregular, even a line for a stanza, a word for a line, often without verbs, or an article. Often there are no punctuation marks in a whole poem. One such poem "Woman" illustrates all the characteristics of Jayanta Mahapatra's early poetry:

> Even
> when she is
>
> Even
> when she is not (*Close the Sky*)

The poem, apparently inconclusive, with no full stops or any other punctuation marks, swaddled in blank spaces at the end of each of the two sentences, remains indeterminate in its meaning. There is no image in this poem. Or, perhaps, the whole poem is an image: an image of the longing for love. The word "even" used twice, provides an esoteric quality to the poem and suggests that the poet's concern for the woman transcends her presence or absence. The absence of the full stop in this poem (as elsewhere in many of the poems in these two books, especially those dealing with the theme of love or woman) suggests that the poem will go on until the mystery of love as well as the male's effort to understand his mysterious concern for the feminine principle is resolved. The absence of the full stop at the end of "Love" is equally baffling. With its theme of love and language, "Love" embodies, as Pushpinder Sayal points out, Mahapatra's "spirit of experimentation, of unabashed freedom in the handling of words" (Prasad 199). He tries to do "something new/to words" and this is evident in the beginning of "Love," the poem in which the title itself is a part of the poem:

like poetry

leave thought alone
to find the meaning

that each one
is doing

something new
to words

in a medium
cut to size (*Close the Sky*)

Besides cutting the words to size, moulding them suitably so that they can dovetail into the framework of his early poetry thematically, he tries to draw an analogy between love and poetry. His strategy to play upon a perceived analogy between the act of making a poem and making love is both a spontaneous and a conscious act. He tries to strike a balance between the heart and the mind in the body of his poetry; he wants his love as well as his poem to be "in a medium/cut to size." Conscious as he is that he "is doing/something new/to words", he is also aware that the creative experience is eventually inexpressible and opaque:

> You stare at
> it long
>
> it will not turn
> to
> a sentence
>
> or sun (*Close the Sky*)

While these concluding lines clinch the equation between love and poetry, they also point to the desperate quest for an individual form and diction. The punch line in this poem is the word "sun". The imagery of sun as an eternal presence and the absence of full stop at the end of the poem hint that every creative effort is an interminable exercise to reach out to a comprehensible articulation of personal experiences.

Like "Love", many poems in *Close the Sky*, *Ten by Ten* and *Svayamvara and Other Poems* are on the art of poem-making and they correspond to the analogous act of love-making. Mention may be made of "The Farewell," Sometimes," "Apartment," "Morning" and "An Ordinary Day." In "An Ordinary Day" passion and objects fuse together and create an intense atmosphere congenial to creative activity. The poem begins with the picture of a room invested with "blackness" and "sleep." The room contains two chairs, a bed and a tumbler. The two bodies seeking fulfillment are so passionate that their perception of the physical objects turns surrealistic: "the walls join themselves." Here the joining of the walls suggests the fusion of the external and the internal world in the process of the poet's working out a poem. "Apartment" begins with the sunlight in the morning ripping the "walls" "apart:"

The poem beginning with a description of a morning in an apartment ends with a note of discomfort at the pressing need to go back to that "captive beginning" to restore the peace of mind, so that he could be on "terms" and "anonymous" with the spirit of creativity in "writing" as well as "building" "an ark."

The three analogous acts of creativity—writing, love-making and building a house meet very often and they help imparting a sense of unity to the book. Not only does the poet arrange them in a like-manner to develop a unified vision of a cosy, creative world but also he sees to it that they have a proper conducive atmosphere for growth. "Sunflower" begins with the depiction of a "mood":

> But, the black mood, angry
> and swelled, comes
> by the night. (*Close the Sky*)

when, he hopes, "my green words fill" the blank pages. He also catches this kind of mood, parturient for writing, in "Bells":

> Every poem cries the gloom; between,
> possessed, hanging about that tender need
> where a gentle touch makes the dark flood ring.
> (*Svayamvara* 16)

Stressing the "need" of a "mood" that is "black" or "gloom" as a pre-condition of every creative effort, the poet draws his images from the coterminous worlds of love-making, house-building and poem-making, though eventually he realises that there is a limit after which activities in any or all of these worlds cease to grow. In order to substantiate this point, the poet once again falls back on the images of these three worlds:

> Yet every time a moment is established
> other moments are waiting under cover
> to reason away the thin line of scar
> that joins our snake-arms; here there the walls
> squeezing in your concealed space of guilt
> will await the sad bout of abasement
> as from an erection hard to improvise. (*Close the Sky*)

These lines not only reveal his early concern for the craft of poetry but also embody the characteristic that Jayanta Mahapatra would have for himself in future: long lines, extended metaphors and free-flowing lyricism.

The act of creation, thus, is a dominant strain in his first two books. The other major theme in Mahapatra's early poetry is loneliness. Loneliness, which is incidentally the title of the first poem of the first book, is pervasive in his poetic universe. In this poem the poet attempts to define loneliness through a succession of images:

> Loneliness is when the ash
> upon the veneered table disintegrates
> from the breath of ruptured egos
> Loneliness is when an act, a word
> hangs undecided and unborn
> in the eyes of longing,
> Loneliness is of a winner
> turned loser, traitor and beggar
> in a centrifuge of possessions,
> Loneliness is of now, of the noises
> of the graves, of the silence of the waves (*Close the Sky*)

This poem is devised as one continuous sentence consisting of six three-line stanzas and one four-line stanza. He perceives loneliness in the very nature of existence. Loneliness emerges from every conceivable act as also from metaphysical experiences, "the noises of the graves/ of the silence of the waves."

There are a few poems in the first two collections centring round the beggars, whose loneliness comes from their estrangement from the society at large. The context of the poem "The Blind Beggar" is a crowded, lighted market place ; "light wanders around him the whole day/where he stands" and the whole poem is lit by the poet's empathy with the beggar, as loneliness is the condition "common to us both". Likewise "Blind Beggar in a Train" is seen against our "bone's blind beggary." In "A Kind of Love" he says, "I believe from blindness." This belief turns out to be the very metaphor of life and its futility; "days that will guide my surface/with braille." Mahapatra carries forward the idea of the vision of the inner eye into his later poetry, the beggars who do not emerge as strong characters in these two books, become an integral part of the landscape in the poems on Puri in *A Rain of Rites* and *Waiting*.

Besides beggars, a few other prominent characters in *Close the Sky, Ten by Ten* are depicted as inexorably lonely. Those characters are Mahatma Gandhi, the peace negotiators and the nuns. Gandhi is depicted as a forsaken leader.

> the multitude
> waiting
> to be born,
>
> bitter:
>
> under his
> tortuous steps
>
> we have burst open his blood
> to bleed
> We are on his side, perhaps
>
> We hate him
> we do not know it (*Close the Sky*)

This poem, "Gandhi," is marked by the absence of punctuation marks and syntactic discipline, which are characteristic of Mahapatra's early poetry. The form reflects a certain kind of ambiguity as we enter a 'bitter' and 'tortuous' world that has "burst open his blood." The ambivalence is clearly perceived as the poet proclaims.

"We are on his side, perhaps." Mahapatra's description of loneliness as "Winner/turned loser" seems quite appropriate for Gandhi bleeds for us as "we hate him."

In "The Peace Negotiators," Mahapatra speaks of the "forsaken" old men who talk of peace in the face of the menace of war:

> Somewhere, across the table
> they talk of it,

under the gaze of war:
crucified bodies
crying out
in the hollows of their palms.

For the time being
they understand.

The black windows look on.

Most of them
are rich old men with dogs:

they have been forsaken. (*Close the Sky*)

As in "Gandhi, " there is an ambivalence in the poet's attitude towards the peace negotiators. The poem begins with the peace negotiators "talking of it" (except for the title, the word 'peace' is not mentioned in the text of the poem, and thus the significance of the talk of peace is belittled by deliberately using its pronoun) while they themselves have lost it in their own lives. They have been "forsaken" and the only companion they have in the loneliness of their old age is the dog. The image of Christ sharpens the ambivalence inherent in the poem. Though the "crucified bodies" refer to the soldiers killed in the "war," its spirit is transported to the peace negotiators who hold out some possibility of saving mankind from destruction. In the characterisation of these old men there is a sense of irony. Those who are supposed to be the saviours are themselves "forsaken." The poet's perception of loneliness as that "of a winner/turned loser" seems applicable to the peace negotiators.

While depicting "the geometric mosaic" of loneliness in the nuns' heaven, the poet is mercilessly cold. This is apparent at the very opening of the poem, "The Nun":

a sun's iciness
rushes
down these hills (*Close the Sky*)

In investing the sun with iciness, the poet suggests the lack of warmth in the nuns' divine love. They lead a sequestered life, but they are further depicted as lonely souls because of their suppression of the libido. Their import is carried out in the images of heat and cold. Like sun, the nuns' virginity is both hot and cold. The heat is generated by such words as 'opens' and 'rushes' and the cold in the word "frozen." The loneliness of the nuns borne in such reflections as "isolate honour" and "isolation of skin" is embedded in the very semantic structure of the poem. As S.K.Desai aptly remarks,

> Isolating some words from their syntactic context and foregrounding them in terms of one-word lines is a technique he is fond of, particularly in his early poetry. In "The Nun," to begin with, one-word lines consist of verbs: 'rushes', 'virgin heat'. In the last stanza, the structure words like 'where' and 'of' replace the content words in these single word lines, suggesting perhaps the abstract structure of the heaven that the nun has fixed her eyes upon, the abstract structure being reinforced by the image of an abstract 'geometric mosaic' and also by the image of a wall of 'whiteness'. (Prasad 119)

If Gandhi and the peace negotiators are lonely in being forsaken, the loneliness of the nuns is due to their chosen way of life and their failure to "reach across" carnality.

Two other experiences which sharpen the feeling of loneliness in these first two volumes are filial relationship and man-woman relationship. The essential image that links the two poems, "To My Father" and "The Report Card" is a sense of "emptying" into nothingness. Here it is worth mentioning that Jayanta Mahapatra's first book, *Close the Sky, Ten by Ten* is dedicated to his father and that this book carries the epigraph from Nissim Ezekiel, "My father, sceptic, rationalist/trying every curse and blessing/powder, mixture, herb and hybrid." Mahapatra, in fact, has written a considerable number of poems on his father and has also widely referred to him in his later poetry. In "To My Father," Mahapatra's early concern with loneliness comes to the fore right from the first line of the poem: "It's the garden he is privately emptying into." With ageing, his father has withdrawn into his self and his son, the poet, who was once close to him—"One summer I remember, when we could yes, /stand together"—now finds himself "push(ed) to tears" at the invisible wall that separates him from his father. "The tree's tightness" that once acted as an embracing warmth between the father and son now gives way to "the expanding void", as the father is about "to die", to "fall to air." If in "To My Father," ageing accounts for the loneliness of his father, in "The Report Card" it is the result sheet that separates the son from his father, and the loneliness depicted here is that of the son. There is "the escalation of greed/ locked within a father's bone" and "the fear of reprimand" in the child at his bad performance in his school. It is now the child who "empties" himself "into duplicity." This leads to a sense of loneliness in the child which is depicted in such vivid images as

> a splintered mirror,
> a shred of silvered paper, or the torn hand
> from some clock's face, these his own. (*Close the Sky)*

While in "To My Father," loneliness is a lingering experience, "The Report Card" resolves the loneliness in filial relationship with the father coming out of his own self and in taking his child to the zoo:

> The card? Foe or friend,
> he only found. I never understand. (*Close the Sky*)

In the poems dealing with man-woman relationship, it is the woman who remains the prime image of loneliness. In "Intimacy, " the poet seems sceptical about the permanence of togetherness:

> For how long can we
> prolong this togetherness
> of being invulnerable together (*Svayamvara* 27)

Of this kind of "intimacy," what will ultimately "remain" is nothing but "the faceless equilibrium/of indifferent silence". This strain of loneliness is intensely felt in the poem "Afterward: Time Exposure." The title, as an image, is derived from the science of photography. As the title suggests, this is a memory poem in which the absence of the beloved is lamented in different terms: "Yet she/ was not there/when the white rain fell" and "she is not there/when I am/mechanically changing trains" (*Close the Sky, Ten by Ten*). Even when he is with his beloved, as in "Intimacy, " he feels lonely. In "A Ritual," the poet calls the act of coming together as a ritual. The cataclysm occurs to the otherwise ritual of coming together when she is found to

> tear off a blade of grass
> with one hand
> while the other holds on to her
> dry earth of day

In the third stanza the loneliness rests on a deceptive quietude: "the quietness is no solace." Their loneliness becomes irrecoverable at the end of the poem when the very hope of it is abandoned: "even this holds the promise of noise." Another love poem "Poem for R.M." records loneliness in conjugal life. The "Poem for R.M." seems, at first, to be celebrating the happy moments of marital life. They are encapsulated in such images as

> you walk over
> to me without a word,
> in the innocent
> trimmings
> of your clean nakedness. (*Svayamvara* 37)

Even when we know the husband is content to have her and gratuitously admits "you are kind, " we do not trust his "trust(ing)" her, for we find him bequeathed at last with "a plain sadness."

The poet's tender tone in love sometimes gives way to a harsh irony. This happens when we find him intolerably lonely with her.

The ironical note in "The Poster" sounds scathing when it ends with

> a pity we will
> not learn to deceive
> each other
> from the very first time

This poem "The Poster" is replete with such dark and bleak images as the children "splatter/the face on the wall" with "slime," "air, " "lays low/the rain of love" and the "restless trees" are "doomed to their roots." But In "How High Your Smile" the poet's ironical perception of the intimate relationship is sharpened once again.

In this poem he considers the lover's "behaviour" as a "craven ritual, " and that what they do is only to "rehearse" what they have already done. The pretension in their relationship is worked out in the pungent image of a dog searching the park for its bone. This irony is heightened when, just after praising her smile, "O how high your smile," he brings her down to the earth. This is marked by an absence of love, whether the lover admits it or not:

> how the dog nips down the park
> looking for his bone
> not believing it is not there ever *(Close the Sky)*

In other words, when the lover, after a frantic search for meaning in his/her intimate relationship with the other one, finds no fulfillment in his or her mad pursuit, he is left disillusioned. It seems from the above analyses, all along his early poetic career, the poet has been conscious of loneliness as an inevitable outcome in every kind of human relationship.

Mahapatra's first two volumes, *Close the Sky, Ten by Ten* and *Svayamvara and Other Poems* are basically experimentations in language and form. The poems in these two volumes achieve a certain degree of lyrical grace which continues to be the hallmark of his later poetry. These poems also project some of the themes and images which are more competently handled in the later volumes.

But his preoccupation with the form coupled with the failure to spell out the nature of his apocalyptic vision make these two collections no more than the work of an apprentice who seeks to learn the craft of poetic composition.

It is indeed surprising that from this state of being a mere novice, Jayanta Mahapatra, by the time he published his third collection in 1976, could achieve not only a firm grasp on language and form, but also a deep insight into the life and world around him.

A Man Becomes the Place: *A Rain of Rites, Waiting* and *A Father's Hours*

Jayanta Mahapatra's leap from the first two volumes to the second three is remarkable. *A Rain of Rites* (1976), the third volume, exhibits a wider range of themes, perspectives and styles than the earlier ones. In the intervening period of half a decade, the poet's growth into imaginative maturity is evident in his vocabulary, imagery and theme. He achieves a uniformity of style with repetition of key words, similar sentence-patterns, use of contrasts and opposites. His language and images grow more natural, less mechanical and contrived. The poems now may be ambiguous in their meanings but are clean, exact and economical in their form. The poems outgrow the vagueness of the early poems and reflect experimentation in tune with contemporary poetry as it had been evolving in America in the late sixties and early seventies. The American poets of this period like Robert Bly stress that the logic of the poem hinges upon its inner relations rather than on the narrative and argument. As Bruce King explains it, "A poem was an image of what one saw, felt, thought and sensed at a particular moment. There was an immediacy, but unlike the immediacy of imagism and the poetry of Williams the emphasis was not on describing the precise appearance of what is seen but on subjective feelings which brought to the surface otherwise unchannelled, repressed, deep anxieties, fears, desires, hopes" (*Modern Indian Poetry in English* 1988).

Mahapatra, like the other poets of his generation—Pritish Nandy, Keki N. Daruwalla, A.K. Mehrotra—explores the world of the irrational. He becomes increasingly involved with the relationship of the outer world with the inner world of hurt, silence, memory and sexuality. Apart from the preoccupations with childhood, history and tradition of his people and their rites and rituals, he becomes deeply concerned with his contemporary social reality. In *A Father's Hours* (1976) he asks "What is wrong with my country?" and provides the answer himself:

> The jungles have become gentle, the women restless.
> And history reposes between the college girl's breasts
> Mina, my pretty neighbour, flashes round and round the
> gilded stage,
> hiding jungles in her purse, holding on to her divorce,
> and a lonely Ph.D. (*A Father's Hours* 27)

A catalogue of contrasting images in the poem "The Twenty-Fifth Anniversary of a Republic" brings out a bewildering picture of his wronged country. In this poem, along with the images of the new and the bright – "The new postage stamp gleams in silver and gray" (17), "The plumes of rice have glossy furious eyes" (18), "There are new statues on the crossroads, newer dead" (19), "new steel mills palpitate in the darkness" (20)—there are also images of darkness and disappointment: "This is a barren world that has been/ prowling round my room, epidemics in the poisoned air, /dusty streets stretching away like disgruntled socialist" (17). Yet, though this poem seems to deal with the concrete subject of feeling the nerves of his time through perceptions of contemporary life in his own country, it also turns out to be an exercise in articulating a surreal world. For example, in the xiv section of the above mentioned poem he gives a concrete picture of a whore, Kamala, who has a village, a past and a name, and in the next section we see him winding through the long, tortuous sentences in a surreal world:

> In my dreams when I fondle Kamala's brazen breasts
> my hands encounter the blind flowers at a desecrated tomb.
> (31)

This is Mahapatra's forte. His concrete themes help him to achieve his vision that encompasses the real as well as the metaphysical and the surreal worlds. Many of his poems use this characteristic take-off. "Old Palaces" in *A Rain of Rites* begins with "In a limbo of things that accept the past/the blood grows softer, glossier, in the shadows" and moves on through reflection—"Trying to go back/ fulfills fantasy, patterns of childhood, the clear bondage"—to heightened thoughts and uncanny images before concluding with an openness and self-questioning:

> What bring us face to face, across the palace's
> golden light locked inside that secret lens?
> Not the thought that succeeds in pushing the darkness,
> evil and ugliness out of my life. (*A Rain of Rites* 5)

The dominating feature of Mahapatra's poetry, in fact, is his skillful juxtaposition of images from the two worlds: the "exterior world of phenomenal reality" and the "surrealistic world" (Naik 99). These two worlds of imagery help him shuttle between the concrete and the abstract and this method of moving back and forth is the characteristic mode of his poetic strategy. Speaking of the use of imagery in the poetry of Jayanta Mahapatra, J.O. Perry says, "they come as a rain of fragments." The act of 'rain' falling on earth becomes, as it were, the very metaphor of Mahapatra's profuse dropping of images in his poetry. Says Perry: "As they strike our earth of awareness some may too easily disappear in the dust and confusion. If erratic rivulets emerge and form a puddle here and there, we may vainly expect and seek a coalescing, or a dominating image, a concrete show stopper. But all the while pattern continues and tolerates our ignorances, defies our determinations and tests them by the pressure of its seriousness not to be overtaken by its own needs, its own limited ways of seeing and speaking. So we are presented with a repeated pattern, an endless process that cannot be harnessed as energy." (Prasad 62)

The title poem of *A Rain of Rites* illustrates the effect of images raining upon the poem. The poem begins with, "Sometimes a rain comes slowly across the sky" (10), suggesting the rain of images across the sky of the poet's kind. This apparently realistic image leads to a surrealistic perception of the rain as it "turns upon its grey cloud/breaking away into light/before it reaches its objective." The images, once they are on the earth of the poem, strike us like sudden lightning. As we are challenged to go near "the edge of answers," we may or may not unravel the mystery of the "rain" of images, but they stay put in the poem: "What holds my rain so it's hard to overcome?' Later trying to explain this poem, the poet says:

> In a poem I wrote about 15 years ago, titled "A Rain of Rites", I found myself once again at the border between two separate regions of the mind; between what, perhaps, I understood and what I didn't, using rain as a symbol for that substance which makes up my life, those blurs of vague light that pulsate with the days, making me ask at the end of the poem
>
> What still stale air sits on an angel's wings?
> What holds my rain so it's hard to overcome?
>
> I suppose such questionings come from somewhere deep within oneself, and that there is no reason or rationale for these things. But such questions and such searching move me and I am unable to resist them in my poetry. For poetry is voice—*vaak*. ("The Quality of Mystery" VIII)

This elaborate statement of the poet offers clues to the style of his poetry of this period, and the later ones as well. The spirit of questioning, the emphasis on having "no reason or rationale" in poetry, the images of rain as suggestive of something unknown, of things abstract, all appear in *A Rain of Rites* and *Waiting*.

The attempt to surmount the boundary between the apparently contrasting inner and outer worlds, is best reflected in "A Rain" (11). Beginning with "If it is a game one invents" and ending with "If it is a game one has made in childhood, /there will be no word to hide in", the poem creates an impression of vastness. In the process of its making, "A Rain" has shuffled the worlds of "desert," "wise eyes of water," "people," "silence," "truth," "earth" and "stone." In encompassing vastness in its fold, the imagery of rain plays a dominant role in evolving the poet's vision of his inexplicable, mysterious inner world. In other rain-poems too, like "Four Rain Poems," rain is associated with vastness. In both these poems two worlds of eternal contrast—body and spirit, infinity and mortality, sky and earth—are bound by rain which is "a linking process." The poet, in an interview with this author clarifies the significance of rain in the poem, "A Rain of Rites":

> There are two things which connect human beings: what is above and what is below. The sky is above you and the earth beneath you and anything that connects earth and sky is rain. It is a bond you cannot miss. It has a process itself. It is a link. Therefore, rain is a linking process, and so, the very act of your living.

In "Four Rain Poems" (23-24) 'rain' evokes all the moods and objects that

> rise and fall in turn,
> in that inner kingdom of consciousness
> which moves each torture of memory into the flesh.

The "boundary" which he tries to "approach" in Section I between the 'flesh" and "the secrets lost" is reinforced in section II. Behind him lie "inexhaustible worlds" of "submerged sun," "ash and bone," "mysterious looking boats on the river's edge," "stale air" and things "of the past." The tone is, no doubt melancholic. But those "menfolk returning from a cremation" cannot luxuriate in the things left behind. Therefore they are "drowsy and rebellious to memory." The "charred mind of the past" of the poet is set afire with the "cremation." Death, including that of memory, becomes a great leveller in the traditional image of grass soon growing over the dead, and in "even slope of blood." With the poet sensing "rain take over" him as the menfolk return from cremation, he finds release from the "torture of memory."

Subsequently, his reaching out for resolution leads him to encounter the inherent mystery in the nature of man and the world without. This mystery, or "magic" as he calls it, arises when he tries to bring his inner self to terms with either the outer or the metaphysical reality. He needs "to return to a condition/for reality" from his world of memory, and thereby overcome, with the help of rain, "amazement that is symbol/of what one left." In this maze he is unable to find meaning in his action, though he soars humbly to such an imaginative height as:

> do I know what really is my loss,
> do I know what I mean when I say this
> while the remembered rain beats against my walls?

The third section, abruptly ending with "this lie has no poem," shows his humility expressed in his honest doubt about his knowledge and his poetry for both are "provisional."

In the fourth and the last section, the poet waits "for the rain to end" as "the forbidden memories" are still "compelling." In waiting for the "rain to end", there is the parallel waiting for the poem to end and the poem that began with "a day dies" nears its wee hour "the day's last sun smoking/in unyielding fields soaked in innocence." The innocence that runs subterraneously all through the poem is consecrated in this last section which soaks up all memory, pain, absence and rain. This innocence is epitomised in "this water, all the star's silence, talking to a child." This innocence in the heart melts everything. It "draws everything to a close." The rain, at last, turns into "water." The memory which was "rain" is now "water":

> Its water rubs softly on my mind.

Though the day is over and everything is drawn to its close, something inexplicably painful lingers in the poet's heart. It sits in his heart, as a haunting image would:

> Where is that absence which pushed an icy rope
> down my throat, so close my heart could have touched it?

Thus, in its end "Four Rain Poems" achieves a marriage of "mind" and "heart," thought and feeling. It all along deals with a single theme of "memory" and carries along with it the striking imagery of "rain." The imagery of "rain" like that of "stone" binds the poet to his earth amid his people, letting him become "one and centre" in his world, both within and without. This spirit is embedded in "Listening:"

> At the touch of stone
> the immensity becomes your own: gods, fathers, sons,
> binding into earth, becoming one and centre.
>
> (*A Rain of Rites* 13)

Like 'rain', the other dominating clusters of images at this stage of Jayanta Mahapatra's poetry are associated with temples like priests, flowers, beggars and crow. The two worlds of eternal contrast like sun and dark, dawn and dusk, innocence and intrigue also help govern form and meaning in his poetry. In his weird world of imagery the real and the imagined coalesce and what emerges triumphantly is "such strange terrain," as one notices in "Dawn":

> Out of the dark it whirls back
> into a darkly mysterious house.
>
> Is it the earth within?
> Does it keep us waking, give brief respite?
>
> Like a hard crossword puzzle
> it sets riddles crowding against one another:
>
> the thunders trailing around the hatchet-faced banana leaves,
> a front gate limp with dew,
>
> the acid sounds of a distant temple bell,
> the wet silent night of a crow that hangs in the first sun.
>
> Is the dawn only a way through such strange terrain?

The frenzy of noise, which a silence recalls

through companions lost, things suddenly found?
There is a dawn which travels alone

without the effort of creation, without puzzle.
It stands simply, framed in the door, white in the air:

an Indian woman, piled up to her silences,
waiting for what the world will only let her do. (1)

"Dawn," the first poem in *A Rain of Rites*, sums up the Jayanta Mahapatra of mid-seventies: a befitting body of imagery sweeping the theme off its illusory ground, a style of crisp and epigrammatic statements distinctly his own and a theme that roots him to his place.

There are, at least, two stages or states of this dawn. The first one is "like a hard crossword puzzle," mysterious, dark, silent, pristine and creative and the second one "travels alone/without the effort of creation, without puzzle," noisy and mundane. He builds up this poem with the help of contrasting images of sound and silence: "the thunders trailing" and "the acid sounds of a distant temple bell" are pitched respectively against "a front gate limp with dew" and "the wet silent night of a crow" as well as "an Indian woman piled up to her silences." This world of contrasts is enlivened with striking adjectives: "hatchet-faced banana leaves," "acid sounds." In a "hard crossword puzzle" we have the image of a dawn which is complex and suggestive of the very complexity of his poems. The dawn returns to a "darkly mysterious house." By asking, "is the dawn only a way through such strange terrain?" he seems to explore the very creative process which begins like the day beginning with the "dawn" full of "riddles." The "dawn" thus becomes also an effective metaphor for the poem itself. It goes on discovering "things suddenly found," like a revelation or a sudden flash of an idea or an image coming to mind in the process of making a poem.

But this dawn/poem does not remain itself; midway it is transformed into "the earth within" and then recedes into a level of hidden meanings. In "Ceremony" the process of transformation ("I have become: a diamond in my eye") also connects the hunting for meaning in the poem with the quest for meaning of his own existence: "(what is there in ceremony, in a ritual's deeply hidden meaning?)" (*A Rain of Rites* 15). In "Old Palaces" "(what can remain to meaning here/deadens gestures, footfalls, faces of our nature)" such receding meanings begin to become an obsession with the poet. But in "Dawn" the other state of mind does not engage itself in creation: "It travels alone" and "stands simply." This sense of dawn belongs to the diurnal world. It has abandoned the surreal "frenzy of noise" and "the acid sound of distant bells" and "thunders trailing"; instead "it stands simply", unfathomably "like an Indian woman."

The woman in "Dawn" "piled up to her silences" is just like those people in a "A Rain" who are "piled up to their silences." The characters do not stand by themselves, but seek support and meaning in others and thus conform to the traditional Indian saying that the poet, the vine and the woman cannot stand by themselves, at all. This passive stance is reflected in various images such as "old brassy bells/moulded by memories" ("Myth" 22) and "A bell trembles/touched by the pain/of countless people ("Listening to a Prayer" 29), "The ten-armed clay Durga/framed in a mythic past" ("Moving" 26), "A whole religion framed by the land" ("Somewhere, My Man" 42). So too does the image of the waiting woman recur in a number of poems:

> a woman
> cannot find her reflection in the mirror
>
> waiting as usual
> at the edge of sleep (*A Rain of Rites* 7)
>
> a large group of stony women in front of a shrine
> silently sit out the whole day waiting to be cured.
> (*A Rain of Rites* 15)

The waiting woman could be the image of the poet waiting for the poem to dawn upon him, and also for the dawn of an awakened world. Thus mysterious inner creativity and the everyday outer activity are connected poetically. For, after all, these two states of dawns are not distinct or distant from each other. There is actually a thin membrane between them which will snap with even our lightest footfalls. In Mahapatra's poetry the boundaries between the inner and the outer worlds eventually evaporate. The poet himself feels

> That one must somehow try to reach the border between things understandable and ununderstandable in a poem, between life and death, between a straight line and a circle. Perhaps this paucity of our knowledge about death, about the nowhere which exists in the mind, about the knowledge of death and of our future and about this boundary when flesh goes and time enters, holds an unusual power that drives one to create the flow in a poem. ("The Quality of Mystery" VII)

This act of coalescing two worlds or two dawns into a single dawn lends unity to this poem and reflects a vision of the world and of the creative moment as both surreal and earthly.

The other dawn which is of the material, day-to-day world, is more clearly dealt with in "The Morning I" and "The Morning II," which are the first two poems of *Waiting*. Like the "Dawn" of *A Rain of Rites*, the dominating images are drawn from the outer world, the world as it exists, full of paradoxes. Here, too the morning is "pristine gold" (*Waiting*). It begins with "the sweeper-girl walking by, /the can of human excrement/cradled/in her frail arm ("*Waiting* 1"). A more realistic and yet deeply moving description of such a sweeper girl in one ordinary morning in Cuttack is found in the poet's essay, "An Orissa Journal:"

> Round the bend of the road Lakshmi appears, walking purposefully, the wide-mouthed excreta bin resting like an infant across her slender left hip. Lakshmi, the fourteen year

> old outcaste sweeper girl, barefoot and smiling, cradling the faeces of the upper middle class with her left arm while her right hand swings in unison with her small, tight, lotus-bud breasts. (*Queen's Quarterly* 67)

In one such morning the "window" is thrown open like "some woman's derisive look." This is the usual picture in real life and the poet is true to his experience in giving a concrete, objective description of it; the sweeper girl co-exists with "a starkly naked Jain monk/calmly walking down the determined road." The transferred epithet, "determined," suggests the determination of the Jain monk to travel his chosen path, without being provoked by either the worldly filth or physical attractions, both symbolized in the young sweeper girl. Concluding "The Morning II" with "It is the morning to his (Jain monk's) mind," (*Waiting* 2) the poet connects this image of the Jain monk's spiritual awareness with his own mind, open and alert to the outer world.

Indeed, Mahapatra has a strong belief in the beginnings and, "dawn" or "morning" serves as an image for his many beginnings and supporting "his sacrosanct instant" (*Waiting* 2), as he says of the Jain monk. We find another "such familiar morning" in "Somewhere, My Man" which begins with the sunrise and with men rising to a world of action. This poem depicts a life that is traditional, lucid, unhurried, meditative; "In familiar mornings . . . things move/ bicycles, buses, idling bulls," "a man sitting down to worship, after a passionate bath," "motionless on a mat," and "here is my man/in the doorway of a dunged street" (dung-cakes are dried on the roadsides for use as fuel). The poet's chosen man sitting in a doorway is symbolic of transition of a world from the traditional to the modern. His people's inheritance instead of being a burden is like a light feather in the crown of their simple living, for "he knows his fathers well." The awareness of their tradition has taught them to float like lotus leaves on the watery surface of their penury-stricken, diseased world. Images of poverty and disease are reinforced in "the rickshaw pullers," "naked children," "the virus of pox," "ailing mother," etc. Like his men knowing their fathers well, the poet knows his men well and this understanding comes out vividly in his minute observation of the activities of the characters in the early hours of the morning—the pious man sitting down to worship or the rickshaw puller:

> An idle rickshaw-puller gets up,
> polishes the thin chromium trappings
> with a rag,
> spits on the ground
>   and sits down again,
> patiently waiting for fares.

The knowledge of his men, his sympathetic views of them, establishes him as a poet of his place, helps him "become the place," the image with which "Somewhere, My Man" begins:

> A man does not mean anything.
> But the place.
> Sitting on the riverbank throwing pebbles
> into the muddy current,
> a man becomes the place.
> Even that simple enough thing.
>
> In familiar mornings
> early summer breezes shake the palms.
> Things move: bicycles, buses, idling bulls;
> a whole religion framed by the land.
> A man bathes at sunrise with passion,
> plucks some holy flowers,
> sits down to worship
> motionless on a mat.
> He knows his fathers well.
> His mind, like the sun,
>
> gently climbs the godly hill of day,
> will not touch or reveal
>
> the many levels

of himself.

Somewhere
a door opens and shuts.
Years elapse quietly behind,
    like things

people have known all along.
An idle rickshaw-puller gets up,
polishes the thin chromium trappings
with a rag,
spits on the ground

    and sits down again,
patiently waiting for fares.

Each year, in the spring,
the same things drift by:
clouds of silk-cotton seeds, more
naked children, the virus of pox.
Here sits my man
in the doorway of a dunged street,
beside his ailing mother

    her pinched aged face
proudly bearing the irrelevance
    of movement.

Here is the hour that will not move.
Is it made up of old stone?
It holds him now as it held his father.
And it watches like an offering
of flowers at the feet of an ikon,
with the past, with true tolerance.

He waits, with his country,

breathing
and that is all.
What use is there,

tearing

a country to bits?
With his body, he loses body,
pales into a place.
Nothing matters,
the river grows,
the hill takes a high face.
This mystic light oozes everywhere,

like sweat.

Absorbing, it eats his mind
slowly around the edges. (*A Rain of Rites* 42-43)

This image of a man becoming the place gets reinforced each time a character is sketched. The characterization culminates with his "paling into the place" for every character is finally shown in the posture of sitting, be it the worshipping man, the rickshaw puller or the poet's "man." The act of sitting moors the characters to their place, definitively, like trees. The poet himself acknowledges this prime importance of a writer's sense of belonging to his place, when he says, "Frankly, I forced myself to write during the four months I spent in Iowa City, but could produce nothing startling or good. I suppose, I felt so cut-off from my roots that I couldn't reconcile myself at all. I wasn't able to sleep for three weeks. A writer (Can I call myself that?) should become the place he comes from." (Raghavan 59)

This concern of the poet with his place and people is more clearly pronounced in Mahapatra's Puri poems where the place, Puri, emerges as a vignette, a living presence like the omnipresence of Lord Jagannath, the presiding deity of the Puri temple. In these poems there is a harmonious existence of discordant things, base and spiritual, of legend, myth and history. Such recurrent images as the crow, priest, flower, prayer, stone and leper associated with the Puri temple speak of the crowded, complex character of Puri, the great spiritual hub of the Oriya people and a centre of pilgrimage for the Indian Hindus. About the bi-cultural character of Mahapatra's poetry, Dilip Chitre says, "he belongs as much to the phlegmatic, self-doubting, emotionally inward English tradition and its more opened out experimental and exuberant American variant as to the spiritually narcissistic and semantically elusive attitude of the elite Hindu mind." (*New Quest* 81)

The poems on Puri illustrate the characteristic of his poetry, the self-doubting and narcissistic. One such poem, another morning poem, is "The Father." It heralds a dawn in Puri that is "indistinguishable" because it is like any other dawn. But "The Faith" itself is clearly distinguishable from Mahapatra's earlier attitudes shown in poems with similar titles in *Close the Sky, Ten by Ten* and *Svayamvara.* "The Faith" in *Waiting* is marked, in comparison with the earlier poems, by the close attention to the experience it relates, by sharpness of images and by the concreteness of the emotion. Its epithets are exact, coming out effortlessly, and its local details are realistic. The characters in this poem, as in other poems on Puri, become the place they live in and, concurrently Puri emerges as a living character.

"The Faith" (*Waiting* 14), beginning with a dissecting image of the "mornings/like pale-yellow hospital linen," like that of Prufock's etherised evening, brings to the fore a world of disease, both physical and metaphysical. Even the simple epithet "wide" bears significance when it is applied to the Puri temple street (called Badadanda in Oriya which literally means wide street). This wide temple road is seen as physically convenient for "a legless cripple" to "clutter up" with "the light crouched in his palms," suggesting the cripple's painful hope of being annihilated by God.

The three characters in the morning temple scene are contrasting ones: a cripple, a priest and the poet, a stanza being devoted to each in that order. In *Selected Poems* (1987), the changes in the last two stanzas in this poem "The Faith" have obviously changed the characters of the priest and the poet:

What sentence of old
moves him toward the furious wrinkled walls?
The Puri priest standing in indulgent sunshine
plays a small ridicule across the melting festival,
safe in place above a pile of hard-eyed ancestors.

Climbing down the stairs into the dark shrine
the sudden light overtakes me,
my blood drowsy in the mosquito-hum of chanting,
and a frail white flower of worship
pays for my sins and watches. (*Waiting* 14)

What silence inside him
moves him toward the furious wrinkled walls?
Priests across the road everywhere
like flies thick over buttermilk, wondering
if their unseen ancestors weren't happier.

Climbing down the dark stairs into the shrine
the stark smell of centuries overpowers me;
of the sweat of bodies quivering for inheritance,
as a frail white jasmine touches my hand
and watches the body's kneeling agony.(*Selected Poems* 20)

The priest in the later version is no longer confident and "safe in place above a pile of hard-eyed ancestors." Instead of "playing a small ridicule upon people" he is "wondering" upon his own unhappiness against that of his ancestors. Moving like the "cripples" the priests are an embodiment of disease, and moral corruption, "like flies thick over buttermilk."

Successfully avoiding the posture of a moralist and social critic, the poet acknowledges the suffering of the world: "the body's kneeling agony." Here the outer world, that is the cripple and the priest, stimulates him to articulate his inner feelings. And in his humanistic preparedness to suffer along with others, he seems to have the strain of "inheritance" from Bhima Bhoi, the late nineteenth century blind, tribal mystic Oriya poet, who declared, "let the world be redeemed even if my life is condemned to hell."

In the Puri poems like "Main Temple Street, Puri," Dawn at Puri," and "Taste for Tomorrow," there is always an association of priests with beggars and cripples, of crows with flowers. "They rise before us," as K. Ayyappa Paniker says, "in all their objective reality and concreteness and then slowly transform themselves, almost imperceptibly, into monument-like images and symbols" (129).

The image of "leper" forms an integral part of the poet's perception of the world of Puri. As there is a palpable presence of cripples in "The Faith," so also in "Main Temple Street, Puri," "children, brown as earth, continue to laugh at cripples and mating mongrels" (*A Rain of Rites* 16). In "Taste for Tomorrow" "five faceless lepers/move aside/as a priest passes by" (*Waiting* 6), and in "Dawn at Puri" there are "leprous shells leaning against one another,/a mass of crouched faces without names" (*A Rain of Rites* 28). These lepers at Puri are presented as faceless entities. Nonetheless, their presence is imposing. With the lepers and leprous shells looming large on the Puri scene, what one is faced with are "injuries drowsy with the heat" (*A Rain of Rites* 16). The physical injuries of the lepers are the image of spiritual injuries in the human soul. Like lepers, most of the widows and old men and women of Orissa aspire for a pilgrimage to Puri at least once in their lifetime, so that, as per their belief, they would get salvation. So it is natural that the poet's aging mother's "last wish" is to be "cremated" there at Puri (*A Rain of Rites* 28). Even "Ram Lal, the grocer" wishes to "gift slabs of white marble to the limbless One at Puri" (*Waiting* 27). Ram Lal does what every pious Hindu wants to do and, in fact, the yard of the Puri temple is littered with such gifts of slabs.

As the people at Puri—priests, cripples and the poet—pale into the place, so does Puri itself come alive, in one short, crisp, poem, "Taste for Tomorrow":

> At Puri, the crows.
>
> The one wide street
> lolls out like a giant tongue.

Five faceless lepers move aside
as a priest passes by.

And at the street's end
the crowds thronging the temple door:
a huge holy flower
swaying in the wind of greater reasons. (*Waiting* 6)

The typical pattern of images woven into the Puri theme is repeated here. But the "giant tongue" and "the holy flower" point also to his deep-laden consciousness of the myth of Kali and the tantric rituals associated with her worship. The poet's use of the myth of Kali in the description of Puri scene and Jagannath also point to his awareness of the culture of Jagannath which is said to be an integration of all the Hindu religious cults prevalent in Orissa. The slow pace of transformation of animate being into object and vice-versa is at work in this poem and this action precisely yet subtly provides unity to the poem. As Ayyappa Paniker says, "This process of metamorphosis of reality into symbol acts as a connecting link between the objective perception of everyday reality and the imaginative leaps of myth creation. The crows of the first line invisibly turn into the crowds of the last section." (129)

The flower, another conspicuous presence in the temple scene, is the image of diversity. The flowers that grow in the garden of his poetry in this period are varied:

When the sun shines the white jasmines
will drop, there will be a net of scars
on the leaves. (*Waiting* 26-27)

The dried, sacrificed
flowers smile at me. (*A Rain of Rites* 22)

A man bathes at sunrise with passion,
plucks some holy flowers,
sits down to worship (*A Rain of Rites* 42)

They close their eyes everywhere
to that end
airing the poise of a flower. (*A Rain of Rites* 6)

In the world it is always I who come back
to myself, that far flower of thought; (*A Rain of Rites* 15)

Offerings of marigolds, fruit and shaven hair
stare like terrified men. (*A Rain of Rites* 8)

The imagery of flowers in his poetry sometimes signifies a romantic inclination while sometimes it helps unravel the anguish of men. The flowers are often symbolic of the rites and rituals of worship and the poetic process itself. In "Performance III" ("*A Father's Hours*") the speaker questions his attachment to the flowers: "yet does the flower I perceive drag me to despair?" (11) He seems to find an answer towards the end of this poem by demythicising the flower with

The tactics and the strategy
of the wind
tearing the white flower apart
without causing harm to its myth of strength.
(*A Father's Hours* 11)

In some of the poems of this period the imagery of flowers delineating the tradition of the temple and its aura gives way to the imagery of stone that is within and without the temple, circumscribing all the characters and inanimate presence described in the scene. In "Myth" (*A Rain of Rites* 22) the essential ingredients, as in the poems on Puri, are "a chanting," "an incense," "a crumpled leaf," "a filthy scarlet flower," "a recurring prayer," "a bearded saffron-robed man" and "brassy bells." The poet stands outside "the dark dank sanctum" into which he does not dare go. His standing outside the temple is made explicit in the final line of the poem, as a saffron-robed man asks him firmly: "Are you a Hindu?" This question is loaded with an ambiguity, an unresolved tension. His standing outside the temple implies that either he is an outcaste or a non-Hindu, yet everything going on there inside the temple where "myth shifts from hand to hand, eye to eye" seems mysterious and attractive to him. This poise between rejection and attraction gives him a critical means for holding back his emotion and imparts objectivity to his observation. The temple rituals embodied in the image of "dried sacrificial flowers" "smiling" at him reminds one of the devadasis who danced on "the stairs that seem endless, lifelong" to their salvation. The mountain peaks of Annapurna, Dhaulagiri and the peaks of consciousness of devadasis point to the metaphysical heights of the poet's imagination. The geological process of metamorphosis of "a crumpled leaf" to "diamond" culminates in the poet's perception of the possibility of his own transformation. Like flowers in "Myth," stone also undergoes transformation from its concrete nature in "Samsara" with "slow stone surging to flame" (*A Rain of Rites* 7) to an abstract one in "The Earth of July" where "a stone celebrates with its wreaths of faith" (*Waiting* 7).

The imagery of stone provides the poet with the scope to meditate on the metaphysical and eternal as well as personal conflicts, to assess his own and his people's beliefs embedded in age-old traditions. The imagery of stone builds the poems, as does the stone build a temple, and in this process poems are like temples with their tight structure, with the rites and ceremonies of the people merging in them, with the poet holding the centre of the poem as does a presiding deity in a temple, and finally poems, like temples, open the doors to many interpretations. The intermediary between the two is the stone.

"Stone is the theme," he declares in the first line of "Bhubaneswar" (*Waiting* 8). The images of stone have varied connotations; its association with the temple scene being the most significant. When he says in "Bhubaneswar" "we build the stone that has overcome men," his historical and mythic consciousness is revealed. In "An Orissa Journal" he traces the fountainhead of this complex consciousness:

> Slowly I release that I am living at one particular instant in many layers of time—the mythic, the historical and the

> present. What one sees in the present is only what has stirred the air of the place for countless generations. (*Queen's Quarterly* 70)

The Oriyas in the past have been a race of temple builders. His poetry tries to evoke and recapitulate what remains of that past, its decayed ruins or its ruinous state. In "Konarka," which begins like "Bhubaneswar" with a declaration of his adherence to stone and meditation upon—"I must carry the stone I found" (*Waiting* 22)—he traces his origin in stone. In this poem his contemplation is both on the mythic "here the little boy in a dream/waved to the Man once" and on the personal level "inside me/is the boy I found/tracked by stone" (23). Thus, the stone is a track to past, valid in its endurance, even if it is in "ruin." The poet draws on its validity through a parallelism with creative work, be it poetry or painting:

> Someone talks of a work of art,
> looking into its little secret:
> chipped fingers, the thin crack
> running slant along the brow.
> So like a word, its blue wings broken,
> palpitating, because one has failed
> to understand. Nothing that is whole
> speaks of the past. Or lives.
> Or can form into a word. (*A Rain of Rites* 36)

The stone as petrified music, the stone that endures, that retains its wholeness even in its ruins, its very act of existence, however slender and slant, is a testimony to the art-form that lives beyond the temporal. The poet internalises both the qualities of the stone, vulnerable to time yet transcending its vulnerability once it is formed into art, when he asserts ruefully that he will "not find/any right to (his) death" unless he stands "close to the stone/trying to smear it with blood/to give it life" (*Waiting* 23). His preparedness to shed his own blood, an allusion to those people who were squeezed of their blood and sweat by the kings to build temples, is a measure of his penitence for forgetfulness of that past.

This enduring quality of stone is also symbolic of the continuity of values and beliefs. In "Ikons" stone is an embodiment of both the aesthetic and the ascetic powers: "Black ikons/a museum of symbols/silence the land" (*A Rain of Rites* 40). The poet's land littered with ikons is a symbol of meanings lost, of silence itself. Lord Shiva, the creator and destroyer, is represented in the form of linga, from which emanates the divine strength. The father in this poem "touch (ing) the linga with his forehead" is not manifesting pain and frustration but asserting his belief in his karma and its consequence. This silent yet communicative phallic emblem animates "Ikons" as it does in "Sunburst": "Two gods (the bull and the cow) copulating in the warm tar" (*A Rain of Rites* 30). To Frank Allen these are "seen as a mysterious public icon but at the same time a manifestation to the school girls and the reader of the troubling yet inescapable identity. We experience a 'sunburst' (epiphany) illuminating Hindu erotic energy of growing up into sex, of experiencing sexual relationships in an overwhelming, undiluted dimension which is both physical and a paradigm of the supernal." (*Parnassus* 340)

At the end of "Ikons" the father is seen petrified, looking around, "like a hill," manifesting Mahapatra's technique of transforming an animate being into an inanimate one. This act of touching the linga is an effort to free himself from the *samsara*:

> And illusion:
> the sacred plant in a Hindoo home,
> cow and scabbed stone,
> a dark rock of answers and air. (*A Rain of Rites* 40)

Of such an illusory *samsara* we have a further glimpse in "Samsara" "where the image of stone and its associative images like "flower," "prayer," "priest" are powerfully reiterated. "Samsara," like "Dawn at Puri," is divided into six stanzas of three short lines each. Each stanza presents complete yet interlocked images of the stages of life, and the whole poem is structured as an image corresponding to the cyclical birth and rebirth. In the first stanza we have with the rain "the first grasses of cirrus." With the onset of "rain"

the year's
newly resurrected gods
move out of their sleep

The monsoon season celebrates the birth of Srikrishna, Janmastami, and Durga Puja. Once the gods come to earth, they are subjected to birth and death like human beings. The rush towards "the temple doors" is accentuated and in the process the wandering begins "around the deserted targets of the soul." The lonely, tormented soul squelched in the mire of *samsara* seeks an escape route through his father's and forefather's path:

offerings of marigolds, fruit and shaven hair
stare like terrified men;
the slow stone surges to flame. (8)

Here again is the metamorphosing tactic of the poet: the objects of worship are gifted with human qualities and life is fused into stone. The stone surging to flame could be the ultimate consummation of life or the hallucinatory revelation of the divine force. However, man is emboldened "to begin again." That brings the poem, at its end, to its beginning as does the man who "sees no end" of his cyclic process. Here, "evident in every cadence is the long over-ripening of a sardonic wisdom, the tired consciousness of too many beginnings the ordeal of *samsara*," says Vernon Young (617).

In "Listening" he feels at home with stone, verily bound to his earth. The touch of stone plays magic, serves like a Midas-touch to his poetry and to the characters in it; they become one with the other: the subject with the content, the man with the place and the immensity with time and space;

At the touch of stone
the immensity becomes your own: gods, fathers, sons,
binding into earth, becoming one and centre.

(*A Rain of Rites* 13)

Here the poet does not hold the centre of the poem; he leaves it to his people and place and is content to be side-lined, passive, to "wait' and "listen," "pinned to the stone." This listening, attentive quality of the poet has always imparted strength to his poetry which has enabled him to stand apart from his contemporary Indian poets in English firmly upon his place. In "Listening to a Prayer" this attentive quality lends serenity to the atmosphere. The scene is set in the temple yard. This short poem develops in three stages: "stone cuts deep," "a bell trembles" and "the wind/settles on (his) shoulders." (*A Rain of Rites* 29) These tactile and auditory images come through silently. The only object that should ring merely "trembles," because it is "touched by the pain/of countless people." What the poet perhaps intends to hear in prayer is the "pain" of people, which he does not seem to find even in stone which "cuts deep" through the layers of his onion-like existence only to reveal after peeling "neither a silence/nor an answer."

In contrast to the bell trembling, touched by the pain of millions there is the stone as whore; "the vermilion-smeared whored stone" (*A Rain of Rites* 2). Like the bell, the stones are also touched by the worshipping people. But, unlike the bell being "touched by pain," the stones are touched by pomposity and "ritualistic coconuts." The wrath felt towards the stone seems to come out of the poet's indignation with "crafty priests" (*A Father's Hours* 19) and resentment against the linga for its indifference to the suffering of the people. Unlike the bell, the stone/linga does not tremble even if a father touches it with his forehead, as is evident in "Ikons." As a result, the suffering woman of "Village" instead of bowing to "whored stone," "shyly bows to a world of her own."

The whore image recurring frequently in the poetry of Jayanta Mahapatra represented his vision of women wronged, who take to this profession out of hunger. They figure as the professionals, as in "Kamala, the three-rupee whore from my mother's remote village/ with an old, hard tradition." (*A Father's Hours* 30) They take to their work with a brazen matter-of-factness as in "The Whorehouse in a Calcutta Street" where at the end of the act, she asks "Hurry, will you ? Let me go." (*A Rain of Rites* 18)

The authenticity and the universality of "Hunger" comes from the very fact that it ably recreates a down-to-earth world out of the imagined one. "The poem is based on a true incident; it could easily have happened to me on the poverty-ridden sands of Gopalpur-on-sea," says the poet and explains why this poem is significant, "because of the theme. . . . *Language plus* using the image to affirm and control at the same time the sexual drive of the protagonist . . . its basic human sequence . . . quiet conviction. The landscape of Gopalpur chose me, and my poem. To face perhaps my inner self, to see my own debasement against the stubborn starvation light of my country." ("about HUNGER and myself")

The images used in "Hunger" (*A Rain of Rites* 44) are a happy blending of the literal and the metaphorical. Throughout the poem right from the first line, "It was hard to believe the flesh was heavy on my back, the imagery of sex interspersed with the things material and surreal like "trailing his nets and nerves," "his white bone thrash his eyes" go on piling until they climax in the ultimate fall. The fisherman's matter-of-fact tone in asking him to take his daughter—"will you have her?"—in the first stanza and making room for him to brood over his next possible move in the following two stanzas amid hush and noise inside, signified by "my mind thumping in the flesh's silence, "I heard him say 'my daughter, she's just turned fifteen'" in the concluding stanza reveal the wilful blindness of the fisherman towards filial values in the materialistic world as well as the protagonist's hesitant surrender to the sensual act.

The protagonist is sympathetic to both the father and the daughter, and has pity for his own self. His inner conflict runs throughout the poem and gives unity to the narrative. The metaphysical wounds inflicted on the protagonist's soul is evident in lines like "palmfronds scratched my skin" and "the sticky soot crossed the space of my mind." The fisherman, however, conceals his anguish in asking him "carelessly," though the protagonist recognizes it when he says "I saw his white bone thrash his eyes," "trailing his nets and nerves." The theme of fishing is symbolic of sexuality which is the poem's central concern. The fisherman's "nerves" like fishes are caught in the net of the situation which leads to the sexual violation of his daughter. The protagonist, too, driven by sexual hunger and pity, follows the fisherman to his "shack," with his mind "thumping in the flesh's sling." As soon as he enters the "lean-to" he finds it "open like a wound." This is the crucial moment of the poem, for the image of wound embodies the agony and conflict of both the fisherman and the protagonist. The "fall," the consummation of the act and climax of the poem takes place only after the father leaves but not without the protagonist being aware of his concern for his daughter and a gored agony:

> She's just turned fifteen...
> Feel her. I'll be back soon, your bus leaves at nine.
> The sky fell on me, and a father's exhausted wile.
>
> (*A Rain of Rites* 44)

The falling of the sky of a father's exhausted wile corresponds to and sharpens the sexual fall of the protagonist and also to a spiritual fall in the enactment of illicit sex. The other "world"/"hunger" lies between her "wormy legs," "The fish slithering, turning inside" in the last line of the poem suggests symbolically that ultimately the protagonist is hooked to unrestrained passion.

Of course, in Mahapatra's poetic world whores represent a mere fragment of women's world. There are also women who are chaste and who have noble and tragic dimensions. They are primarily characterised by their quality of patience, waiting, suffering and silence. These characteristics of women are reflected in the figure of an anonymous woman in "A Missing Person":

> In the darkened room
> a woman
> cannot find her reflection in the mirror
>
> waiting as usual
> at the edge of sleep
>
> In her hands she holds
> the oil lamp
> whose drunken yellow flames
> know where her lonely body hides (*A Rain of Rites* 7)

The loneliness of the woman is suggested in the image of the mirror not giving back her reflection in the dark. Her staying in the dark signifies her mysterious quality. Her world, characterised by darkness, disease and dirt, is reinforced in the images of "oil lamp," and its "drunken yellow flame." As in "Dawn" in this poem also she waits for her dream world. Her loneliness comes from her "waiting" down the ages ("as usual") for her man and children to come back and make her world whole again. Recalling the circumstances that went into the making of this poem, Mahapatra says:

> So this house of mine became substance, as did my mother, physically ill with the passage of time, moving back and forth in the listless darkness, my younger brother at her heels. We had no electricity in the house (it was a luxury for us) and the long verandah with its adjoining courtyard seemed to float about in a ghostly light, filling me with a sense of insecurity I could not overcome.
>
> And the picture of my mother, swathed in a sari, holding on to the oil lamp in the shadows, the sooty flame swaying in the breeze, seemed to establish itself firmly in my mind.
>
> Strangely these evenings stayed as though carved of black and polished bone. An inexplicable loneliness linked itself with the sad-eyed oil lamp of my mother. They came to mean something to me. Coupled with this was the frustrating, numbing pity I felt for my cousin who was battered by frequent beatings from her drunken husband. Perhaps I began to understand what a symbol was, without trying to go deeper into the meaning of events, without my trying to become wiser. And as the years went by and I grew older, this image buried itself in the heavy undergrowth of the mind. It was only later, much later, when I started to write poetry myself, that I found myself abandoned in this past, the past stretching before me, and it was as if I had stepped on a small twig that snapped to make me articulate:

> In the darkened room

> a woman
> cannot find . . .
> . . . where her lonely body hides.
>
> Probably this was how the brief poem came to be, and I titled it "A Missing Person". (*Contemporary Authors' Autobiography Series* 141)

The suffering and mysterious quality of woman is limned in "Summer," another brief poem like "A Missing Person." "Summer" (*A Rain of Rites* 14) wades through two contrasting images—the harshness of summer and the tenderness of girl suggested in the "green mango." The poem begins with an image of a mango tree and cold ash under it. Then, immediately after the question "who needs the future?" he says, "A ten year old girl/combs her mother's hair/where crows of rivalries are quietly nesting." And in the end, the mango falling from the girl's mind to earth completes the division of the poem into two different worlds. The "cold ash," and "crows of rivalries" (the image of the "crow" is appropriate keeping in mind the atmosphere of the poem—summer, mango, crow, all suggesting a literal summer) cut across the innocence of "green mango." The poem begins with "Not yet," that is, there is still time and hope for the girl to redeem her future when "the home will never be hers."

Another aspect of woman, as wife, is dealt with in such poems as "Indian Summer," "The Indian Way" and "Idyll." These poems present the Indian concept of wife as something pious, full of dignity and fidelity:

> We keep calm; the voices move.
> I buy you the morning's lotus. (*Waiting* 44)

This Indian way of life is made explicit at the end of the poem when the husband reassures his woman of the serenity of his love:

> You know

> I will not touch you
> like *that*
> until our wedding night. (*Waiting* 44)

Thus, the sexual touch is not a desecration: it is sanctified by marriage. The image of a contented wife, her love tested in fire like Sita's, is presented in "Indian Summer Poem":

> The good wife
> lies in my bed
> through the long afternoon;
> dreaming still, unexhausted
> by the deep roar of funeral pyres. (*A Rain of Rites* 35)

The image of the wife in bed with the husband, as on an all-consuming funeral pyre, is striking in its evocation of a happy and faithful conjugal life. An interplay of visual and auditory images is evinced throughout the poem in such images as "over the soughing of the sombre wind," "chant" of the priest, and "the mouth of India opens." The vowel sounds, especially of "o", dominating this scene produce a dark resonance as in a sanctum sanctorum of a temple. The sudden surprise in the image of "the mouth of India opens," gives the poem a twist in its significance by alluding to the mouth of Krishna, which he showed to Yashoda, his mother. In the ultimate reality of existence everything merges: time ("morning" and "afternoon"), space ("midden" and "bed"), love and death ("wife" and "funeral pyres"). In effect, they merge into one complex symbol, "crocodiles move into deeper waters," which is central to the poem which is nothing but entering into the ultimate consciousness. In this poem one detects, as does Dilip Chitre, "the incantatory rhythm of Sanskrit chants and devotional songs in modern Indian languages" (81).

However romantic the image of Mahapatra's women, his vision of women is basically that of a sacrificial and suffering lot, destined to be a living human offering to god and to men's world of carnal need. They are, somehow, deep under man's skin with their passion and hurt, quietude and mystery, all of which are brought out forcefully in the images of lake and snake.

> and the women
> not answering to their names anymore,
> and usually lying like unexpected lakes
> deep within the wooded hills,
> break their calm surfaces
> like wild water-snakes
> let loose from the yearly floods. (*Waiting* 5)

Children serve as a key to his identification with the place, because the childhood he depicts is more local than universal and a few universal elements in it are connected with the unhappy aspects of his personal life. The childhood in his place is, till now, primarily marked by poverty, disease and negligence. The poems dealing with or having reference to childhood are "Sunburst," "Hands," "On the Banks of the Ganges," "Five Indian Songs", "An Old Country," "A Twilight Poem," "Learning to Flow Free in the Chariot Festival at Puri," "Main Temple Street, Puri." In "Sunburst," the reader's attention is, at first, directed mischievously towards two twelve-year-old shy school girls watching "surreptitiously" "two gods copulating on warm tar." These two girls form a part of the composite scene and the poet, at the end of "Sunburst" summing up their world as "part growing up, part sacred, most part lust" is not a prude, for he declares in the fifth stanza, almost epigrammatically, "It is only human mirrors/which shape an embarrassed scene." Other than celebrating the Hindu erotic energy in "Sunburst," Mahapatra here also presents his contemporary India. He achieves this effect by bringing in two school girls into a gathering of faceless crowds to witness a bull copulating with a cow in the street. Two Indias are juxtaposed in this composite scene. The one is rural traditional India represented in the owner of the cow who "coaxes her softly/by name: half woman, half goddess" and the other one modern and urban represented by the school girls who "stare at the road, learning to close their eyes." The children recurring in his poetry at this stage are not healthy or happy. They represent typical Indian childhood marked by disease and deprivation. This brings him to his place, the surroundings in which he grew up. In a poem like "A Country Festival" one gets such a picture when it begins with

> Now the evening shadows creep,
> the scorching, the slow sleep,
> the squalor squealing in despair,
> and the inaction dancing in a circle
> like naked children round their sheer fingers. (*Waiting* 4)

Likewise, whenever he refers to children they are treated either as a burden, "Each year . . ./more naked children, the virus of pox" (*A Rain of Rites* 43), or as sick: "The air smells of sick, mortal children" (*A Rain of Rites* 9) and paralytic: "A man begs for alms, sitting under an old tree/holding his paralysed boy with damp, awkward arms" (*A Rain of Rites* 55). This sickness then seems fatal. In "A Dead Boy" the critical attitude of the poet towards an impersonal childhood gives way, confronted with the death of a boy, to tenderness":

> At times this is a paper boat
> memory survives to launch. (*A Rain of Rites* 25)

The poet's effort to seek a metaphorical release from the physically sick world of children takes a symbolic flight in the poem "Learning to Flow Free in/the Chariot Festival at Puri." This poem refers to the famous Car Festival of the Lord Jagannath at Puri. His references to Puri have mostly been associated with beggars and priests. But in this poem the poet has a positive outlook, as he stands bemused as one of the teeming crowds at the Main Road at Puri. The presentation of the festival occurs through the internalisation of the process and the image is one of lost children which is a common phenomenon in huge gatherings:

> My eyeballs hang uncertainly from the corners of my grace,
> like drifting, helpless children when they are lost.
> (*Waiting* 32)

This literal loss of a child signifies, and points to, the spiritual loss of man from the god's "grace." To make up this loss, the poet prefers to stand "beyond darkness" where "nothing else shall survive."

This spiritual craving to go beyond the limiting and mundane childhood takes on a mystic and agonizing dimension when the poet comes to his personal childhood. In the poems on his own childhood the tone is nostalgic and elegiac and the images are one of dark and pain:

> As a boy I learned to come in
> by the back door. Sad
> houses now, clean and leaning
> against one another, full of sleep.
>
> My old rag elephant is
> smothered with small screams. (*A Rain of Rites* 47)

With the "old rag elephant" smothered, the poet feels within him a playful childhood choked to death. About his childhood, Mahapatra says: "I told you I did not have a happy childhood.But I remember a few joyous moments of my childhood that are connected with rain." (Transcript: This author in conversation with Jayanta Mahapatra, 13 March 1987) What the poet says on himself and on his long past are manifested in the concluding couplet of "A Rain" where he equips rain with the game one played in childhood, or the game one played in the rain in childhood: both these worlds being coterminous:

> If it is a game one has made in childhood,
> there will be no word to hide in. (*A Rain of Rites* 11)

Here again is the rain. The "rain" as a childhood game is a refrain in this poem and the game, in other words, is the play of words in his poetry. Obviously, the mood expressed here is enchanting and it shows the escape-route from his childhood, but he cannot wrest himself free from his infatuation with words that come to him like rains, or to put it otherwise, his love for words is as old as his love for rain, way back to his childhood days. In a way, "word" and "rain" have co-existed in him from his very childhood, often one merging with the other. Finally, it could be said that whether he speaks of childhood in relation to his place or to his self, or to his locale, he inevitably turns to the water-related images.

In this most intensely formative period, Jayanta Mahapatra came to terms with the form and language of his poetry. His decisive departure from the abstract worlds of his first two volumes is easily perceptible in the poems in *A Rain of Rites* and *Waiting*. He is now more specific in his choice of themes and use of images and shows a sensitive awareness of his place. At the same time, there is a pervasive sense of introspection, a disposition to turn inward and view the people and the milieu around him through a subjective consciousness. *A Rain of Rites* and *Waiting* thus strive to achieve an interweaving of the objective and the subjective, a concern which is explored to greater perfection in the next volume, *The False Start*.

Novas of the Self: *The False Start*

T*he False Start* was published in 1980, though some of the poems included in it were published as far back as in 1974. The poems written in that period were also collected in *A Rain of Rites*. It is, therefore, the selection of poems for *The False Start* that lends the book its unity of vision. The poet's attempt to accomplish an inner world, true to his self, safe from the assaults of the external world, is an unsure journey through falseness to beyond, through body to spirit. In other words, it is a journey from external reality to internal reality, a journey in which he takes into account every little delicate, minute gesture in life, even in its falseness and pretension. *The False Start* is divided into three sections dealing with the apparently linear biological growth of life in terms of childhood, middle age and old age. Here the poet's attempt is to respond to life lyrically while at the same time trying to escape into his select world where he can realise the intrinsic truth of life.

Although *The False Start* contains the preoccupations, perspectives and styles of his earlier collections of poetry, here the emphasis is on the relationship of his inner self to the outside world and the outside world in relation to his inner self. The dominant images that help him explore this relationship are mostly water-related ones: rain, cloud, river, water, sea. The other dominating images are moon, ash, voices, heart, silence, blood and earth. The whole corpus of images employed in this volume can fairly be divided into two clusters: body and spirit, dream and reality, the marriage of which he sets out to achieve in order to reach his cherished state of "silence."

His tone throughout this volume is that of disbelief, uncertainty and quietude, projecting itself through innumerable questions which sometimes answer themselves. The thematic unity of the volume comes through dividing it into three sections. In part one are the poems on love, friendship, unfulfilled desires, absences, memories and secrets. In the middle part, the poet takes stock of the things in his middle age when along with accepting the world as it is given to him, he questions its purpose only to find no answer either in friendship or in the past or in his house/world. Even at this stage, life remains as elusive as before. The poems in the last section reveal a struggle against death and decay, imparting to his vision of life a solidity and a sense of tragic reconciliation. As the past here holds no promise "Of what concern to me is a vanished Empire?/Or the conquest of my ancestors' timeless ennui?" (*The False Start* 70) he tries to give meaning not to life but to death: "to give to death's livid flesh its possession and its time" (76). Through these divisions, dissecting the life he sees and lives, he gears his way into his tragic vision.

The poems here are more closed and less experimental than the early poems of *Close the Sky*, *Ten by Ten* and less ambiguous and less obscure than the poems of *A Rain of Rites*. Also the loose structure of *Waiting* is here overcome with the tight stanzaic patterns. The neat divisions of the poems and of the book itself gives a transparency to the themes. The poem, their line-lengths and verse paragraphs, are longer and marked by a meditative, melancholic mood which strengthens his tragic vision of life. Through all the poems in *The False Start,* Mahapatra tries to bring to the surface the inner recesses of mind and articulate an inexplicable feeling in seeking quietude within the self. In this there is the expression of anxieties which are of universal concern.

In *The False Start* an elusive "you" is all pervasive to whom Mahapatra goes on addressing consistently. The poem "Suppose" beginning with a stark, bare statement—"Suppose I write a love poem/to the world"—glides across the physical plane of reality into an interior landscape: "The present is not what I believe./A blind habit gropes/against the walls/barely touching your human face/ with my outstretched fear." (11) The poet gives this "you" a feminine quality. This mysterious "you" takes different hues and colours in different contexts. In "Something Spreading Itself" the "you" is the poet himself who is being addressed to

> There is always the feeling
> of something spreading itself inside the chest,
> like blood or sweat
> or the smell of iron on iron
> after the train has left,
> and it says:
> you are here alone, and you are happy. (38)

If his you's absence is nostalgic and endearing with "your absence/is a part of growing older" in "Another Evening," (19) its presence could be traced to the dark recess of mind associated with death in "A Certain Refrain":

> I look for your voice everywhere,
> but nothing is heard
> above the lapping of water. (79)

This poem, gathering momentum, paragraph after paragraph, finally forces the poet to admit its intrinsic strength, "your presence is only part of a plot/to destroy me" (80). Here the poet is not just commenting on the objects or concepts, or absorbing them, he is rather showing a gesture of intimacy, an inevitability in his belonging to them and his participation in their processes.

The objects and senses embodied in "you" grow up to be palpable presences. The speaker in the poet addressing "you" is not only a speaker, the hearer in "you" sometimes gets animated to take part in the process of making a quasi-dialogue poem. "You" also sometimes remains a vast mass of emotions and muted expressons as in "Like the deck your small look tilts and sways./What you would have wanted to show the world/is your stagnant silence that falls away/from the wind" (25) and in other contexts "you," instead of just being a silent hearer, an audience, acquires voice in the process of the interchangeability of the hearer and speaker in "you"; sometimes the ultimate difference between Mahapatra's "I" and "you" extinguishes, leaving behind ashes; ashes of the words uttered, ashes of the voice, even that of the silent one who thinks yet refrains from expressing.

His you's participation in dialogue-like poems is clearly audible, and in these cases "you" emerges as an image of the ultimate silence of all the voices: "You said: the heart stretches on for ever" (27), "you said: hold me just once, tonight, /before you leave this land. /But then these were words again/pieces of silence people merely tell/one another" (18). John Oliver Perry rightly dismembers 'you' from a particular name in "Poem for Angela Elston," "the misleading individualised name demonstrates how this 'you' is everywhere, and not anywhere: 'Did you sense falseness as you/ crossed the orderly seconds of time?'" (Prasad 57)

The acquiring of voice of his "you" or the search of his "I" (in fact his "you" and "I" merge together to create not only a poem but a personality) is significant, for the sought-after "voice" is a strong force that binds together his characteristics and needs. This "voice" is emblematic of his own self and this image of "voice" also merges with the elusive "you," the inexplicable perfection, the ultimate goal. The hunting after this "voice"/ "you" grows to be an obsession with him, bearing with it the strain of his steady movement from physical reality to a world within which has no definite contour:

> Is it all
> if I refuse to heed that voice,
> which hides the essence of my guilt
> behind the old moon as it crawls across
> the grotesque museums of remembered silence? (28)

An analysis of this "voice," embodiment of his "you" and "I" will bring into focus the other qualities that will explain his fond act of situating himself within his inner world. The search for a personal "voice" is the driving force of "A Day of Rain," the opening poem of *The False Start*, which inheres the overriding thematic and stylistic concerns of Jayanta Mahapatra. "A Day of Rain" beginning and ending with "rain" is truly a day, and poem, of rain. This first poem of the volume opening with "rain" marks the poet's persistent imagistic obsession with "rain" and at the same time, suggests a progression towards realising a vision of life's immense possibilities. In fact, the images of rain pervade the entire volume, *The False Start*: patter of rain, fleeting clouds, water and blue waves. The poems transcend the stolid physicality of rain into a lyrical evocation of a mood, of a state of mind, like "the water flowing in my veins" (62), or "the endless blue waves of your body," (54) or

> Like the fleeting clouds, you appear to chase
> an invisible soul in the sky. (74)

The rain that by its very nature seeps into the earth, also seeps through Mahapatra's poetry. He himself concedes: "I think I have always written one poem. That is rain" (Jayanta Mahapatra in conversation with this author). If in "Time Drawing In" there is a feeling of the immensity of rain as is evident in the poems of *A Rain of Rites*, in "Poem for Angela Elston" there is a tenderness in "rain":

> It was cold now, and stiffly silent;
> a silence that has been kept away
> too long from words. Here, I thought:
> this is how it is before the soft rain
> comes, before a certain memory
> streams into our eyes, or death. (18)

The kind of rain that occurs in "The Rain Falling" brings "relief" to the poet from the "frightened eyes" (32). "Rain," indeed, acts in Mahapatra's poetry on multiple levels of meaning and evocation. The images of rain may set the scene, create a particular mood, represent a situation or may help the poet to reflect on life and death, love and absence and silence.

"A Day of Rain" sparks in the poet a chain of reflections. The images that follow the first one are extensions of that feeling in various modes: the sound of step like that of rain on earth, a summer behind the hills like a haunting dream whose meaning escapes him and mimosa, seeking that "touch" which is for ever "lost." All these auditory and tactile images perceived in their bare physicality acquire a human dimension when the poet brings in abruptly the motif hidden so far: the initial exclamation turned at the end into a question:

> What thin air your face is now,
> now that I touch it? (13)

Soon after 'touching' the external world of tangible reality through such images of the mundane world as "the stupid code of cricket" and "the wind's low whine" he recedes into the layers of subjectivity. These layers of subjectivity are achieved in doubling the questions and complicating the apparently clear beginning:

> who knows
> what's dying underneath
> a growing blade of grass?
> Or what habit palpitates
> inside the dark pit of love:
> art, ceremony or voice that lies
> under my aimless hearing of the rain. (13)

Now the centrality of the poem makes itself felt. What is central to the poem is what is there "under aimless hearing of the rain." While life goes on as usual in this world, another world which "is dying underneath a blade of grass,"—which is deep within one's self—seems to get submerged. The poet shows concern for that world which is within him and which, for him, is real.

The scope of the poem, "A Day of Rain," is further widened with its double-question which leaves it tentative, open-ended. The second question in the above quote asks for the knowledge of what he expects from his aimless hearing of the rain: "art, ceremony or voice." Ceremony being already explored in *Waiting* and *A Rain of Rites* and art almost always woven into his act of writing, it is the "voice" that motivates and conditions his aimless hearing of the rain. Thus, the "rain" ultimately becomes a vehicle of search for "voice": voice of his own, a voice of humility revealed through questions addressed to the self. "A Day of Rain" ending with an assertion but with a question is significant. It determines the tone of *The*

False Start. The questions through which he tries to articulate his voice takes him round every nook and corner of his body, heart and mind to reach his pure, lyrical being.

His hearing to and search for "voice" are symbolic acts. In them lies his true being. That he cannot but listen to this "voice"—listening to the rain shifts to listening to the voice, or rather they become coterminous—is evident in "The Secret":

Is it all
if I refuse to heed that voice,
which hides the essence of my guilt
behind the old moon? (28)

This very questioning leaves the poem open. The answer to it can be both affirmative and negative. Towards the end of this poem the poet himself seems to find an answer to his own question, as it rises above him, goes up into the sky, and from there he hears, "the cracked voice/of secret's thunder." The voice of his secret, at the beginning of the poem, which, he was afraid, might reveal the things he wanted to hide becomes the secret itself at the end of the poem. The image of this unknown secret of the poet is well embodied in one strikingly original image of a "morning" which is "like a woman who hadn't done many things." This "voice" he is after is an inward feeling which he tries to define in a poem titled "The Gradient of Dreams"

Nests. And a net thrown
neat around my neck.
It is night the concealed
voices are looking for.

Words are working out
against the napes of cries.
A withe of moment draws
me to an unknown throat.

In the dark a white, a

> grief of lost. What is grace,
> how dead, in this wanting
> to be enough to reach across. (21)

The "Nests" with which the poem begins is analogous with his search suggested by the "sudden need for life" as he states in "The Retreat." "Nests," which are his poems, are also symbolic of shelter for the poet, the world of his inner being where he likes to nestle. The apparent obscurity in the next image of "net thrown/ neat around my neck" is answered subsequently in "words are working out/against the napes of cries." If the neck is something physical, a limb of his body, "the napes of cries" are his urges to write poetry, something non-physical. He sets one against another to create an effect where boundaries of these warring worlds meet. The voices seek to tàke concrete shape: "It is night the concealed voices are looking for." The voices are looking for that dark dwelling place in the poet's mind where it can take shape and flourish. Indeed, he would like to express this in another context: "Like some shape beside my body; a presence, flourishing." (53)

As the net around the neck in the first stanza becomes words against the napes of cries in the second stanza, the voice looking for night becomes the poet, while another voice is drawn "to an unknown throat." And thus in voices seeking "the throat" ("Nests") and the poet seeking a voice there is a complementarity similar to the complementarities between his speaker and the hearer, the "I" and "you." Also the territories of his physical, mental and dream worlds become interfused. They change, and, in fact, are exchanged. In one intense moment in "The Rain Falling," he is convinced that "words can be taken off/and replaced by others, similar and true." The same strong conviction is felt, though in his humble manner of self-questioning, in "Tonight I Hear the Water Flowing in My Veins":

> Was I merely a drunken man who needed
> his morals like intoxications to bring
> the real and imagined worlds together? (62-63)

or in "Time Drawing In" where he strives "until reality and dream become one" (35). In the final stanza of "The Gradient of Dreams" he suggests this need of weaving the world of dream and reality together, and the need "to reach across" it, even across the sheltering, complacent "Nests" of his already achieved world of poetry.

The voices he looks for usually leap from within. Even "the wet pigeons' voices on the naked ledge" (31) or "the voices of leaves and water/curl like a tongue" (80) have about them the secret strength of the other world rather than the "voices of the living" and of the mundane world to which the poet turns his back:

> Still I cannot grasp what this distance is,
> dripping with the blood
> of the perfumed voices of living (35)

These voices are as varied and as multidimensional as

> my eyes have climbed long the shapes of trees
> to find only breathless voices trapped inside (17)

> voices echo from the damp vein walls (15)

> My voice crouched in the shadow of spilt blood
> hangs on a branch like a droplet of water
> and quivers only to become
> secret star, slow flower, again (36)

> The shaped flower-beds expose a cry that bears no voice
> (78)

He pits these voices of his own and those of the others against "silence." About silence, he says, "What appears to disturb me is the triumph of silence in the mind; and if these poems are inventions they are also longings amid the flow of voices toward a need that I feel is defensive" (*Ten Twentieth Century Indian Poets* 59). The silence comes out of all these voices that emanate from memory, hurt, love and contemplation of death. When his eyes climb, as it is evidenced in "The Gift of Night," the shapes of trees, they find the voices silenced, trapped inside. The "breathless voices" have double inscription. Climbing the trees they have become exhausted and breathless. The breathless voices could also denote lifelessness; voices without breath. His search for voice thus ends up in silence which he takes finally as "the gift of night." He is "surrounded by stars' vast silence," "the sky's emptiness" while he is beset with an urgency to find a "voice." (17) All these earthly silences soon drift into his body and mind, to clear the "mist of metal butterflies" (74), to alleviate "hurt" and "pain" inside, as when we "sit hurt under the trees" (50) or when the silence grows "easily into the pain of our bodies" (23).

This silence inside bodies grows into images, embodying the past of his own or of his native land, as in "The Abandoned British Cemetery at Balasore, India," and nostalgia, "What must come, speaking of impossible things, is an indulgence" (55). The poem, "The Day After My Friends Became Godly and Great," filled with emptiness, hurt, inconsequence and sullenness—"What use is history if it gives sanction to certain things"—is worked out in such telling images as "clock ticks wildly against the widening dawn," "trunk full of old papers and things," "the mirror" that robs him of "reflection" and "worn-out world on fire." The summing-up line that typifies Jayanta Mahapatra is "It is memory alone that makes one a silent part" for it is the silence that crowds inside him and out of this past he cannot "make an instrument of his glory" (44). If at all he ever tries to make an attempt at that "its call drives (him)/ over the boundary (he has) built in (his) flesh" (44).

The silence inside grows stronger as it moves deeper. Even the past in "The Rising" glides inside and over "the magic slopes and hamlets of the mind" (44). This silence arises out of the thought of past and death, out of his attempt to measure them to feel their presence deep inside him which is almost palpable like blood: "the sunsets floating darkly inside our breaths/describe without irony the feeling of death" (75). The physicality, the outer world along with its objects, gets transposed into the inner silence. This is the kind of reality with the poet. It is the process of internalisation which is the reality of the creative act. In the poem "The Accusation" (45) "that distant field, the blur of green" gets closer as his "face lies heavy on the grass." This world he comes across has "firmly used its rules upon" him. The analogy of the earth and his body gets progressively blurred until in the last but one stanza the parallel lines of body and earth reach towards a point "at the edge of the field where the old heavy feeling/hangs in the air" and finally in the last stanza, 'that distant field' has turned out to be "that inner field." This retreat of the poet into his self is succinctly articulated in the poem "The Retreat." It begins with apparent statements that gradually accumulate mountainous weight upon itself through slow bringing in of extending images:

> It is always the war. The clash of symbols
> that drifts into the body. (60)

A powerful image of the body for Jayanta Mahapatra is the house which, again, stands for the place within where he feels he belongs properly. He declares timidly in "The House": "perhaps here is your real life". (58) For a poem dealing with the house, to begin with the "child's first drawing with the door" is pertinent for it is the house where is the beginning of all beginnings. In the house, as in body, as in heart and mind, or in writing, "it is always the war." "Every house is the same" despite the presence in it of the warring elements yet "house is not a plaything," the poet realises, or rather admonishes. Rather, "innocence" of a "child," "the first days, the believing," "serious attention," "order," "dream," "false look of tranquillity," all these qualities taken together, make a house a house:

> But bring in a lie when you are sure
> no one is watching, some dishonesty or a scheme of
>   adultery;
> such things will tie the house to black secrets
> making you grow in strength. (58)

A house is gravid with meaning, importance, vigour if only it has grace and sympathy about it: "How would you measure death/but by the house that comes to deny sympathy?" This image of house illustrates his inner world, lends it reality yet at the same time imparts to it a dream-like halo; that is the quality that Jayanta Mahapatra always tries to achieve in his poetry in describing a certain object or concept.

The most persistent images that signify the poet's realisation of the eternal reality through its internalisation are the water-related ones: "water," "sea," "river," "cloud," "boat." Like "rain," water is a recurrent image in Mahapatra's poetry. The purport of the image of water is well carried in "Tonight I Hear Water Flowing in My Veins." His hearing "the water" instead of the blood in his veins is significant. By substituting water for blood he has changed the perspective of the poem. Once more the emphasis is on passivity and meekness as suggested by the image of water. He is not strong enough to withstand the outer world:

> each time I found the empty seat beside me
> dripping with worms and excrement; each time
> the demands of a war, a flood, a murder or rape
> startled me with the salt taste of my blood. (62)

His withdrawal into his cocooned world marks the culmination in the last line, "I am not fulfilled as I think of the long lines of water behind." (63)

In "Woman in Love" the poet draws an analogy between earth and woman. She carries inside her "a river of sunlight" while "water sobs through the tangled rocks of relationship." (24) Again the poet invests with her body "the endless blue waves" and sets on those blue waves "a touch, a boat." The woman's body acquires a cosmic dimension wherein the physicality of the sea, rock and boat is dissolved. As in "Woman in Love," in the poem "A Sailboat of Occasions" woman's body is compared with water-related images: "like the deck your small look tilts and sways." The boat here carries nothing anywhere, and here "the noises spin, like gull cries, like the love of other men." (25) Like the other men, the poet has also staked his lot in it: "in it I have staked those my precious years" (54). The kind of atmosphere created in "A Sailboat of Occasions" with "sea," "water," "boat," "deck," "wind," "sails," "gull cries" and, of course "savage solitude" recurs with cumulative emphasis in "A Kind of Happiness" with those and other associated images like "creek," "reeds," "keel" and "moss." Here again there is the same feeling of being adrift—"The boat I've laid my mind on/is adrift"—the same feeling of unfulfillment and uncertainty, "I fear it may never reach the promise of the sea." (54) It precisely draws the contour of the kind of happiness he is after. It comes from something unknown, from an aimlessness, be it hearing of rain or from

> a swift tenderness that makes one wander aimless
> among the ruins of an enchanted country (16)

or from "a late afternoon" that itself is "an aimless look:"

> like moonlight,
> or of a marble iceberg, drifting in an unknown sea. (78)

All these images and suggestions make one point clear: his search for happiness has always been elusive except that it does occasionally well up in one's heart. Here in this poem "A Kind of Happiness" the poet considers the pros and cons of living in his elect world:

> barely escaping happiness I thought I knew of it,
> but would I recognise it if it really came?
> What use would it be if I'd tie the boat to a tree
> and lie down in the heart of its demand? (54)

After three such consecutive questions comes his prime concern richly suggested in: "What would tell me at last where I belong?" (54) The most probable answer to it is to fall back on "the heart of demand." It is his heart where he, by choice, belongs; it is his real dwelling place of consciousness, where lies his voice and what lends him his voice. In that secret love of his heart the speaker and the hearer in his poetry meet. It is to that place that his incessant addresses are directed. His drive inward is ever dictated by the wish of his heart.

Jayanta Mahapatra is, indeed, a heart. Through the verbal space he tries to probe into his own dark heart, to explore its secret dimensions. From his speaker's voice he has the assurance of an indefinite expanse of his heart: "you said: the heart stretches on for ever" (17). Dwelling in his heart he tries to make up "the loss of innocence" (15) "to understand the star's vast silence" (17) and from there to emerge as a renewed being: "my heart's beating makes of me a survivor" (51). Thus, his "heart makes its home" (34) in the inner world he has chosen to live in, where there are "silence and pressure only, /multiplying, adding, subtracting" (41). The joys and sufferings to which his heart has stood as a witness, or through which it has undergone, are a rich tributary to the mainstream of his poetry.

One of the most telling images of the heart is "moon" which frequently occurs in *The False Start*, and it is nowhere better illustrated than in "The Moon Moments" (50). Giving a brief picture of the sky and stars and the women outside with "clouds passing across their eyes" he gets the slow feel of "always there is a moon that is taking me somewhere." Then suddenly comes the questioning, the inverted leap: "Why does one room invariably lead into other rooms?" This question could simply be re-read as why one poem leads to another and why one image leads to another? In the case of Jayanta Mahapatra, it "invariably" occurs because he always tries to privatise the outer world, "the visions of childhood . . . the socialism and the love," to heed the voice within, to respond to the moon/heart that is always taking him somewhere. And this process of privatisation of the outer world happens to him through questions, especially more with self-questionings. Here in this poem "The Moon Moments" he asks explicitly:

"How can I stop the life I lead within myself? (50) The deeper he moves inside, the sharper becomes his self-questioning. "The Moon Moments" like "The Accusation," "A Kind of Happiness," "The Day After My Friends Became Godly and Great" ends with a double-question:

> How can I stop the life I lead within myself—
> The startled, pleading question in my hands lying in my lap

> while the gods go by, triumphant, in the sacked city at
> midnight? (50)

This serves the purpose. The poet ends up within, with self-analysis. The questions become the image of his attempt at creating a self-sufficient as well as a self-critical world. He probes into his heart time and again. But all through, there is a certain sense of a tentativeness. Even when he asks, trying to affirm his belief, "yet don't I know it is better to leave the boat alone?" he does not give a finality to the answer for immediately he questions "what would tell me at last where I belong?" This question of where he belongs to finally haunts him because in his heart a great cosmic upheaval and a stillness are played upon in the final answer: "the cracking keel, the bold green moss." And he does not know which is his heart, which is the universe. And the self-questions he leaves in the parentheses are most enigmatic as they do disarray all he wants to believe in himself, in the very inner world he craves for:

> I know how to defend myself
> (yet really can I when the moment comes?") (48)

The spirit of questionings or self-questionings transports him to a lyrical world, towards a world of resignation where he won't feel like defending himself and his activity, where he would feel at home.

All through *The False Start,* there is a pervasive sense of inwardness, a withdrawal into "the sad shut tufts of mimosa." This leads to the pensive and self-retrospective mood in the poems of *The False Start*. Considering Jayanta Mahapatra's chronological development as a poet of the locale, *The False Start* may be taken as an interregnum. In *A Rain of Rites* and *Waiting* Mahapatra's concern was mainly with the locale. In *The False Start*, the locale is transformed into metaphoric and symbolic dimensions that reveal an inward quest. This quest of the inner self, through perception of the physicality of the objects, is further reinforced in *Relationship* in which two worlds strive towards a unified vision embodied in the body and spirit of his beloved land, Orissa.

The Tapestry of Stones: *Relationship*

Nothing that is whole
speaks of the past. Or lives.
Or can form into a word. (*A Rain of Rites* 36)

The closing lines of Jayanta Mahapatra's poem "The Ruins" open up vistas into his *Relationship. Relationship*, being a long poem after six volumes of short lyrics presents the whole of his experience. In *Relationship* Mahapatra's earlier strategies such as contrasts, opposites, obscurities, private symbols fall into place. His concerns with the past, with the locale of Cuttack and Konarka were in a great detail articulated in the poems of *A Rain of Rites* and *Waiting*. Prior to *Relationship,* he had also attempted to go beyond the fragmentary in such poems as "Twenty Fifth Anniversary of a Republic" in *A Father's Hours* and "Measuring Death" in *The False Start*. There was already the suggestion of the need to achieve a total integration of experience: "There is somewhere a great poem I have to write" (*A Father's Hours* 21). In spite of their concern with integration of fragments, these two poems were rather like collages: they lacked the sublimity and compelling unity that make a long poem. In *Relationship*, there is a propelling force, as themes evolve section after section and the conceived unity is achieved through repeated use of particular images and motifs. Mahapatra's *Relationship* is in the tradition of the works of Whitman, Pound, Williams, Eliot, Stevens and, above all, Neruda. Like them, Mahapatra has tried to create a wholeness out of the fragmented world and to offer a world view of his own.

Mahapatra's *Relationship* has a striking resemblance with

Neruda's *The Heights of Macchu Picchu.* Both the poems are divided into twelve sections and are centred round a monumental historical ruin: "tall city of stepped stones" of Macchu Picchu (*The Heights of Macchu Picchu* 25) and "a flight of steps" of Konarka (*Relationship* 29). The irresistible obsession of both these poets is with death, and regeneration. The ruins form the axes in both the poems upon which the perceived worlds revolve, and evolve. The mythic motif of journey and pilgrimage in both the poems binds together all other myths, motifs and images related to Latin American and Orissan past. These two poems deal with the identical aspects of nature, the "ruins," "stone" and "rain." In *Macchu Picchu* "there remained a precision unfurled/on the high places of human dawn, /the tallest crucible that ever held our silence, /a life of stone after so many lives" (30-31) and in *Relationship*, Konarka "is marooned on the stone, on the dark chariot of the sun/whose fevered granite wheels claw desperately/ at the strangled earth in our lives" (22). These two passages amply demonstrate the spiritual kinship Mahapatra has with Neruda in syntax, tone, diction and the way of comprehending reality.

Relationship is a long poem that shares some of the traditional characteristics of the epic such as sublime manner of speech, announcement of the theme at the beginning, invocation of the muse, division of the book into twelve parts. But the essential feature of *Relationship* is the relationship of self to the quality of life and time rather than a linear narration of a legendary event of historical importance. In the process of exploration of the self vis-a-vis the land and its culture, the poem moves through the fuse-like gathering of images through a dream-like pilgrimage into the past that unburdens guilt, both racial and personal. This poem as Emily Grosholz says "recounts a journey into the source of darkness or guilt, a personal burden and an historical blood guilt" (*The Hudson Review* 330).

The relationship of the poet's self with reality and with the land forms the matrix of *Relationship*. The epigraph of *Relationship,* derived from Walt Whitman's *Song of Myself*, suggests these two basic concerns of Mahapatra. Humble as the poet is, nurtured in the ancient Indian sensibility, he does not proclaim anywhere in

Relationship that "I am large, /I contain multitudes" though the import of the statement is felt all through the work. Rather the second statement of Whitman, "I exist as I am, that is enough," seems to support Mahapatra's stance of the centrality of the self in the creative process of interpreting reality and myth.

Like the preceding volume *The False Start*, *Relationship* opens with the phrase "once again" but this taking-off is into the "earth," in consonance with his proclivity to turn into his inner self. Here the earth is in the literal sense his locale, Orissa. This fondness for the native place is in the tradition of Poe's and Whitman's America, Hardy's Wessex and Valery's "Cimetiere Marin." In *Relationship*, the setting becomes physically concrete and metaphorically crucial.

In the opening stanza of *Relationship,* the poet asks the reader to concentrate on this land, its variegated forms of existence in order to comprehend in its wholeness, to have an integrated experience of it in space and time. The images that describe Orissa, the land of "forbidding myth," are: "the phallus of the enormous stone," "a vulture's shadow" "caress(ing) the strong and silent deodars in the valley," "the tensed muscles of rock yield(ing)" to the river Mahanadi, "slow steps of stone," "old men curling for warmth/in the winter sun" and the "young ochre-clad prophets" (9). These images gradually weave into a symbolic pattern that represents Orissa in all the complexities which is dotted with innumerable temples, including a large number of Shaivite shrines centring round the worship of the "phallus" (9). One has to turn repeatedly to this land at a time when the shadow of death—suggested by the images of deodars, vulture, valley is as much a reality as beauty and tenderness are, like the presence of "the time of the butterfly" "inside the fierce body of the forest bear" (9). This "tensed muscles of rock," in coexistence with the landscape ("the virtuous water of the hidden springs of the Mahanadi") and its mystery ("secret rights that make up destiny)." (9)

The poet seeks to "clasp the slow slopes of stone again." The stone of the land, like the land itself, embodies another paradox. It reflects the "quiet faces of sorrow" as well as the "silent fulfillment of tomorrow." The association of sadness with the stones gets explained in the second verse paragraph where he describes the life of artisans of the sun temple of Konarka who left their families for twelve years to build this massive structure. The bright future he envisions in the young prophets has an oblique reference to the legendary Dharama, the son of the chief artisan, who put the crowning slab into place on the temple and, in order to save the name and honour of twelve hundred artisans who had already failed to do so, sacrificed his life "to the night in humble brotherhood." (Dharama becomes, for the poet, a symbol of the dream of an emerging generation imbued with the spirit of sacrifice and fraternity).

The poet goes on to draw the contours of his physical land. Its geography spans "from Chilika to Chandipur" (10), its history evinced in the "ruthless emperor" Ashoka who massacred lakhs of Oriyas at the feet of the Dhauli hills and, out of remorse embraced Buddhism and "carved peaceful edicts on blood-red rock," (9) as well as in the maritime traders who were the carriers of Oriya culture to the Far East. All these aspects of Orissa constitute an environment in which he tries to set his feet firmly so as to become the poet of the mother-earth, Orissa.

In the course of limning the landscape he becomes one with it, and with its people. By beginning the second verse paragraph of the first section with "We have come," the poet becomes the persona of those "twelve hundred artisans" (9). The poet's passion, as the passion of those artisans realised in the intricate artistry in stones, flowers through long, winding lyrical sentences of *Relationship*. The ancient wisdom of the land symbolised in the image of "aerial roots of a centuries-old banyan tree" has taught us to "take our lives seriously" (9). Though he nowhere propounds a systematic philosophy of life, the vision is often apparent as when he points to the paradoxical nature of existence "inside our watery skulls" (9). "Water" is one facet of enduring quality and eternity. The other one is "stone" into which the poet glides: "my existence lies in the stones" (10). The poet's hearing "the old voices drift into silence/and yet my existence lies in the stones" speaks of his two-fold existence, in both space and time. At one point of time he traverses "infinite distances" (10) from the coast of Chandipur to the dense forest region of Western Orissa and to the woods. This expansion of the poet's self corroborates Whitman's claim endorsed by the poet "I am large, I contain multitudes." But he is uncertain as to whether this realisation would help him envision the vast mystery of the earth:

> I continue walking back and forth
> not knowing whether the earth
> would let me find finally its mouth. (10)

The "mouth" of the earth perhaps alludes to the child Krishna's mouth which had revealed the universe in all its vastness and glory.

Section I ends with the poets's uncertainty at unraveling the mysteries of the "forbidding myth" that his earth is. He "wonders whether he can tell the tale, whether he is worthy of the poem" (Corseri 20). This indeterminate tone determines the entire work.

The second movement of the poem turns personal and familial. If the first section is an attempt to "clasp the slow slopes of stone again," to unearth the mysteries of the land, the second section tries to understand the "wounded pools of our living," our present life which is full of "hurt and loneliness" (11). The slow beginning and development of private memory soon grows out to be the racial memory of the past. Even when the memory acquires the nature of the public, he does not disown his personal burden. When he says "my blood becomes to share his (father's) curse," (12) the curse is racial as much as personal. So also is the case with his "I" in *Relationship*. As the poem develops section after section, his "I" turns out to be more of a racial psyche. Like the famous Oriya poets of the late nineteenth or early twentieth century, such as Bhima Bhoi and Gopabandhu Das, he chooses to carry the burden of the suffering of the world on his own shoulders:

> and the suffering of the world returns
> like winter's persistent asthma
> year after year. (12)

Likewise, "the swords of forgotten kings/rust slowly in the museum of our guilt" (11). Here, the "guilt" referred to is our forgetting of the past and the valour that characterised the fifteenth century kings of Orissa who later almost gave up war by surrendering themselves unconditionally to God under the magic spell of Chaitanya. Thus, section II becomes the struggle of memory against forgetting: forgetting of the smooth idyllic creative past which is evoked in such images as of "old village's pelt, glistening with rain," "stillness of my gentle daughter's skin" and "the desire/oozing out of the hewn stones of Konarka" (12). This spectrum of the past is also cited in section I: "cruelties of ruthless emperors," "groans and cries," "gunsmoke and smouldering flesh" and "the tactic and the strategy" (9).

The images that he has for memory are of road, voices, bewilderment and rats: "memory takes a road vague with the distance/of loneliness and hurt," "the man with many memories/doesn't know what to do with them," "my memories are just voices/of another world, /pretending from the throat" (11) and "my memories are rats scampering in the dark." (12) All these facets of memories characterised by emptiness, pretension and unease are mirrors of the present as well as its countermeasures. Memory releases him from the tension that he undergoes while trying to juxtapose past and present to find a way out "of wounded pools of our living." Even his watching bewilderedly, like "a member of some magician's audience," his "mother's" "grave" (11) or aping his father's way of living does not serve any purpose. Still then his "mother's grave," "childhood" and "aging father" are established as leit-motifs of the poem and grow in strength through repetition and re-structuring.

Section II ending with "the tranquil hills in the rain" (12) and section III beginning with the declaration "here is the tapestry of the year's first rain" (13) show the interlocking of the sections in the poem. "Rain" being a recurring image, the other one is "stone." In section III, each of these two images occur thrice. He wonders "how the age-old proud stones/lost their strength and fell," (13) imagines "a cloud drops its rain/onto the great silence over the stone of fire" and cherishes to go beneath "the dark crevices of stone" (14). Likewise he also "yearns for rain" (14). Thus, his yearning to go beneath the stone and his yearning for rain itself are an attempt to touch the earth, the land and the sky, to move into the past and the future, all at the same time while the present is populated by "gigolos and pimps and cocksuckers/(who) jabber excitedly in a language of monstrous flowers" (13) and in this kind of the present his yearning for rain "catch (es) only the jagged lightning of this new cult/and its messianic gain." But this much is not the total turbulence for him. Added to this turbulent time of his society is his disturbing personal relationship with his friends who exhibit selfishness, "doubt," "envy," degradation and anxiety. These characteristics of friendship he comes across in his life also get mention in section IX and X. In section IX his friends know only "how to keep walking towards themselves" (24) and in section X his "friends/ have become friends of others/writing poems, abject and anxious" (28). He had also dealt with this subtle theme earlier in such poems as "The Whorehouse in a Calcutta Street," "A Rain of Rites" or in "The Day After My Friends Became Godly and Great" in *The False Start*. His concern for his friends, his incomprehension of their distancing of themselves from him, land him in a "painful exile." This is an echo of what he had said in section II: "wounded pools of our living."

The relationship with the past that always haunts him, his uneasy relationship with his time and people leave him indecisive as to what he should do to move out of the impasse he is in. He has already pitted memory against forgetting to revive the past; now to return from the "painful exile" (13) he seeks succour through remembering his parents.

His relationship with the mother-figure is unambiguous: "Mother's grave/defends my dream" (14). He recounts all the happy moments in the past associated with his mother—how he clung to his mother's "dry and drooping breasts," how he read "epics in the lamp light" to his elders (13).Those "enchanted" days of childhood are now irretrievably lost. Further, all that the poet speaks of his father reflect genuine care and concern of every father for his child. This gets an apposite suggestion in the image of the growing moon:

> These nights of the growing moon
> fill us with the feeling of good:
> that is exactly what you wished for us,
> didn't you, Father? (13)

The father not wanting his son to write poems on and of violence is only the secret wish of the poet. His withdrawal into the self, "shut(ting) out the wind, "his renewed faith in the cycle of birth and death carried in the image of "age-old grass" and beyond "its withering," reveal his concern with those aspects of life that make it eternal and enduring, not with "those words which spit blood and vomit/and speak of malice" (14). He puts what he himself would have liked to say in his father's mouth: "Now you don't even want me to write my poem/of those words which spit blood." (14)

By the fourth movement, the poet establishes his father as a major force. In section IV he concedes to his father's wish, voiced in the previous section, not to write "words that spit blood and vomit." Here the poet yearns for the "peace" of his father. It is this search for peace that was "the burden" of his father and his father's father which, in turn, becomes the poet's "theme-song of (his) life" (15).

Indeed, he is a child of the earth and the sea, sun and wind, of the tradition in which he is brought up. All of these taken together have richly shaped his Oriya sensibility. The various aspects of Orissa, its flora and fauna, its enchanting landscape vividly summed up in the image of "the indigo waters of the tropics" and "the eternal half light of rain" which exist amid the squalor, poverty and the drudgeries of daily life, its customs and festivals which have enriched his sensibility, find sensuous and detailed expression in an apostrophe, sweetly addressed as "my ancient love of a hundred names."

> And now, you, my ancient love of a hundred names,
> of rains and endless skies and thought,
> of wind-beaten evenings of owl-calls and of rice-harvests
>   in December,
> my love of gold nose-rings and laughing earrings,
> of towering ruins of stone panting in the dark,
> of loyal lions guarding the diamond navels of shrines,
> of amber breasts and secret armpits,
> of cries and the soft steel of thighs,
> and of the old emptiness of my own destiny (15-16)

How else could one have expressed his love better and raised decoratively "the altar" of one's "origins" (16); how else could one have imparted transcendental beauty to one's own words, or how else could one have, speaking of the object/concept of his love, identified one's own sorrow with one's land? It is indeed significant that the poet's own destiny with its "emptiness" gets identified with the "towering ruins of stone panting in the dark." The exterior world and the interior world dissolve into an intense perception of being alive:

> I know I can never come alive
> if I refuse to consecrate at the altar of my origins
> where the hollow horn blows every morning
> and its suburban sound picks its way
> through the tangled moonlight of your lazy sleep. (16)

This awareness of the poet of his need to go back to his origins is a compelling force that drives his poetry inward. This act of consecration will enable the poet to rise "like a flame which sings on the altars of the dead." This awareness also includes his fear of his own aging in which there is not much chance left for his creative efforts to realise his cherished vision of comprehending his existential reality in its totality. As soon as he realises the need to consecrate his self at the altar of his origins, he resolves to "finish (his) prayer" (16). His prayer is directed at drawing "his body out of a thousand years" and to retrieve "the earth's lost amplitudes" (16), a two-fold declaration which has already been stated in fragments in the short lyrics of his previous volumes.

With the poet's overcoming his father's "burden of peace," and his realisation that his relationship with his land is best achieved through a filial awareness in terms of "father"/ "mother," he now enters into the world of "sleep" and "dream." The motif of "sleep" dominates sections IV, V and VI. The "sleep" in section IV turns out not to be a rewarding one because it "will not reveal the truth of that secret miracle/of the darkness," (15) whereas the kind of sleep described in section V would let him see "the miracle of living." (17) The failure of sleep in section IV in finding the path for the poet to realise his vision is attributed to its lack of "dream" and "colour," while the "sleep" of section V is more fulfilling. Here in "the sleep-habit of the golden deer" (17) he hopes to fare forward in his journey towards attaining a vision. The mythical golden deer that tempted Sri Rama into a world of illusion now tempts the poet to diffuse himself into worlds of different hues. The "sleep-habit" of the golden deer is one of the private symbols of the poet. Here in the "sleep-habit" of the poet's "golden deer" is the tangled skein of associations of the mysterious qualities of life. Through this sleep habit, the poet would be able to explain his heart's vast expanse, like a "forest," the miracle of living, "the lies and betrayals" of one's own people, the power associated with Siva, "the enchanted regions of boyhood and dignity" (17), the suppleness and fecundity of life as carved on the walls of Konarka. The motif of sleep as formulated in the final stanzas of section V is "the largest circle" of the poet's vision that encompasses the poet's imagined world of the "frightened virgins" and "gold quarries" as well as the real one: "scarlet in the mind" and "heart's skies" (10). When he begins with "This sleep is a song" (18) he acknowledges the driving force of his creative urge. This sleep spans in space and time in an infinite scale. It is a "cage" which contains the unravelled mystery and history of his land, "a hiding-place" (18). This sleep is stretchable like time "in the mind", not in the body. This "sleep" is "coarse," it has also "grace" in it. This sleep is also

> a blind eye that creates the special vision
> of our poignant significance. (18)

The image of "a blind eye" of sleep could be read as the sixth sense. Sleep provides the poet with a sixth sense. The closing of the eye to visualise what the naked eye cannot see gives the poet an insight into the poignant significance of his land and life. The motif of sleep in section VI moves a stage further in his continuing quest for vision: "how shall room be made for sleep?" (19) His obsession with "room" recalls his groping for form and vision in the first volume *Close the Sky, Ten by Ten*. As a step further in the extended meaning of sleep, it becomes another house of accommodation for his poetry which will not only contain the themes declared in the beginning but also carry them forward with "the lioness's roar", "the endless ritual/ of the black kites" (19) silenced in the clouds, so that what is seen and what is hidden shall merge into a surreal shape which he strives to achieve.

His next move is his contemplation in the dimensions of time and his search for strength in stone. He hopes to withstand the onslaught of time through endurance and "waiting" for a "miracle" that would redeem him from his mire of *samsara*. The mysterious and ominous presence of time is worked out in the images of the clock's hand in "a cobra's tongue," "an unknown bird/ brushing past with a flap of wings" and "the unseen wind"/"in the bleak cremation ground." The poet's struggle against the immediate surroundings in the beginning of section VI is thus at the end, directed towards the ravages of time. Still then the poet's streak of optimism lies in his faint assertion "no, there is room enough for cries and whispers, . . . for another kindredship of spirit."

In section VII the poet deliberates on the paradoxical nature of existence, the duality of body and spirit and his relationship with the past. The subtle delineation of philosophy through folklore, physicality of existence, spirit of the Buddha and "the elephant of the six blind men" (20) comes through forcefully, with intensity. Here are also the images of sleep and rain but with different shades of implications. For example, as against the "cutting rain" of section VI, here is the soothing "green rain of centuries" (21).

This section begins with the poet's awareness of the body. The body is only a witness-box where the soul stands to defend and justify life:

> It is he who is standing there,
> alone by himself in the witness-box
> of shackled pink muscle (20)

The image of "shackled pink muscle" gives the impression of our imprisonment in the body of the indispensability of physical life. The physicality of body leads to the poet's perception of the physical dimension of time manifested in "the weight of shadows of sick relics," "venison," "the seated Buddha" and "the subtle bird of night"

(20). He is pulled by "the five shadows" (20) which most probably are the five physical senses. By bringing in the folk tale of "the elephant of six blind men" in which each of them touching different limbs of the elephant give their own perceptions of the animal, the poet seems to suggest that it is the individual perception of the world that determines for oneself what the world is like. The folk tale goes like this: six blind men asked to examine an elephant, give their individual impression of it, one by one, touching its different limbs. One touches its trunk and says it is like a rope, the second touches its ear and says it is like a winnowing object, the third touches its legs and says it is like a pillar and so on. Unlike "a blind eye", which is the image of sleep in section V that "creates a special vision," the blindness of these six people has only a narrow perception of things and is suggestive of prejudiced views. This prejudiced view of the world in man is put forth in terms of

> the rules of our song
> that can only move back and forth
> like a galvanometer needle
> between the zero and the hundred of gloom. (20)

In order to overcome the limited vision of the frog-in-the-well, the poet suggests one should move to the abyss of suffering to sense "emptiness" in life, and then only can one come out of it:

> for only by conquering them
> can one conquer the rest of the road. (20)

The poet's immediate shift from this present gnawing emptiness to the heroic past is in keeping with the norm the poet has established in *Relationship*. Pitted against the past of a chivalrous race, he is now left with a sense of emptiness, with "the shadows of (his) world" "waving their pretentious hands" to "the wooden soldiers marching" in "thick insomnia" (20). These soldiers marching in accompaniment "to the beat of drums/heralding the periodic invasions of the enemy/into the vanquished city" is an addition in the 1982 edition of *Relationship*, published by the Chandrabhaga Society, Cuttack. This addition in the text to the already existing references to the foreign invasions on his land such as Ashoka's Kalinga War and the loss of the military and maritime glory of ancient Orissa reaffirm the poet's obsession with the defeat that his race met with.

Reviewing *Relationship*, M.L. Raina says, "Konarka to an Oriya poet symbolises the peculiar mythical ambience with which he must come to terms in order to be able to write." In Notes to *Relationship* the poet describes the temple as a "monumental chariot" and "the figures in (its) innumerable niches and panels, many of them erotic, show the moods and phases of human life compellingly. Its gods and goddesses, the women with their entwining serpentine bodies, the elaborate lattice work—all these represent the Orissan craftsman's search for the beatific vision in the realm of art and aesthetics." (32) As the ancient Oriya craftsmen sought their aesthetic fulfilment through sculpture, Jayanta Mahapatra seeks poetic fulfilment by evoking the figures and events depicted on the walls of the Konarka temple. His process of identification with the object of his contemplation reaches its culmination in this section:

> It is my own life
> that has cornered me beneath the stones
> of this temple in ruins, in a blaze of sun. (22)

In the succeeding lines he addresses the "sun-lions," and questions them as to whose return to life they are waiting for, since he knows that their waiting is an exercise in futility.

In this section VIII the poet scales metaphorically the height of the Konarka temple "where the air is moist and soft in the smell of the sea." The height of Konarka temple turns out to be the place from where all else makes sense: his past and his land. The poet's passionate description, with a sweeping lyricism of the life as it is carved on the stone reflects his concern with the totality of life whose realisation alone would lead to an experience of poetic fulfilment:

> there swills about us

the spacious body of woman, the fruit and the flower,
the gentle leaf, the folded belly
                    and the sweeping fire,
like the warm waters around fish,
like the velvet down about the floating breath of fledglings.
(22)

In order to be able to comprehend life in its fullness, one has to go through the varied experiences, through the three kingdoms of "the mineral, the vegetable and animal" that roughly correspond to three worlds of the Sattva, the Rajas and the Tamas. Going through these three dimensions of life one will "experience the fever of love/and the deeper undulation of the earth" (22).

Like the meticulous depiction of the *linga* and the *yoni* and the various poses of congress, as described in the Kamasutra, on the walls of the temple of Konarka trying to embody a harmonious fusion of the Prakriti and the Purusha, the poet evoking "those moods and phases of human life" strives to achieve a "secret order," a harmony of grace and meaning, form and vision. The world of love, lust, sex and fertility is recreated through the images of "raging pachyderm" with its "crazy testicles," "lusting god," "cloud of my sweat," "valleys," "stricken muscles" and "violent splashes of sun-sets" (23).

Mahapatra's question in the middle of the section, "would meaning remain/in merely that a thing exists, on a single plane, /in the helpless sips of loneliness we have made, /marooned on the stone, on the dark chariot of the sun/whose fevered granite wheels claw desperately/at the strangled earth in our lives?" (22) is indeed vital in terms of poet's own perception of the poetic world. As for his kind of poetry, he has the probable answers in the subsequent question.

Even if "these things"—the themes of the Konarka temple and of the relationship of his self to his land—serve as the backdrop to *Relationship*, the poet takes imaginative leaps beyond the thematic boundaries and reaches the mysterious working of the mind, the unexplored corners of experience and existence, which would reveal "an absent dimension of the blood" (23).

Thus, section VIII beginning with the picture of his life "cornered beneath the stones" which is reminiscent of the fate of warrior Karna in the *Mahabharata* whose chariot got stuck in the earth and finally ending with the poet's attempt to "pull you out/of the centuries of fallen stone" (23) and thus encompassing in a lifetime an imaginative experience of centuries, is, in itself, a well-knit poem apart from being a fragment of the complex texture of *Relationship.*

In section IX the poet captures the mood of the present, his relationship with his immediate surrounding which determines the course and tone of his poetry. The past that he has dealt with in the previous sections is epitomised in the symbol of the Konarka temple. Now he gives it almost a final touch:

> The colossal temple had crumbled in the unknown past,
> onto the sandy bank of a vanished river
> which once had dominated the heart of the wind. (25)

His present world is crowded by "shadows over body," "structures which flank the river," "Sundays with savage afternoons," "prostitutes," "malice," "daggers" and "shameless fevers" (26). He seeks redemption from these forces of negation through "the myth of sleep and action" which he hopes will soothe him and reveal "the deepening nature of all things" (24). This deepening nature oozes from one's heart which makes one love his neighbour, causes a mother to give milk to her neighbour's child and accepting one's friends "who have known only how to keep walking toward themselves" (24).

His defensive stance of 'the myth of sleep and action" which seems apparently contradictory is illustrated in the myth of Savitri, "a dark-eyed woman (who) climbs the endless stairs." By virtue of the fidelity to her husband, Savitri was able to bring him back from the hands of Yama. The steadfastness of her faith and action enabled her to bring her husband back from the realm of dead, "turning back/the triumph of death with the power/of her faithful silence." The myth of Savitri affords further hope of getting back the lost glories.

In the last section, the poet gets over his intoxication with the past. He tries to step out of his clogged fate. Here in this section, the poet "stand(s) among these ruins/waiting for the cry of a night-bird" (28) for deliverance. He is out of the past. He is optimistic about his friends who are now endowed with creative force. As for himself, he comes to believe that

> We are delivered by the myth
> which exhorts our sleep and our losses. (28)

Thus the modes of redemption are myth and sleep. In section IX he spoke of "those who survive the myth/have slipped past their lives and cannot define their reason" (24). The meaninglessness and purposelessness of their present life are "like brooms" which "wait oddly on their unstable heads" (24). The spirit that was insipid is now fortified in section X. In the beginning of section X the poet is proud of that rich past which smacks of a pervading sense of futility: "Waters flow past without their purposes"; instead of monumental architectures, only "replicas of temples lie scattered everywhere" (27). We can, at best, only repeat "humiliating episodes" (28). If at all we "wake," it will be waking into a life without creativity and energy, "like toys springing out of a box" (28). The sense of defeat and passivity of the present life, the "darkness over us," is reinforced in corporeal terms like "the mossed walls of my life" and "my volcanic flesh."

The poet's search for meaning through myth leads him to a perception of the present in terms of the past which finds symbolic enactment in "the fairs and festivals, feasts and fasting" (7). The mystery, the spiritual blend of mind and a belief in pantheism are all manifest in the Dussera Puja celebrations in Cuttack:

> scores of women waited, their heads
>   covered with devotion,
> like the leaves, shaking as though possessed
>   with spirits malign,
> and the town of Cuttack where I was born,
> its lanes scarred by ruts from whose clay
> the goddesses take their sacred shapes

year after year. (27)

Like Lord Jagannath, whose idol is carved out of the wood of a neem tree every twelve years, the Goddess Durga takes her shape from clay every year. As the poet tries to identify himself with the myth and legend of the land, there is an attempt to merge himself with the crowds he hopes to resolve the duality that dwells within him, of his being born to a Christian family and his psychological assimilation into a Hindu ethos. The resolution in effect annihilates the conflict within his self. This resolution makes him an integral part of the "mysterious inheritance/in which roots stick out here and there from the dung." (27)

As the poet moves towards the closing of the poem he grows anxious and at the same time, confident. He begins to draw all the diffused themes and tensions together into an order that embodies a stable relationship between the past and the present, between his self and the world outside with its people, its ruins, its glories and ills. Section XI beginning with an image of "mirror" in fact mirrors what have gone by. They are "hollow, unreal space of stone" and "the flesh hollowed out by the years in a woman," and "fragrance of old sandalwood and the dawn light of fish." These reflections of the past connect him to the present and assure him of the temporal continuity in terms of the "twenty-four blue spells" (29). The twenty-four blue spells are the twenty-four hours into which the stone wheels on the chariot of Konark temple are divided. Those wheels finally stand out as a symbol of eternity, of the co-existence of past and present. They are "what one endures."

The poet's awareness of the present is brought about by a symbolic descent down "a flight of steps" (29) from the heights of the temple of Konarka, by abandoning myth and dream to savour the essence of being.

The "trembling" stone at the beginning of the poem has eventually led him to the "trembling with the being" (29). In the image of "each woman's breath of moist grass/and her thresholds of milk" (30) at the end of section XI, the poet sums up his vision of life and its continuity and endurance. His final vision of relationship between what was, what is and what will be is one of "grace." (30).

The poet finally bids farewell to the feeling of the personal and the historical guilt consciousness:

> Fear of my guilt, I bid you farewell. (31)

This becomes possible through the poet mustering strength from the "stone" which emerges ultimately as the symbol of unity of all the diverse elements as well as the symbol of perfection in art" "a song rises from the honeycomb latticework of stone" (31).

Mahapatra now invokes the "dark daughters" on the friezes of the Konarka temple in this final section, seeking shelter in their "dance" (31). Here the dance of the *naika* is positive in contrast to the dance of "shadows" in section II. This dance is the cosmic dance, like that of Siva, in which the whole of creation participates: the poet's personal and racial existence, the green hills of the land, the "crows that quicken the sunlight in the veins" and even the "stone" which contains "sadness" and "deaths" (31).

Towards the end, along with his sighting the dawn coming to the earth with the "crows" that "quicken sunlight," along with bidding farewell to guilt, the poet watches the "sadness fly in and out/ of (his) death" (31), which encompasses interpenetrating layers of relationship. To sum up, in the words of Vasant A. Shahane, "Thus, memory becomes a pervasive mode of comprehending relationship—between personal self and society, the creative self and the arts, sculpture and architecture, which in turn embody the meeting point between life-giving impulses and the poet's quest for comprehending different levels of relationship between art and life." (Prasad 178)

Jayanta Mahapatra's earlier themes like the delineation of his place and people and images like rain, sleep, stone, memory grow more forceful in *Relationship*. The lyricism which was prominent in *The False Start* reached its peak in *Relationship*. But from the peak of *Relationship* Jayanta Mahapatra once again comes down to the plains of day-to-day life in his next collection, *Life Signs*. But it is only in *Burden of Waves and Fruit* that his own bodily concern gripped his attention, and in order to articulate the struggle between his body and soul, he went for the images of the very physical elements that constitute the body.

The Centre of the Web: *Life Signs* and *Burden of Waves and Fruit*

"Mahapatra's poetry forms a continuous work revealed by his titles. After writing *The False Start* and having established *Relationship*, it is appropriate that *Life Signs* should follow," says Bruce King (205). In his post-*Relationship* phase with *Life Signs* (1988), *Dispossessed Nests* (1984) and *Burden of Waves and Fruit* (1988) Jayanta Mahapatra embarks on a confident search for a personal myth of his own. While in *The False Start* he was groping for a form and a vision, in *Relationship* he achieved a firm grasp on the medium and a profound understanding of the self and the world. Now he is more confident and self-assured. He is more direct, communicative and conscious of his role as a poet.

The myth-making process starts with the abandonment of direct allusions and reference to myths. In the three volumes proposed to be discussed in the following pages, there is hardly any reference to myths as he used to do in his previous collection. Instead, he tries to evolye, mostly through his deliberations on the creative act, a personal myth in which he is at the centre. In this process he moves slowly but steadily towards what he calls "the centre of your web" (*Life Signs*19). This centre is the meeting point of the self and the world. His creation of a personal world—his drive towards the "centre of your web"—is achieved in this period through two distinctive phases. First, in *Life Signs* and *Dispossessed Nests*, there is an emphasis on the physical dimension of the external world vis-a-vis his inner feeling. Secondly, in *Burden of Waves and Fruit,* his dilemma and confrontation with the process of ageing are examined profoundly. This second move may be said to be the most personal of all he has ever said in his poetry.

As regards his technique, in these three volumes there are no major shifts in terms of syntax, or voice, but only renewal of spirit, imagination and perception, "simply a flight of birds," as he admits in his essay "The Inaudible Resonance in English Poetry in India" (27-36). But the dominant images at this stage are vigorous and violent, such as darkness, wound, and in the second phase old age, death and decrepitude, which symbolise a pervasive sense of bleakness, melancholy, fatigue, ennui, defeat and ultimate destruction of body. Nonetheless the poems continue, as Bruce King aptly observes, "to bridge as epistemological, phenomenological gap—to know, be part of, enclose, experience—with the world and the other, whether it be a woman, temple stones, a Hindu priest" (King 206).

"The life signs in Jayanta Mahapatra's book [*Life Signs*] are the expected ones, the archetypal symbols of religion and art, but given a sombre power by the bleakness and compassion of the poet's view," says John Barnie (*Kunapipi* 107-22). The signs of life in his world as captured in *Life Signs* include temple priests, solar eclipses, life by the river and sea, devotees and hippies, desolate rice fields, fireflies, ancestors and ruins. The description of these sites and everyday situations, inherited religion and lived life, sublime and mundane moods, acquires the proportions of vignettes. Water-related images, with which he had always been involved, here once again are effective tools to explore the patterns of life around him. The sea, the river, water and rain that ran through the expanse of his poetry like veins and arteries now attain new dimensions.

Life Signs opens with a drunk sea spitting out "the gauze wings of shells along the beach" (1). Breaking himself out of the spell of the "captive air," the poet asks:

> Who can tell of the songs of this sea that go on
> to baffle and double the space around our lives?
> Or of smells paralysed through the centuries,
> of deltas hard and white that stretched once
> to lure the feet of women bidding their men goodbye?
>
> (*Life Signs* 1)

This too short and narrow space, too laconic yet lyrical passage, makes room for a proud chapter of Oriya history associated with Chandipur. Although this ancestral, historical obsession with Chandipur was revealed in *Relationship*, it now points to the poet's response to the individual, humane aspect of it, the sorrows and suffering and heroic sentiment that goes with it and its charm that owes to the archetypal sexual pattern implied in the metaphor "deltas hard and white" which in fact forms the axis of the poem, "The Captive Air of Chandipur-on-Sea." The sensuous description of woman combines in it the landscape and history of the land:

> Of salt and light that dark and provocative eyes
> demanded, their shoulders drooping like lotuses
> in the noonday sun. (1)

With the end of the first stanza is the "drooping" of a chapter of history. So, in the second what follows is only "the shadow of this proud watercourse" (1) which is clipped at the end with an interrogative mark, to express the poet's humble way of putting the fact straight. Again the similar question "who are you, /occupant of the silent sigh of the conch?" can be clearly understood when one knows the cultural compulsions that went with those "women bidding their men goodbye," who blew conches as an auspicious sign. Those life signs are now extinct. So, the question set in the second stanza of the poem is as much an eulogy of the past as a contempt of the culturally orphaned present. While he resigns himself as "the ground seems only a memory now, a torn breath," he also waits "for the tide to flood the mudflats." But his act of waiting, as he perceives in "Evening Landscape by the River," is a "familiar but useless ornament" (2). This bleakness is also evidenced in his very act of writing, as he questions, "Will a Poem of Mine be the Only Answer?" Out of this sense of futility in writing comes his sense of desolation and loneliness. The images of the river is one of the modes of comprehending this desolate feeling: "Images of the river form a framework though, no two images of the river are alike, but all convey a sense of permanence, co-mingled with a sense of sadness," says Uma Parameswaran (255).

"Evening Landscape by the River" speaks of a six-month-old child of a fisherman crawling in the shack by the river. The poem "River" is "memory" and "Dead River" is

> like a father left with a picture
> of his traceless son, perhaps dead,
> grey with determination, and infinite skies. (6)

"Dead River" is dead tradition, supposedly. Brooding over the loss of a common past he feels "a rope of familiar water" "making a desultory circle round" him (6). And towards the close of the poem this surreal river bends towards "the sluggish centuries" (6). As the title suggests there is no water in this river. So, whatever is depicted as taking place upon it is either a hallucination or a rumination of memory or an archetypal imagination. It is a "tamed temple god." The "boat" is "silted" and women, imagined in this context "dreaming on after all intention had died" (6) could be interpreted as bathing after all water had dried. Nonetheless the picture described here is a strong reminder of the past, of what is lost: "life's persistent symmetry" (6). This dead river, above all, could also suggest Chandrabhaga at the feet of the Konarka temple:

> a vanished river
> which once had dominated the heart of the wind.
> (*Relationship* 25)

Tradition is one dimension of the image 'river'. Another possible significance is suggested in the phrase, "river of my life" (*Life Signs* 38) in which life is depicted as a river running into the sea of death. This traditional image of life is however expressed as a complex metaphor, taking on multilayers of correspondence to the geography of his land and that of his mind. They get fused into the chaos, loneliness and restlessness in him. The unrest is reflected in the reference to the recurrent cyclones along the Bay of Bengal that affect the coastal region of Orissa and render life miserable:

> Absently I turn and stare toward the east,

toward which a river flows, deep in the hills
of my blood; I remember
it is summer's end,
and far out, a storm is about to begin,
crying from the lonely places of the sea. (*Life Signs* 33)

The other "river" is a futile course, like his act of writing poetry. Like the rain "that doesn't wet the earth any more/lost of purpose, like a benediction" (*Life Signs* 13), the river is,

swallowed up by deserts before
it reaches the sea. (31)

River is also an image of regeneration and rejuvenation. The poet describes a scene on the river bank of Mahanadi in a neatly crafted poem "Again, One Day, Walking by the River." It begins with a Neruda-like earthly solemnity," "The same river, the same sun, the same town." The barges loaded with hay are moored to the river banks. They are "trapped like a leaf in a basin of water." Likewise the minute observation of details, like women workers tarring the road, lepers going home, "their helpless looks/drawing fantasies on the town square" and tar smoke scattered upon the river imparts vividness to the landscape he evokes. All persons seem to be tied, like barges, to their places as the poet would like them to be. There is, in their fixed and conventional life, a strange sense of freedom. The last dreg of the poem, loneliness, is the poet's. Even though the poet identifies himself with the people and place, there is nevertheless a corroding sense of loneliness:

I can't remember hearing anyone
saying he will mourn for me when I am gone. (39)

This feeling is reinforced further when he speaks of the "light wind, so weak and thin/ I can't say where it came from" (39). Thus with this springboard of external details, he leaps into his inner world of void. With the bright sun, active town and limping river, he creates a dream-like effect and asserts his inexplicable loneliness. Reviewing *Life Signs* Daniel McBride says: "Nothing more powerfully develops the sense of tenuous meaning in Mahapatra's poetry than his inversion of the ordinary. "The same river, the same sun, the same town," the first line of "Again, One Day, Walking by the River," conjoins a feeling of familiarity with unutterable strangeness. The latter feeling is perhaps not yet ennui, it is more a vision of perspicacity attempting to derive meaning from the simplest event, only to come away empty handed." (88)

In Mahapatra's poetry water is often associated with the bleak shades of mind, darkness and violence. These metaphoric suggestions of water get themselves tuned to the perception of violence inscribed in the images of wound, death and darkness, of the hunger-stricken men, women and children. In "The Wound", we plunge headlong into darkness that sprawls like an infinite expanse of water, that is both literal and spiritual:

> do we dare ask of one another those questions
>
> that go on searching
> the secret places of the soul? (3)

In such a wilderness in the body and soul, there are only the "old terror" of "water," "obscene wounds" in "mind" and a "silence." But this silence is only a warning that "the world is not ours." So we should just "endure one another" and all that is subsumed in "the existing structure of order." (3)

The poet's drive towards the centre of darkness occurs violently in one poem explicitly named "Violence." The darkness, that hovered earlier on the periphery and was somewhat abstract, now takes on solidity and resides in the heart of a "bullock-cart-driver" and of the children in the classrooms, "shrunk like caged slaves" (5). "Violence," beginning with a short, elliptical sentence "The day dims," then with the darkness being popped into the poet's mouth, "when I open and shut/my mouth/ the darkness chokes inside," wading through the "black pressure/of dragging ribs" of the bullock-cart-driver and through the restlessness in the school children, is a slow glide into the labyrinth of darkness, violence and wound that reside at the centre of the soul. Through the images of darkness the life signs glimmer fitfully as in "Firefly" in which "the cry of the dead" refuses to be quiet, or glows fiercely as in "In a Night of Rain." As Daniel McBride comments: "The incessant images of darkness throughout the work depicts a cosmos essentially random and ignorant in nature within which, to echo Sartre's 'man is condemned to be free'. The poem "In a Night of Rain" metap- horizes men's spiritual concerns as an empty gesture born of an ineluctable ennui." (89)

The juxtaposition of the two apparently disparate images of darkness and rain in the poem "In a Night of Rain" seems rather baffling. The poem beginning with "A time of rain, and the old town/stinks of mould and wet dog's skin" describes the lot of "homeless women" driven to the river banks and to the rain. But the poet's compassion, the sense of hurt and humility makes this poem a symbol of life-force, a struggle against penury and pain. This sense of involvement fills the poem with a warmth of love. An "evening jasmine" blossoms and then there is love and a fructifying rain. The erotic feeling is aroused and suppressed in one single line "the sound of satisfaction after love has been made." But this hope goes against its grain because the destitute life of homeless women won't let their love endure time. Equally, the rain becomes ambivalent in being a catalyst to love and misery. Above all, the poet seems to be well-meaning and sympathetic to their lot though he cannot do anything to pluck them out of their surrounding. All these paradoxical resolutions glide down sadly and serenely into an ultimate pact of futility, the core of our existence;

> Here
> a man's heart is moved, but the feeling is needless
> like that of serving one's country which hangs
> like a tall, rosewood-framed portrait of an ancestor
> that had lost its light and meaning:
> man's mourning dispirited, his concern a stale caress (13)

Darkness is one of the predominant aspects of life signs around the poet. In "The Lost Children of America," the poet says, "In this time of darknesses, the lost ones and I/ will dim like lamps and go back to the moments . . . /to balance ourselves." Those life signs that inhabit "this time of darknesses," are the "bigbreasted hard-eyed whores," "the corrupt politicians," "mangled lepers," "the lost children of America," "she-jackals" and "hunters," "virgin woman" and "grotesque god" "the priest's pomaded jean-clad son" and the raped "squint-eyed foruteen-year fishergirl." These are the types that crowd the streets, "malarial lanes," "slums," "the Town Hall" and the "cracked stone-platform" of the Hanuman Temple (23-27). Like the poem "Again, One Day, Walking by the River," "The Lost Children of America" is another one on Cuttack. It is charged with a socio-political-cultural significance. The immediacy of the bleak human condition—considered against the backdrop of the Third World—is felt even with the opening of this poem: "Here/in the dusty malarial lanes of Cuttack." He describes the familiar characteristics of his place, like hunger, disease, poverty, immorality, corruption," as Uma Parameswaran observes, "at length with Miltonic similes and Ginsberg's breath. Every line is rich in visual images which cumulatively build up their somnambulistic movements to the point of universal void" (Parameswaran 257). Its import could be aptly noticed in the way the poet describes the movement of the lost children of America:

> like the languid movements of mangled lepers
> around a temple of the goddess Chandi at dawn
> like a wounded whale drifting away
> sadly in unknown seas
> like the dark winds of Asia
> which murmur joylessly in slums but do not answer
> they wander, these lost children of America. (23)

Their movements compared with that of mangled lepers, wounded whales and unanswering, dark winds of Asia amply indicate how the place in which they sought their "succour" is flushed with fear and uncertainty. Finally, when the poet encounters the lost children of America, one suspects the lost child to be no other than Mahapatra's doppelganger:

> We gaze at each other in silence, the lost child and I;
> who knows who is playing a joke on whom?
> What can drive me from these mean, sordid alleys where I
> live? (26)

The darkness of his "mean, sordid alleys" is echoed in other poems, in other ways. Like "river," "darkness" is another forceful image that at this stage of Jayanta Mahapatra's poetry seeks to convey the spirit of his locale as well as the morality of his people. In "A Night of Rain" one gets the picture of the wretched life of the homeless women who have "put up their huts" on the dingy river banks. As the poet depicts their world as one of darkness in which the houseless women lead their lives of little sorrows and joys—"There is a sound of crying in there, /of an evening jasmine being born, /the sounds of satisfaction after love has been made"—there is the suggestion of their dehumanising condition:

> Here
> a man's heart is moved, but the feeling is needless. (13)

This sense of dismay takes its root deeper in the poet as he becomes more and more conscious of this pervasive presence within him. One such portent metaphysical usage of darkness is noticed in "Beyond the Himalayan Ranges." This poem dedicated to Andrei Sakharov only heightens the "indecipherable words" (13) that he came across when he was face to face with the unpleasant reality of his surroundings in "A Rain of Night." The indecipherable darkness of "A Rain of Night" tends to be the darkness of the soul that the poet attempts to share with the scientist in a spirit of comradeship in creativity. That spirit of fraternity is embedded in his fond image of stone where darkness serves as a link:

> when darkness falls the stones come closer
> toward us. (8)

The darkness in "Total Solar Eclipse" set against the backdrop of the poet's familiar locale, "the foetus of Puri," is played upon through the image of the hunter and the hunted. Though here the locale is Puri, the images used for its characters give a more lively and intense dimension to its characters than the ones used in the poems on Puri in *Waiting* and *A Rain of Rites*. While the pilgrims now are "peering here and there like hunted dogs," the priests are depicted as crocodiles:

> And cautiously the crocodile
> pushes its long snout from the deep water
> like the fearsome Brahmin priest in the temple (22)

Another addition in this poem to "this new image of night" (21) is

> A banner of pale human skin
> fluttered on top of the temple of Jagannath. (21)

In this dark image of man-god relationship we have a co-mingling of the political and the religious, the unanswering god of bricky words, insensitive to the misery of his devotees and the vulnerable, suffering and believing populace. When the world has come to such a state where the banner of God is made of pale human skin, where "cobra" and "hyena" and "vultures" pile up as "corpses," the tone of the chronicler of such time is bound to strike its darkest note, and the "Total Solar Eclipse" is bound to occur.

In "A Country," where "hunger keeps growing," a girl dies of starvation before her "breasts are swollen with milk" (29) and out of hunger a girl turns Naxalite. This poem is an attempt of the poet to come to grips with the prevalent spirit of his land that encompasses revolutions, protests and suffering. He realises much to his chagrin that the age-old myths are no answer to the stark reality of hunger that post-colonial India faces today. In the colonial period, the year 1866 was the darkest year in the history of Orissa. It was the year of the Great Famine that not only caused millions of starvation deaths, but also led to the erosion of socio-moral values. While an inheritance of guilt still troubles him—his grandfather walked into the folds of Christianity to keep his body and soul together—his son is not troubled as much. For there is the distance of time: "A conscience of years is between us. He is young" (20):

> we wish we knew what it was to be, against dying,
> to know the dignity
>
> that had to be earned dangerously,
> your last chance that was blindly terrifying, so unfair. (20)

The poet describes this Great Famine of 1866 in Orissa with accuracy, precision and an insight into the psychology of its victims in the autobiographical poem "Grandfather" which begins like this:

> For you it was the hardest question of all.
> Dead, empty trees stood by the dragging river,
> past your weakened body, flailing against your sleep.
> You thought of the way the jackals moved, to move.
>
> Did you hear the young tamarind leaves rustle
> in the cold mean nights of your belly? Did you see
> your own death? Watch it tear at your cries,
> break them into fits of hard unnatural laughter?
>
> How old were you? Hunted, you turned coward and ran,
> the real animal in you plunging through your bone.
> You left your family behind, the buried things,
> the precious clod that praised the quality of a god.
>
> The imperishable that swung your broken body,
> turned it inside out? What did faith matter?
> What Hindu world so ancient and true for you to hold?
> Nervously you dreamed toward the centre of your web. (19)

The unnatural laughter of the victim of famine, his compulsion to bury his Hindu identity, to sell his morality and to desert his religion in the face of hunger, echoes the laconic question that the poet had raised in *The False Start*, "Where is the good reason that says a moral cannot be sold"? (63) When in *Life Signs* he speaks of the inheritance, willy-nilly, he speaks of this spirit and of his personal agony of a rigid Christian upbringing, around the throbbing life-centre of a Hindu socio-cultural ethos.

While Mahapatra has always tried to take stock of the lives of the people around him and of the place where he lives, he has never forgotten his persistent struggle to evolve a poetics and diction of his own. This attempt to evolve a distinct style of expression which was evident in his very first volume, *Close the Sky, Ten by Ten* now is clearly an obsessive preoccupation in *Life Signs*. Though there is no systematic formulation of a poetic creed as such, *Life Signs*, thus, raises certain crucial questions relating to the role of poetry in the realisation of an ambivalent vision that encompasses the real and the unreal, the self and the physical world.

Those poems that deal with the creative act of poetry are "Will a Poem of Mine be the Only Answer?," "An Impotent Poem," "Last Night the Poem" and "The Quality of Ruins." The life signs embodied in these poems are also the characteristics of his poetry, or his belief in what a poem should be like. In "Will a Poem of Mine be the Only Answer?" the poet asks

> And if the heart doesn't overflow with love,
> will the spirits of poetry stir out
> of the walls of my bone? (46)

He suggests that the poet believes in the inspirational basis of poetic composition. Earlier in this poem, he confesses that he has been "defeated" by his own "*tactics, my poetry*" (italics mine) (45). Thus his poetry is of tactics as well as of an "overflow." He is aware of the "impotence" as well as the wayward nature of words that often threaten to subvert the process of realizing the self and the world:

> Let not words fill you with fear,
> those that trap you like an animal in your heart.
> Those that claim you like insects of the night . . .
> those that run down from snow-capped mountains . . .
> those that contort themselves to tangled rivers . . .
> those that blind you with your own impotence

and then crush you with the desire
to make things right in the world. (14)

Yet at the end the poet knows that he cannot escape from the compulsions of poetic articulation, for his "grief/is to endure the words of the living" (15) despite their impotence, despite their waywardness. The effort to negotiate with words to get over their residence to self-realisation, eventually leads him to the paradoxical feeling that

when all else has failed
the poem's words are perhaps justified. (34)

He realises that despite their subversive act, it is only through the words that he can peep into the "tomorrow" of his life, of his poetry and of the world in the inevitable process of ageing with all its concommitant burden. The process of ageing and the problem of coming to terms with it through poetry becomes his agonising ordeal in *Burden of Waves and Fruit*. His poetry, as has been already observed, is marked by his shuttling constantly, phase by phase, from the inner world to outer world and vice-versa. As a result, he takes up the images from both the worlds: in *Life Signs* speaking of the lives and conditions around him he had made use of the signs of external world and now that he is back to his body in *Burden of Waves and Fruit* his attention is arrested primarily by the elements and working process of the body itself. In this context, Jayanta Mahapatra's views on death indicate the move his poetry would take:

JK: What are you writing about now?
JM: I am writing about death. Not in the way I used to, the day of death being an ending, death giving movement to life, not in that sad, closing way. I want now to write about death in another way.
JK: Death as another level of being ?
JM: Yes, death as another transformation, as another kind of life.
JK: Death as in the traditional Hindu way of seeing it?
JM: Maybe, that way, seen through poetry, maybe, yes, through

the eyes of poetry (Kemp, *Kunapipi* 49)

What the poet expresses here is largely reflected in the poems in *Burden of Waves and Fruit*. In this sense, this volume becomes a watershed in the career of Jayanta Mahapatra by distinctly marking a fundamental concern of an ageing poet, that is, the relationship of the self to the ageing, alienating, slowly turning decrepit body and the ultimate death awaiting it.

By the time this volume was prepared for publication the poet was around sixty. So it was natural that his poetry should have responded to the immediate and urgent demand of exploring the ageing body. In trying to meet this demand the poet turns the gaze of the "centre of your web" towards the inside of the body. Body, then, becomes the centre of attention as well as the centre of his poetic world and consciousness. The body now emerges triumphantly as an overpowering image:

> I touch my shoulders; they are bare, contrite.
> Like the shape of a deserted park bench in the rain.
> (*Burden of Waves and Fruit* 52)

The shoulders of his ageing body are "contrite": they are "bare" "like a deserted park bench "in the rain." The signs of ageing on the poet's body are conspicuous, but "contrite." The body that has started holding his attention deceives his very self. Now that the body is slowly becoming a burden, intruding into the terrains of his consciousness, he is getting increasingly obsessed with it: "shoulders," which he might have considered obnoxious a decade ago, have replaced the heart. Of his heart he is growing diffident, sullen: "The heart has nothing to learn," (*Burden of Waves and Fruit* 39) whereas a decade earlier, he has said:

> Where is that absence which pushed an icy rope
> down my throat, so close my heart could have touched it?
> (*A Rain of Rites* 24)

The preoccupation with "absence," with "waiting," with a haunting sense of unfulfilment continues through these years. What has intervened is the shadow of ageing demanding for itself an exclusive attention from the poet. Given all the changes in theme, his mode of giving shape to the immaculate feeling, and dissolving the existing shape of things into a flux, continues. The shape about which he was very uncertain, and to which he was trying to give a concreteness as when speaking of the moribund hours of a man in "A Summer Afternoon"—"time drawn like a thin wind/to the shape of pain" (40)—has come to acquire a body-form. So, the shoulders are not just "like a park bench" but "like the *shape* of a deserted park bench" (italic mine). Ageing as the theme of this poem "Waiting" was of course more avowedly declared by the poem's original title, "A Poem at Fifty-One," which had first appeared in *The Hudson Review* of Summer 1982.

Old age has come to him like a "weary night bird," (51) like "a grey owl on a branch of (his) breath" (53). The presence of this bird is ominous. The soul is now about to depart like this bird and he is aware of its consequence: he will be left as "a soiled shirt as though it were empty of its body" (50). The indelible signs of old age make him feel that he is being reduced to a mere "symbol." His "poem taunts (him) like a discarded bone" (29). "The naked truth of ageing is that," as Kathleen Woodward says, "while we usually associate young age with arms and legs and reaching out into the world and old age with the interior organs, we think of the young as moving into the world. We think of the body of the youth as the symbol of social interaction, while we think of the immobilized, infirm elderly as turning inward, preoccupied with the invisible working of the body's internal mechanism." (Woodward 54) These reflections on old age, as against youth, are abundantly, noticed in the recent poetry of Jayanta Mahapatra. See, for example,

> Here I lie, watching
> the summer of my body
> trembling over the grass (12)

Here we find the poet watching "the summer of (his) body," instead of the exterior worlds of stars, sky and fullmoon night around him. He is preoccupied with the dark workings of the inside of his body. His gaze is inward, bodyward. "Grass," which is an image of youth and vitality, now seems to be merely a shred of memory, overlooked, existing on a different plain, a thing of the past. Where there was once suppleness and tone—"grass"—now there is dryness, "absence," loss of colour—"summer" (12).

In a recent interview to the *Indian Express* Jayanta Mahapatra says, "I have been working hard somehow feeling that I don't have much time left. The morbid streak you find in my poetry is also there within me. The idea of death has always been with me." (Sept. 5, 1987) Of course, elsewhere, he had already equated death with poetry: "It has sometimes been said there are two main things poets can write about: love and death. For in poets dwell Man, this biological being, easily hurt, easily destroyed. And if one thinks a little on this, one will come to the conclusion that in reality there is only one subject all poets talk about—and it is death." ("Poetry: Climate for Renewal" 7-16)

The imagery he uses for ageing body is bare, almost brutal. This imagery speaks of lives and of things beaten up, chopped, battered, ruined and empty. They are: "as though I was no human, only a turd," "a leper's mutilated hands," (29) "the carcass of night" "damaged drums," (31) "dark pitchers of bodies," "battered stone walls," (18) etc. Whatever he looks at, whether at the historic river of Daya or at the ruined "Shivaji's Fort at Panhalla" (18-19), or at "Love's Fragment" (34), the imagery comes filtered through an ageing man's eyes. So his poetry carries with it the burden of physical decrepitude.

> The rusted body of a mutilated automobile
> watches me behind closed eyelids.
> With barely a whisper my blood shuts the door. (20)

He cannot close his eyes to that "something/that stands eyeing you from the opposite shore" (43). He faces death calmly as he knows it is the biological destiny of life. Jayanta Mahapatra is not only disturbed by his own corrosive age, but also is shocked by the diseases and unnatural, premature deaths in his world. "The fleeing children of Nellie" "shaking their mother's slashed stomachs" (10) an insane "mother cradl(ing) her child's head/that lies without its body" (11) and "children struggling with their last summer (22) make him feel ill at ease.

His images now speak of a kind of life which has met its end or is nearing it. Granted that the same life had a goal, a determination to follow, is it not death that has strangled all its possibilities? Old age subverts the very possibilities of existence, sometimes a value system. Where, today, is that significance of 30th January, the day Mahatma Gandhi was assassinated? In "30th January, 1982: A Story" the poet draws up characters and situations that are pock-marked, as it were, with unhealthy signs. On Gandhi's death anniversary, the butchers become active, the postman clutches his hernia and a "rich woman" "cursed the Government" when "the mobile loudspeaker van/of the Department of Public Relations swept past/pouring out the words of Gandhi's once favourite hymn" (26). The same morning, "Neighbours both, Amar Babu and Sham Babu smiled sweetly/at one another as they chose/their choice of cuts of meat hanging from the hooks/in the marketplace." (26) The country in relation to this poet "makes (him) more embarrassed than lonely" (32). In "Stand By, Memory" reacting to the Emergency of 1975 he does not exhibit a youthful rage but a slothful, self-resignation; his protest is in the gesture of a silent endurance:

> And slowly I return, embarrassed
> to meet the one in me, feeling the same colors
> play upon my consciousness, as the spectrum
> breaks down, always, as though in anticipation
>
> of the brutality of the oppressor,
> unable to escape the trances
> of my place, my endurance
> simply creating gestures of magnificence. (45-46)

If this country with its political and economic disorders, so deftly articulated in *Dispossessed Nests*, make him more embarrassed, it is his own ageing that makes him lonely. He thinks of himself as old, his hand too feeble to change the world. As a result of either, or both, his turning inward seems to be an impulsive growth. If youth is narcissism, old age is the reverse of it. Mahapatra's poetry consequently opens his eyes inward. One evening he sits down to ponder over a "part" of his self that plays like a fish and slithers down into him, thereby making itself "hard to recognise" (53). Likewise, "this evening a part of (him)self closes in on (him)" (53) filling him with "shame and pain of defeat" (53) as a result of which he turns compulsively inward to reach towards his own elusive self.

Ageing is usually viewed with some sort of prejudice. The elderly are looked upon with sentimentality. Jayanta Mahapatra's way of looking at his ageing body is in a manner of dreaming, of looking back at his former, irrevocable self, and with that, hoping to re-establish what is lost, as the following poem, "Harvest" illustrates:

> What does my world say?
> I follow the substance of my shadow
> in the procession of light on the leaves;
> and I watch myself, standing in the shadow,
> afraid to step out of it.
> But then the sun comes down on me.
>
> And I sit all alone, waiting
> for my joys to come back.
> Ah, the monarchy of the morning lily,
> its eyes narrow with love!
>
> Can one grow strong ever
> in such a constantly resurrected day?
>
> The sky that teaches one at night
> when the day is done.
> So often I hide, playing a game with myself,
> my suffering the only thing that's hard to bear.
> Leeches of stars keep sucking my blood.
>
> Just *my* world, the odors I've become immune to.

> Goatherds, jasmine, this woodsmoke of pyres.
> Have I not told you
> that I see myself, hear myself distort the truth?
> My name never getting worn, never frayed and dead.
> The sun hanging out of the window, a leering face.
>
> Ah, these eyes of mine, narrow with love! (28)

Undoubtedly this is an old man's self-contained world. A flower, after full blooming, is about to wrap itself within the darkness of its enveloping petals. The world of lilies will go on. Thus the poet does not find old age antithetical to beauty. He is only worried about his ageing and its resultant pain and suffering: "my suffering the only thing that's hard to bear." That is, he is not disturbed as much by the loud suffering of the outer world as by the imperceptible suffering inside his body and in his own inverted world. Before his eyes there is a world of the young that haunts him: "leeches of stares keep sucking my blood." In the world outside him he sees light and festivity, "the process of light" on "leaves," "sun" and "stars," but he sees himself standing in shadow, "one at night." Though he is now a citizen of the dark zone of his body, there is a lone streak of light within him which comes from "the woodsmoke of pyres." Brooding over it, he is burdened by an immense self-pity:

> Have I not told you
> that I see myself, hear myself distort the truth?

And yet, this is not mere self-pity as he would make us believe. Before the poem is about to fold up, the poet almost pounces in self-defense upon that part of his self which takes him by the collar of his instinct like the elusive golden deer of his quest. In order to protect his feeble self, his illusion of immortality—"my name never getting worn, never frayed and dead"—he dismissed the mighty sun as a mere "leering face," as though he is stronger than it. At the end, he ends up narcissistically, abruptly:

> Ah, these eyes of mine, narrow with love!

Ageing as he is, how does he look at another ageing body? Does he accept the other ageing body, or reject it? The onslaught of ruins on the decrepit body of the society has made him feel "embarrassed." He has an implacable sympathy for the victims and pity for his own helpless self. Rather than himself or his people, he has someone else to blame for the degeneration of the society—Lord Jagannath. He, along with the suffering children, scoffs at "the atrocious innocence/of Jagannath/ in his sheltered shrine" (40). The irony intended here is that the Lord who should shelter others, finds himself contentedly sheltered in his shrine. The poet almost asks himself: of what use is that lordly "innocence" which cannot mitigate human suffering or ensure poetic justice? In the context of such a society, the poet recoils into his self and to his personal relationship. Speaking, for example, of his old father, he speaks of himself by putting his foot into his father's shoes, without moralising, without sentimentalising:

> My father, sad-faced father! How very far you are
> from this empty room filled only with myself!
> Tomorrow maybe I'll hear my father is dead,
> but he might bear the face of my son.
> This is the hour when there is no distance
> between the two of them. (51)

The poet here observes his aged father with a cool, detached eye. The father is away from him and he is isolated, like an island: "we now echo our father's dignified voices." This shows how far his father has receded from him. The father's voice remains with the son, or rather within the son. But the poet is not willing to concede the fact of his father's distancing away from him. Instead he finds his father's ageing-process reasonable, perfectly in the usual course of things. In order to achieve this effect, he adopts the strategy of distancing his father's body from its possessive noun "father," thereby enabling himself to feel pain and sympathy for his father and a simultaneous disgust for the ruinous body. While the body must wear out in the natural course, the spirit of fatherhood must prevail. He too shall be the father of his son. This almost physically bridges the generations:

> he might bear the face of my son.

Thus, the poet is able to establish an unseverable umbilical chord of which each, his father, himself, his son, is a constituent thread. The dignity of life—despite its receptacle and obstacle, the body—continues undiminished.

Now that the poet is ageing, the awareness of death flashes before his eyes in elemental images: the sky ("dead whiteness of the sky" 14), the earth ("swollen feet that make my body/bite the dust" 31), the stone ("the wounded letters in the stone's arms" 21), the fire ("wood smoke of pyres," 28) etc. The poet comes to realise that his body is about to go back to its elements and so, his poetry tends towards the physical and elemental. His sensing of death occurs through both the auditory and visual images: he sees "a pariah kite from another world" and hears "a voice far away/but strangely familiar" (14). Now this body, which consists of elements, in due course of ageing begins to witness a widening gap between the spirit and itself. Ageing is a physiological process but the self does not grow old. It usually never wears out with the decaying constituents of the body. Yet both these two processes, of the self always feeling young and the body wearing out in due course, sometimes come to clash:

> dreams strangling the hearts of old men
> who feel they were always born old. (37)

But ultimately the self remains undeceived, for it knows the truth of living, the reality of corporeal decay:

> it is not that I face
> a total stranger suddenly sometimes. (53)

Jayanta Mahapatra finds himself in the mirror before him "a total stranger," an interloper, a trespasser on his own familiar body. Here there is nothing uncanny indeed: the poet shows no dread at the creeping horror of the ageing body. This happens due to the poet's insight into the indispensable act of ageing. He has never been blind to his self, "that part," alienating itself from the ageing body. He is not unprepared to meet the stranger that he has become to his self because of his old age.

It is the insight into ageing that has saved the poet from vanishing into the dark pit of his frigid self. Once he accepts his decrepit body, he comes to terms with his self and with that he feels a sense of abandonment within him: "a careless memory inhabits my walk" (17). This endearing relationship between the self and the ageing body is amply illustrated in "This is the Season of the Old Rain." His favourite image of 'rain' seems to have grown old along with him and his poetry. This poem almost sums up the poet's struggle to come out of the quagmire of ageing. The declaration to this effect is made in the very first line; "This is the season of the old rain/always with much to answer before time is done/with decay and death" (27). The season, that the poet speaks of, is the season of his body and "rain" is its image. If now he imagines rain as "green on the grass" it is by falling upon memory that he envisages an escape from the torturing ordeal of the self, to explore the moorings of his self: "Traveler, where is it you belong?" (27) To body or to mind? In his effort not to belong anywhere which is a prison, be it body or mind, he takes resort to the act of writing poetry. He prepares himself with the wisdom of his experience to be taken in by the natural course nonchalantly, indifferently, his soul steeped in creative effort:

> And now, it carries one away,
> the seen miracle in those eyes, closing and opening,
> revealing neither sorrow nor hope nor loss
> and cutting down the fruit of my silent season. (27)

If "silent season" is his old age, death is its "fruit," the ultimate end.

The Sleep-Habit of the Golden Deer: *Dispossessed Nests* and *Temple*

With *Dispossessed Nests* (1986), Jayanta Mahapatra shifted the locale and the centre of his poetry. In *Dispossessed Nests,* the poet attempts to capture the mood of violence in the Punjab and the industrial disaster in Bhopal. *Dispossessed Nests*, with its lack of intellectual rigour, looseness in structure and its elaborative pattern is indeed an interregnum between 1983 and 1988-89. The 1984-poems in this volume mark the poet's shifting of gravity and broadening of his horizon; thematically, the poet goes beyond his province. In that year's violence in the Punjab and the catastrophe of gas-leakage in Bhopal, Mahapatra responded to the mood of the time, condemning the barbaric madness and bringing in God to question: "Must you dry up the river to hear the sands/breathe? Is your hate of man your ultimate fate?" (*Dispossessed Nests* 15). Mahapatra now ponders over the loss of human concern: "to be human/is to see in a dream perhaps/the one who can never be seen" (20). In such a state one is left to wonder about "the dispossessed nests" "in the mind's expanding nova" (23).

The poet articulates the suffering of people in the rhetoric of his country's turbulence. Though the images are traditional like riverbed, sea, sky, land, they are seen in the context of a suffering community. "The rainbow chokes/at the end of its leash" (25), "the torso/looking about/for its missing head" (18), "two rippped-out eyes/ shaking their tears" are all testimonies to the bloodshed in Punjab. If in the context of politico-religious violence in Punjab it is the knife, the gun flashing, the images that denote the gas tragedy in Bhopal are "dance of bejewelled snakes," "smell of burning leaves," "clouds of paranoia," and "sinister shadow of the Minister." These ominous presences ironically constitute a "dream city." Amid the bloodshed and gas-leakage in places far away from Orissa, the poet has an encounter of a different kind, in terms of the revelation of innocence:

> Once, I remember, I was awakened
> by someone's laughter outside the window.
> It was evening, I did not recognize
> the voices. Was it true what they were saying
> about me? Innocence was revealed to me
> in a land less barren and ruinous –
> *not my own.* (*Dispossessed Nests* 58, italics mine)

So, it is in the search of innocence that the poet goes places. The "innocence" that he found revealed to him in *Dispossessed Nests*, through a perception of pain and suffering, is transcended to a sublime level in *Temple*. While in *Dispossessed Nests* the suffering was on a mass scale; in *Temple* it is on an individual level. Notes to *Temple* announces "the plight of Indian woman" (36) as its theme.

Temple, a long poem of over nine hundred lines, longer than *Relationship*, inevitably demands comparison with the latter. Unlike *Relationship*, *Temple* is more varied, more forceful in its philosophic intent and more social in its context. Here in *Temple* there is no indulgence with self and obsession with his locale; rather the poet's attempt here is to go beyond his people and place, to transcend all the barriers and divisions. His obsessive preoccupation with self is overcome in *Temple* by the use of different points of view and constant variation in tone and structure. *Temple* has many resemblances with *Relationship* in its use of images and its structure. *Temple* echoes such images from *Relationship* as "messianic sleep," and "sleep and action," (24). In *Temple* the very image of "the trail/ of the sleep-habit of her golden deer" (46) is driven to the core of the poet's central concern. While *Relationship* is divided neatly into twelve sections, each of equal length, *Temple* with its clear-cut division of three parts is deceptive. The first part is divided into seven sections, the second into eight and the third into four. Besides the text, *Temple* begins with a news item and ends with another.

Instead of following the traditional epic pattern of dividing the long poem into twelve sections, or its multiples, Jayanta Mahapatra, in conceiving the body of woman as temple and constructing a poem out of it, has made arbitrary inner divisions in *Temple*. Yet, he has kept the main structure of his long poem intact. The structure of *Temple* is clearly in the pattern of the architecture and the spirit of the Orissan temples. These three parts of *Temple* are: "The Hall of Dancing," "The Hall of Offering" and "Sanctum Sanctorum: The Shrine." And, then, there is "the Prologue". This structure is suggestive of, at least, two things, textually, the three-fold division corresponds to three broad stages of a woman's life—girlhood, marriage and motherhood. Secondly, the movement from one section to another denotes the reader's gradual realisation of the ultimate vision where, as the poet puts it, "the real and imagined calmly coalesce," (*Temple* 18). The poet clarifies the nature of this vision in the note appended at the end of the poem: "Hindu mythology states that the ultimate consciousness and the divine force are one and the same. A woman represents this divine force, *shakti*, and the ultimate consciousness. Man is only able to forge ahead through this force, accomplishing whatever he sets out to achieve. (*Temple* 56)

Temple begins with a news item, which speaks of an octogenarian, childless couple belonging to the weaver's community, Ramanujam (85) and Chelammal (80) committing suicide. The poem ends with another news item that speaks of a twelve-year old girl being gangraped and murdered. These two items suggest the endless suffering of the Indian woman which is indeed the basic concern of *Temple*. These two news items form the social context against which the poem is built. In the former case, the police believe that the couple committed suicide on account of their poverty and loneliness. From this brief outline of a double suicide the poet picks up Chelammal as the protagonist of his long poem and projects her as a poor, suffering and lonely woman. Here it is significant to note that Mahapatra chose the woman, not the man, as the protagonist of his poem. Here, the mysterious and complex character of woman is woven into the text. Woman, who plays a crucial role in the poet's evolving vision, is perceived in this long poem in the image of the temple. The ruinous temple and the ruined woman, hold the key to Mahapatra's vision in *Temple*. The very fact that he chooses woman as a symbol of suffering and possible redemption is an indication of his inclination to explore the féminine psychology or the "feminine principle," as he concedes in the Notes to *Temple*. (57)

Although the poet states in "Notes" that the plight of Indian woman is the theme of *Temple*, there is no attempt at story-telling or character building. Instead, the poem concerns itself with the very depth of feminine consciousness, with the psychological and spiritual plight of woman smitten by poverty, illusion and disillusionment. The poet perceives the multiple facets of womanhood, base and exalted, through disparate images that fuse into the imaginative portrait of Chelammal. The images employed in *Temple* emerge as a complex pattern embodying tenderness, the violation of tenderness and subdued violence.

As is customary in the prologue to the epics, "The Prologue" to *Temple* hints at Chelammal's character and the eventual culmination of her life at a blissful moment when the entire cosmic spirit participates and acknowledges her sublime act of suicide in reverence: "a nameless jasmine/burst into a silent white" and there were startling "tranquillity" and "a wisp of air." (11) If Chelammal's act of suicide conforms to the story of the news item, here in the prologue, there is also the equally conspicuous suggestion of the sense of vengeance that Chelammal's death symbolises. The poet addresses Chelammal as "savouring a pledge you had made," "You watched *the* vow cast its scarlet net in which destiny/tumbled and turned" and "now in a new reason of awakening/stirred a frenzy to force into the moments of your fantasy." (11) These two streams, the suicide and its symbolic sense of requital, run parallel, because, as the poet warns us in the Notes, "to all accounts, *Temple* represents a dream narrative." (57) What imparts to her story the epic grandeur is her being a pawn in the cosmic design: "everything had been planned, yet it was no plan" (10). That is why the "Prologue" ends with the suggestions of the protagonist's wish fulfilment:

> now in a new reason of awakening
> stirred a frenzy to force into the moments of your fantasy
> something that, even in fantasy, you did not possess,
> something other than the fearful flashes of human goodness.
> (11)

The prologue, thus evoking the destiny and the ultimate triumph of the meek and of "human goodness," sets the tone of the poem. The whole poem is an odyssey from the "fearful flashes of human goodness" to craving for the "fearful hunger for human goodness." (53)

"The Hall of Dancing" comprising of seven short sections shows Chelammal's early stage of life, her growth in the lap of nature, her sexual awareness, her consummation of the physical passion in marriage and, above all, her sense of helplessness are being a poor woman in a male-dominated society. The images that go into the making of the poem are those of tenderness. They are drawn from the rural landscape, reflecting the protagonist's innocence of mind and body. The images of innocence and tenderness are all-pervasive in the psyche of Chelammal and in the landscape she inhabits.

The very first section is a memory poem in the sense that it alludes to her past life, the life that ended with suicide. It speaks of the meek and futile lives of the women of Chelammal's kind who lived before her, or like her, committed suicide. The images that carry the burden of memory are "mirror," "wind" and "a river flowing backward" (14). This memory of failure and futility in life makes Chelammal more "conscious of being alive" (14). She is aware that "the instrument of incarnations fails to work" and also that there is "an avenging god wanting to share its offerings with others" (14). When the gods in different incarnations have not come to her rescue, when the scores of women before her have taken her kind of path, now it is she who is to determine the course of action she is to take to overcome the numbness that has been traditionally imposed upon her. The course she is to take, as is evident towards the close of the poem, is that of Putana.

By the second section of "The Hall of Dancing," Chelammal is seen to have got a faint awareness of her coming to age. The age she has reached might be "thirteen" (15), or "eleven" (16). Her initial awareness comes when she stands by the village well:

> By the old well, the first darkness
> caught her awareness, in the failing light.
> Perhaps she was thirteen. Underneath
>
> her growing breasts two swells of pain
> felled the first touch. Then evenly it spread
> its humid fever into the waiting brain. (15)

This description shows that she had her first knowledge "unawares" as much as she "waited" for it. This "humid fever," now associated with her age, was also hinted in the opening section, aptly put in the image of a paddy: "like a paddy in heat before it bursts into fruit." (14) The other images that bear the suggestions of tender age as well as of the sensation associated with it are: "the secret of the uncarved cup of flesh," (15) "new-born breast's slow rise," (16) "she/surfacing like baffled fish from hidden depths," (16) etc. The landscape upon which the story of her life is set is also befittingly described. The images that evoke the rural landscape are also in correspondence with the psyche and body of Chelammal. The elemental images correspond to and incorporate in it the being that Chelammal would be at her early teens: "the silvery monsoon took her for the ochre earth" (16), "The moon hives in her body" (17) and the "scattered footsteps of virgins" are "like gritty cattle-bones, dry ordure." (17) If in section II she senses her own growing body unawares while standing by the old well, in section III standing upon the river bank she fully realises the growing demands of her body. Chelammal's shifting of awareness occurs with the poet's shifting of emphasis from the dark of the narrow old well to the vastness of the open river:

> One afternoon, as the river
> brooded over the burning corpses on the bleak bank,
> Chelammal felt herself wake.

> inside her own shadow;
> she saw it all, the shallow ponds
> of her body strangling
> to the mauve tissues of hyacinth. (17)

Her being fully aware of her sexual need is signified in the images of the "burning corpses" which is suggestive of the consummation of sex. With this knowledge, the kind of abandoned, unbridled childhood of Chelammal, now gives way to shyness and mysterious fear suggested in the image of a "chameleon" running briskly and halting and then staring, "faint with a fear in the sun." (15) She now realises "that legs were not mere things to run with." (20)

In the fourth section, luminous sensuousness and mystery are imparted to her grown-up body. As she is now ready to be married off, her sitting like a bride is portentous:

> Now, like a mound of freshly-steamed rice
> she sits, in the white-haired vapour
> of a new hour, an ambiguous presence
> on a reed mat,
> as the drowsy earth anchors once again. (18)

The pre-marriage ritual that she would go through with her "two aunts, a distant cousin," applying turmeric to her "growing limbs" and her being bathed in the open—"her intimate secrets public spectacle" (19)—which is whetting like the "mystic hunger of a country" is yet to be "resisted" (19) with "the unappeased lust" settling down "like shallow backwaters in her mind" (19). There is a clear movement towards eventual consummation. The last part of this section, beginning dramatically with "that first time, she remembers," clinches the act of sexual consummation:

> As she moaned under the weight
> of the equation of flushed and unflushed tides
> of her body's promise,
> watching the lacquered spread
> of peacock feathers of her arms,

and the lure of vivid colour
suddenly turned sea-grey and distant,
making her scuttle inside
like a small stranded crab. (19)

But Chelammal is not privileged to live these ecstatic moments for a lifetime. Soon after this happiness, in section V, "grey mist of rain, dark cumulous/ flapping in the winds of July" (20) hover over her sky. These images of darkness, as against the images of her previous buoyant life, portends an evil future. She is led to realise that what her life has hitherto been "was play, mere play, /a game of leap-frog or snatch-the bride" (21) which she used to share with her childhood friends. Instead of those happy days, she would now be beset with the "fanatic sunsets" (21).

Before she meets her pre-ordained fate, Chelammal gets its premonition. She recounts her past life and wonders if at all she would meet the "promise of paradise" (23). The reminiscing of her past life brings back the memory of the simple village, its poverty, "the mud floor damp and sweaty," "earthen rice pot" and her mother who "would smile and nod and bend to the work, resting awhile/ to catch her breath" (22). It is only when she begins to question the belief that was imposed on her, that her inner self tries to come to the surface and she shows herself as a self-conscious woman:

Our minds were tied to the myth
that womanhood was pure. (23)

This self-consciousness unshackles her mind from the numbness of life she has lived so far. This attempt at achieving her freedom is first seen in her questioning: "But had I no right to dream? (25) With her "breath" startling her with the "promise of paradise" (25), she shows her preparedness to find the way out for herself, although it is not hinted at this stage what course she would ultimately take.

In the last section of this part of *Temple*, in "Chelammal's voice," the tone is exuberant, sensuous. She has in her voice the inclination to face the challenge of the myth of ideal womanhood, though at the end of her version, there is a conspicuous sense of despondency.

It is significant to observe that the voice following Chelammal's is the poet's own, in the first person. Pondering over the fate of Chelammal, the poet remembers the death of another girl in Kaveri. The suffering of the girl-child, and of women in general leads the poet to discover "a corner for myself/ where a dismal Asian silence looks up at me/from newborn mimosas in the grass" (24). The poet is moved to question his own self, in a mode of addresssing himself:

> Even in this remote, slack and wrinkled village
> on the bank of the Kaveri, the breeze
> trembles to the last breath of a drowned girl,
> yet you move about, Jayanta,
> as though nothing had ever happened here. (24)

This confrontation of the poet with his self brings forth further discomfort, further dismay. He finds himself helpless and, like his protagonist, the poet perceives himself as another pawn in the cosmic design. This fact of the poet, put in his own voice, conforms to his warning in the Notes: "*Temple* represents a dream narrative; and perhaps Chelammal *is* a character in someone else's dream-unaware herself that she is a main figure in this dream, unaware too that this dream might restore her to the world of reality." (57) The glide from "The Hall of Dancing" to "The Hall of Offering" is clear and definite in the former's concluding group of images like "old trees/shiver at the memory of birds that have long passed by" and "out of the river's silence/the breeze, with the eyes of the hunted, /begins to cry plaintively to get out." (25) These images foretell the loss of innocence and the violation of Chelammal's tender life that would constitute "The Hall of Offering."

"The Hall of Offering" asks for the sacrifice of Chelammal's chastity as it happens to the temple dancer, once she attains puberty. Her being "raped" and then "left to her fate" (29) is symbolic and is compatible with the spirit of "The Hall of Offering." Against her preordained life what at best she can do is to go dreaming, and in that process, "confuse memory with reality" (28). As in "The

Hall of Dancing," here also the poet frequently uses rural image in order to create an atmosphere befitting her plight. The images that depict her plight are predominantly those of the violation of tenderness.

The first section of "The Hall of Offering," with its "darkness of the day" (28) sets the tone of the ominous story. Once she has reached "the stage of ripe thighs of the temple dancer," her mind becomes "storm-riven" and "clowns/in turmeric-yellow and hibiscus-red" (28). The impending threat now strikes her—she is "raped". The entrapment to her fate is best worked out in the image of fish caught in drained terraces in the rice fields:

> like the fish spawned in rice fields,
> wasn't she fated to be caught
> when the terraces were finally drained? (29)

After she is "raped", the loneliness of her agonising life is further heightened when she finds that "her father, brothers all move with the sadness of men./ They belong, but not to her" (28). The image of laxman-rekha reinforces her isolation, because in the whirling embrace of this laxman-rekha "she sees all purpose elude her and disappear" (28). Now her isolation becomes complete with the family ties having been snapped from her. With the "rape", Chelammal's "life is made smaller" (28). She grows more withdrawn and lonely.

In the next section the poet draws a picture of her isolation which, apart from emerging from the prevailing ethos of male chauvinism, is inherent in her own race: "there is no woman/ who is not alone" (30). Or, rather, there is no other woman, as the poet says, "who is sure/she has found her way/ to her real purpose of life" (30). He sounds deterministic when he thinks that each time a woman suffers, each time she is "raped" or she commits suicide, another woman "chasten(s) the vision of her own death" (30). One cannot get rid of this thought so long as "the rough noose/of ownership" (30) of men is there round the throat of women. Woman's frail existence gets its apposite picture in the image of "origami crane in the wind" (31) and the stubborn attitude of men:

While the Man says:
It's the same story. The same one
we've heard a thousand times. (31)

Chelammal's violation of chasity, tenderness and, above all, of womanhood itself are summed up poignantly in the following lines:

Like a clock that has broken down
perhaps long ago,
she has no time, no answer
one day.
She simply fuses into a pale, thick smile,
a faceless shell on a beach. (31)

Section III continues to articulate this kind of suffering, lonely, inconsequential life of Chelammal. In this section we get to know her own version of what she feels about her catastrophe. This section, opening with her questioning, reveals the essence of her character with the questioning of her own state of being "condemned . . . to the legacy of possession" (32). She shows her preparedness to walk across the laxman-rekha, and rise to action with the hope of happiness "in the lives of my children to come" (33). But this hope is merely a dream in the sense that her child would never come, for at the end of this section we come to know that she is barren: "night scours my womb/with the ashes of solitude" (31). She now invokes the "solemn Ayodhya skies," and "savage dens of Siva" (33). Her invocation of Siva points to the evil potential of Putana. She would finally be transformed into an ogress to wreck her vengeance on man. Although by this stage of development of the story, she is slowly getting prepared to go for action, she is not completely without tenderness. With what has already happened to her, she is still able to dream and to wish to go back to her childhood days which was gentle as "susurrus of summer breezes," "golden doe's eyes" and "as a dream/ after consciousness is dispossessed by sleep." (32)

Section IV and Section V take Chelammal's story to "the centre of the arena" (34). In these sections when the poet says "she saw them search," he imparts to her an insight that enables her to see into the working of men's minds and thereby get an edge over them: "she stood among them, . . . a riddle on its pedestal" (34). Then follow the questions that reveal Chelammal's confrontation with the dominating male. She is filled with "light" in her shut eyes; she "reaches blindfully forward" (34). With each step, she is seen "reaching" (34) closer to her goal. The closer she comes to her goal, she is more certain of her possibility of being "free" (35). Her death is to set her free from the cycle of birth and death.

Section VI contains the last "Chelammal's voice" in *Temple*. In this final version, Chelammal opens up her secrets. She recalls how she had happy moments of sexual union: "Often, I recall, he made love to me/when we were sleeping" (37). Chelammal now thinks of a redeemer: "To my mind/ comes another exhausted man/ seated in an ill-lit prison cell" (37). That man is Nagabhusan Patnaik, the Naxalite leader. Nagabhusan Patnaik comes to her mind because, in her own words,

> He has seen the anguish on our faces,
> tried to lift us out of ourselves;
> I seem to know him so well, without ever
> seeing him. He could have been my son. (37)

Chelammal's picking up the image of Nagabhusan Patnaik as the instrument to attain her visionary state of womanhood is in itself a significant act though her dream remains only a dream because, Nagabhusan Patnaik with all his concern for the poor and the downtrodden, is nevertheless a fallen hero, who fails to redeem Chelammal and her tribe of the poor and destitute from the tyranny of social discrimination. He is now in "the dark prison cell . . . thinking of the time he was ready to kill, ready to plunge, ready to make the spider bleed to death; but now he whimpers as saliva drips, from his lips and his mind forgets when he was last sure of himself" (39). Chelammal's last monologue marks the end of her wistful reminiscences and her turning towards the end of her life.

The final section of "The Hall of Offering" prepares Chelammal to rise into action. This section, beginning with "her quickened pace in the ominous jungle" (40) and closing with "the light passed/ into the rotting jungles," (41) is in essence, a poem of darkness. The creation of such an atmosphere is conducive to the upsurge of Chelammal's inner strength to face the domineering world of men. She is now ready to carve out a world of her own – "her's wasn't a land without a flag" – because her once "tender" life has turned "ashen" (41). She finds "the pure eye of the earliest dream waking within her, driving her on, / this refulgent, unguessed" self that was inhibited so long would finally purify her life. That fire, it turns out, is nothing but the end of her own life that would lead to her *moksha*.

"The Hall of Offering" ends with a cynical note. Chelammal could not in reality find her ways out of the mess she was in. It is only in "Sanctum Sanctorum: The Shrine" that she discovers her inner self and hidden strength to combat the calamities of her life. Only when one reaches the bottom of suffering that one feels the urgency to come out of the pit. Chelammal, at last, discovers that she needs to rise to the call of her spirit, the source of her ultimate strength, the dwelling place of her consciousness. This dwelling place of Chelammal's consciousness corresponds to the image of "shrine" in the structure of the temple. In the opening section of this last part of *Temple*, the poet asks:

> In the hour of tearless grief
> what can lead one to the truth? (44)

Then the poet goes on searching for its answer. He puts one possible answer to the above question again in the interrogative form and the answer is "the light of guilt:"

> Can the light of guilt clarify,
> seeming to answer to one's happiness? (44)

As he does not seem to be satisfied with this answer, he goes on to put another answer, which is "the habit of sleep" and it is again in the question-form. As this question, whether "the habit of sleep" will ever serve the purpose of venting her pent-up wrath by "raising that inner self right where it belonged" (44), is not followed by another, this question is posed as a possible answer to the problem of reaching the true self. The poet puts Chelammal's changing of her course of life in the befitting image of "unmapping its boundaries/towards something greater than faith" (44). The poet employs this method of the habit of sleep because it would help Chelammal achieve her ultimate freedom, help her to "build into a myth" (44) of her own.

Chelammal hopes to build a myth of her own because she does not want to follow the submissive path traditionally followed by the Indian women who have been idealized as chaste and loyal. Instead, Chelammal wants to be aggressive, and if need be, she would even take the evil course to justify her righteous action. The evil role she is to take is that of Putana. The great mythical women like Sita, Savitri and Draupadi are basicaly of numb, docile and surrendering nature. On the other hand she hopes that if she takes recourse to the violent path, maybe the rage within, that comes of humiliation, can be assuaged, even if she is defeated at the end, the poet endows Chelammal with an aggressive role to raise her character from the traditional concept of illusion with which an Indian woman's life-pattern has been closely associated. The image of the Indian woman's illusion is usually taken from Sita's wish to have for her the golden deer. The poet discards this myth, as he also discards the myth of Draupadi—"probably the tale of the woman/ who could not be disrobed/ was a myth" (48)—and proposes the myth of Putana as a redemptive symbol of the Indian women's assertion of dignity, happiness and power. In proposing the role of Putana for Chelammal, the poet does not go for any other image than the one which Sita followed: wishing for the golden deer. But he reinvests this image with an altogether new dimension. This new dimension to "the habit of sleep" is aggression. Chelammal's donning this new role is in keeping with the story line of *Temple*. This "habit of sleep" is generative of energy which is otherwise known in the Hindu parlance as Shakti. The image of this "habit of sleep" finds its true expression in section II of "Sanctum Sanctorum: The Shrine" which begins with

> All through the house she followed the trail

of the sleep-habit of her golden deer
all through her need she followed the trail
of the sleep-habit of her golden deer . . .
on this most naked of her days
as she followed the trail
of the sleep-habit of her golden deer. (46)

The image of "the sleep-habit of her golden deer" carries the forceful energy of Chelammal that finally catapults her into action. This is the method through which she can think of fulfilling her secret wish, of actualizing her illusion. Here Chelammal is depicted to have followed the illusory path of Putana, not of Sita. While Sita's illusion was rather a romantic yearning, Putana's was one of action. Putana had also illusion, because when she ventured to kill Krishna, the child, she did not know that her prey was not mortal. Even if she was in illusion, the poet approves of her kind of illusion rather than Sita's. Putana's illusion has nonetheless a redemptive function because in her attempt to kill the child-god, she herself is killed and thereby she is released from the cycle of birth and death.

Here in *Temple* Chelammal follows the path of Putana. The illusory path of Putana suits Chelammals's character because living a life of suffering all through, Chelammal finally rises to action, or she thinks so, knowing very well that her action might not bear any fruit. The news-clipping at the end of the text bears testimony to her failure; despite all the steps taken, all things said and done, women's fate remains the same:

Khagaria, January 5, 1986

> A 12-year-old girl was allegedly gangraped and murdered in Biribasa Tola near here last Wednesday, according to the police. The police recovered her beheaded body. No one has been arrested so far.
>
> In the last two months, six rape cases and five murders of women have been reported from different places in the Khagaria district.
>
> *The Telegraph*, Calcutta (*Temple* 56)

Commenting on *Temple*, the poët himself concedes the importance of the role of illusion in the text: "It is difficult not to be influenced by the Indian doctrine of illusion, and I appear to have been taken in by it" (57).

Chelammal's following "the trail of the sleep-habit of her golden deer" clears all the web of complicity from her character and so from the text. At this stage of *Temple*, Chelammal rises again like a sleeping volcano, spitting live lava. Her sleep is not the mere literal sleep; it is

> the messianic sleep of womanhood
> which was only playing on herself
> to spend her hours of impotent rebellion. (49)

The portent of this magnificent sleep is pushed further when Chelammal

> wanted to found through mysteries of sleep
> the country of the infra-red delirium of memories
> that could hold no hidden designs
> where exotic birds played their parts
> and the great hooves of death lifted and fell. (47)

This 'sleep' of Chelammal serves as a mode of metamorphosis for her to take the role of Putana. Once she is possessed with the spirit of Putana, possessed as she was with her own story—"her story took possession of her" (47)—she enters "the unfathomable temple." This unfathomable temple is the secret clove of Chelammal's consciousness, of which she is now fully aware:

> And now the ogress,
> transformed into a lovely woman,
> her poisoned nipples
> the *moksha*-centre of her own martyrdom,
> awakens the woman of *the* mind. (48)

The image of breasts as her *moksha*-centre is pertinent because when Putana gave her poisoned breasts to the child-Krishna to suckle so that he would die, he sucked the breast so hard that he sucked not only all her milk but her life away. However, with her death as the legend goes, Putana attains *moksha* since she had acted as mother, even though an evil one, to the child-god. In the text of *Temple*, the death of Putana is described in the compelling images of the lofty and agonized, the virtuous and the redeemed. The great shadow of death is suggested in the images of "ash" and "dust". The lines describing her death, with no full stop at the end of the tortuous sentence, move incantatorily and finally reach a crescendo when, at last, Putana achieves her desired martyrdom:

> Writhing under the disastrous stroke of her fate
> she stopped, miraculously revealed:
> svelte and slender, mysterious in venomous virtue,
> set free by the unmistakable aura of rebirth
> the weapon of youth flashing again, lifted blade
> more terrible than the agonized mask of *shakti*,
> yet feeling the thirst that cauterized her insides
> her melancholy breasts stretching their shadows
> across the sacked hours of ashes and dust. (49)

Then comes the sudden denouement: "for this remains my obsession, terrifying metronome/ to come to you as cosmic mother" (50). This obsession is Chelammal's as well as the poet's. This role "will build the future myth" for Chelammal (50). As Chelammal is here raised to her martyrdom, to the spirit of "the cosmic mother", the poet hopes to raise his poetry to a level where he can hold "the tiny glint of innocence to infinity" (50), where poetry like a true mother feeding her child, can nourish the mankind. That is why Putana's death emerges triumphantly

> to become the razor's edge dividing two worlds
> and at that precise moment to allow myself to die. (50)

In Notes to *Temple,* the poet states that "this dream restores her to the world of reality" (57). As the world of dream and illusion merges with the world of reality of *Temple*, the section following the meaningful death of Putana, begins with an epigrammatic statement:

> *For only when you dream, reality begins* (52)

The very dream of Chelammal playing the role of Putana restores her to the world of reality. This preparedness of Putana to rise into action dissolves the boundaries of the real and, in the case of Chelammal, it transforms her from the traditional numb, surrendering type of woman to a woman of action and transposes her to a world which is gleaming with "the fearful hunger for human goodness" (53). The story of *Temple* reaching this stage of the "fearful hunger for human goodness" completes its journey which began with the search of "the fearful flashes of human goodness" (11). With the completion of this odyssey of a woman in the story of Chelammal, the Indian concept of the body of a woman as temple, finds "the revelation of the Circle" (54). The image of temple in the story of Chelammal culminates in her reaching the ultimate dwelling place of consciousness which, as the poet says, is the Shrine, where the eternal opposites merge in a divine union

> The saffron that trembles of the heart's cry
> savoured from both the perfume and the stink
> from love and despair, virtue and vice—
> a circle which returns the endless shrines
> to the soul from their crumbled temples
> and brings back all shapes
> to light from the nothingness of space. (55)

On another level, the poet wishes to merge life with art, act with belief, in order to achieve that "blind orgasm of epic and song," (55) which integrates action and feeling, body and soul, sense and sensibility, sin and redemption.

The Sentient Being: *A Whiteness of Bone* and *Shadow Space*

The senior poets in Indian English writing have almost produced their best work, and are now falling silent. A.K. Ramanujan is no more. We have been hearing the unsettling news of Nissim Ezekiel's Alzheimer's. R. Parthasarathy has been silent for a long time. The peak is getting thinner. Only Shiv K. Kumar has a book of poems, *Woolgathering*, published in 1998. A.K. Mehrotra, of course, has sprung back from his obscurity and an inscrutable silence of thirteen years with *The Transfiguring Places* but then he is not in the age group of those amidst whom he grew up as a force to reckon with. At a time like this we have Keki N. Daruwalla admiring Jayanta Mahapatra's prolific writing: "Jayanta Mahapatra stands among the sterile Indian crowd of English language poets who dry up after an average of two volumes. *Shadow Space* is Mahapatra's fourteenth or fortieth (I forget which) volume of poetry." *(Biblio* 28)

Only a Keki N. Daruwalla can come forward to embrace Mahapatra because he himself is in the league of these flamingoes. His latest book *Ministry of Permanent Unrest and Other Stories* was published in 1997. In this decade itself, Jayanta Mahapatra has published two volumes of poetry, *A Whiteness of Bone* and *Shadow Space*, *The Green Gardener*, a collection of stories and three books of poems in Oriya, his mother tongue: *Bali* (The Sacrifice), *Kahibi Gotia Katha* (I Will Tell You a Story) and *Baya Raja* (The Mad Emperor). This essay deals with Mahapatra's *A Whiteness of Bone* and *Shadow Space* and the three books of Oriya poems.

The sudden demise of A.K. Ramanujan in Chicago shocked us

all but the way it touched Jayanta Mahapatra had to result in the birth of a poem, "A Day in Marburg on-the-Lahn." This moving elegiac piece will perhaps remain as a milestone in Indian English poetry. "A Day in Marburg on-the-Lahn" is very much unlike Jayanta Mahapatra in the sense that it has no complex metaphors, no private symbols. In fact, like death baring life, any talk of death in poetry would strip its ornaments. The hearts of two men as such, of two poets come to the open. Here is the portrait of two poets, the homage of one to the other, the scrutiny of one's self and on the whole, speculation on the ultimate silence. Here one is struck by the intimate sharing of each other's world:

> Suddenly you said you had something to buy.
> "Birkenstock sandals," you went on to say.
> I had never heard of this brand before. "They are
> the best, you know, Jayanta." I didn't.
> A Bata was all I knew. You smiled, as you rose . . .
> (*Shadow Space* 47)

The two poets were meeting for the first time after twenty years since they knew each other. Even after that, they did not have any correspondence which speaks of the reticency and a lack of proficiency in pushing themselves forward. Says Mahapatra, he never wanted to ask Ramanujan "about poetry or peace or love."

In his keynote address delivered at the annual conference of Indian Association for Commonwealth Literature and Language Studies, held at Bhubaneswar, Jayanta Mahapatra spoke about the "bad heart" of a poet, his own: "Poetry makes me write poems with a bad heart. I don't know what that exactly means, but it is the heart that makes one turn secretly into someone—a leader or loser perhaps—pushing one to choose values, attitudes, and to do the not-so-obvious; this heart as it keeps on trying to hide the wounded walls of its house, and at the same time asking itself for a meaning to our lives." (*Haritham* 8)

In other words, "bad heart" for Mahapatra is being dismayed at the impact of television commercials over the people; "bad heart" is the wish of a poet to "see a just and fair society" though he cannot be "a social reformer"; "bad heart" is realising that all these wishes are "tall orders" and all that one hopes for through poetry brings one at last to the sad conclusion that exercise in poetry is all futile.

So, what kind of a poet's role does Mahapatra envisage for himself? In a poem "Last Night the Poem" in *Life Signs* he had an inkling of the futility of poetry: "But what use is a poem, once the writing's done? . . . Like the sound of a match striking, then over; I know that much." In *Shadow Space* poems are often referred to as countermeasures to overcome the feeling of guilt, of impotency at not being able to do anything corrective or constructive with his poems when the world is not as it should be:

> Indefinable, like life, with the government wrong,
> the thinking wrong, the world wrong.
> But the irony is beautiful. . . . (*Shadow Space* 49)

The variation of the reference to poetry, his own or poetry as a genre, questioning its efficacy occurs in as many as fifteen poems in *Shadow Space*. Those references are, like, "A hundred years hence/poems will still be luxuries." "I write my futile poems," "Poetry stumbles and falls" and even there is a title, "The Colourlessness of Poetry". If in one moment of quietude he muses "through words I try/to recover my balance," in one moment of rage he is willing to "trade" his poetry if it could stop the trading of innocent children by their starving parents in the drought-affected districts in Orissa.

In *A Whiteness of Bone,* the references to the role of poetry are no less disturbing. In "Light" one is given to believe that the sad fate of a poem is to be questioned of its worth:

> Let not the meaning remain behind
> as a poem, to be questioned. (20)

One gets the same vein of thought when Mahapatra terms poetry as that "Of a Questionable Conviction." This poem beginning innocently, talking of "A man" "who talks of pain", who "waits" night after night finding "excuses to live", trying to capture "light" that would come through the "empty window" to light up his heart, ends meaningfully because the man referred to was first painted as one in the present tense—"Maybe he *is* a poet"—but at the end of the poem he is pushed to the past tense: "They say he *was* a poet." But the concluding line "Such a harmless pastime never ruined anybody's sleep" is not that harmless to the kind of those authorities who have rewarded death to Osip Mandelstam or Benjamin Moloise. In the poem "The Rage in Those Young Eyes" which is dedicated to the African poet Benjamin Moloise, Mahapatra feels a deep pain but then he is aware that that will serve no purpose:

> Perhaps the rage in those young eyes of yours
> will never serve any purpose, great or small.

Moloise's poetry, like his consequent martyrdom at the altar of poetry, might not have served any purpose in any tangible way. Nonetheless, can we at all ignore his contribution however little that might have been to the movement against apartheid? Yet, one cannot be sure. Mahapatra might extol the power of poetry at the hands of a Jack Mapanje of Malawai where he is perishing in "some remote jail" ("Someone in My Room") but when he thinks of himself vis-a-vis Mapanje, he is not that sure of the force of his poetry:

> Someone in my room twenty years hence,
> and something suddenly born shall nudge me
> to convince my poem it should better stay dead.
>
> (*Shadow Space* 79)

Ineffectiveness, impotency, futility, inaction, death, these are the portentous words and worlds in which Mahapatra traces the origin of his poetry, into the sands of which the ostrich within him buries his head as a defense mechanism. His position is such, his confrontation with a hostile world is to no avail; he knows it yet he cannot ignore it. This complexity informs the art of Jayanta Mahapatra. A poem dealing with this dilemma or with the dissolution of it is "All the Poetry There Is" in *A Whiteness Of Bone*. In this poem Mahapatra's stand on the role of a poet is clearly pronounced. It begins dramatically with "All the poetry there is in the world/appears to rise out of the ashes" that echoes the Biblical wisdom: "Dust thou art, and unto dust shalt thou return." The world it goes on to create is a quiet and sombre one where one is humbled as one comes to know its cruelties. In a world like this "twenty persons were gunned down" for no fault of theirs. He cannot restructure the world out there. He builds a world of his own, in his poetry consoling himself:

> Poetry simply wants to know what sort of thing
> war was, or a sunset, even a bizzare crime.
> (*A Whiteness of Bone* 9)

If this can be the way with poetry, it "doesn't have to raise its voice." (9)

How ostrich-like the poet is! However hostile, like a desert, his world might be, he cannot live elsewhere. He will live in the world yet bury his head in the act of writing poetry. It is through this paradox that he hopes to alleviate his pain and agony. For this the poet needs to have an inner-detachment. With Mahapatra, earlier it used to be the pure, uncontaminated inner-world, the socio-cultural and mythic details of the past and the pastness of the present economic and political world. Now, like Brecht, he constructs his poetic world on the bad news of the present rather than on the golden past. *A Whiteness of Bone* is a collection of such poems that creates a catalogue of catastrophes that have ripped India into shreds, emotionally. Some of them are violence, mindless bloodshed in the province of the Punjab, thousands dead due to gas-leakage in the Union Carbide factory at Bhopal, assassination of Indira Gandhi and the riot in its trail in Delhi and the self-immolation by fire of students protesting against the implementation of caste law. All these dark sides of life in the present time find expression in such apposite metaphors as:

> Night is where slavish stars move,
> where darkened roads grip the heart
> in dumb cries of rage and fear.

> Yet one falls back on the idea of happiness
> balancing oneself, with words, a spinning top.
> (*A Whiteness of Bone* 44)

This is how Jayanta Mahapatra responds to the Bhopal-tragedy: not going into the details of it but creating an aura of "rage and fear." His heart—the same "bad heart" as referred to earlier—is in the grip of "the darkened roads." Again in another poem "The Hill" "its own darkness" "swallows" the hills of Bhopal. Intimidated by darkness, all his cries of rage and fear go "dumb." The only way for the poet to escape from this impasse is to "fall back on the idea of happiness." And he can gain access to it by balancing himself with his words like "a spinning top." A spinning top, which is the synthesis of movement and stasis, storm and calm, is a metaphor for the condition of this poet who lives in a world that is unconducive to his act of writing poetry. In order to achieve this condition of being he tries to become "a spinning top." Therein lies his idea of happiness, his sanity which is, as he puts it in the poem "Death of a Nameless Girl in Bhopal, December 1984" "necessary" for him to write and to live.

Only in a state of mind like this can a poet sanely approach that period of student unrest in which many of them chose self-immolation by fire as a sign of protest. In this case the poet does not feel "sad or angry", but "worn". Since he cannot stop anything, since he has to live, he seems to tell himself, why not create an ambience of lyricism that would make life less painful and why not balance himself with the words? The metaphor of a balanced spinning top finds its twin in the metaphor of the dancer merging in his dance although in this context the dance is that of death enacted through the students:

> They are dying, dancers in the air, like birds, almost human,
> adorned with the sunshine of youth,
> their hearts consumed with purpose,
> their hands folding their flame like festive ritual lamps,
> gathering wings— (*A Whiteness of Bone* 66)

What Jayanta Mahapatra says in another context in "About My Favourite Things" could be applicable here, supplementing the irony embedded in it: "But the irony is beautiful . . ."

What is still more significant about this irony is that the tragic incident occurred on Mahatama Gandhi's birth anniversary. The way the poet describes the day it resembles Mahatma Gandhi: "This day, lean and naked." Thinking of Gandhi, he feels a pain in his heart; he is amidst "an uncertain, misled glory." He asks himself, will life be ever the same again?" Thinking of the grim present he cannot but think of Gandhi but what does he give him in return?

> The photograph of Gandhi in the new airport lounge
> is more than forty years old.
> Everytime I look into the old man's eyes
> he calmly hands my promise back to me.
>
> (*A Whiteness of Bone* 50)

This love for Gandhi dates back to his youth, when he was eighteen. Then he used to attend prayer-meetings of Gandhiji at Patna. That must have left an indelible impression on him. Although he is having a good number of poems on or referring to Gandhi, now he has embarked upon a long poem on him. In an interview to *The Hindu,* asked about what he was doing now, he said, "I am doing something on Gandhiji. The Mahatma has always fascinated me. I am doing a sort of long poem (on him)."

Why should Gandhi, who sculpted freedom for India, hand the poet's promise back to him? Is the poet's land that unredeemable? So many fissures are now cropping up in the country. Dismayed at it, he laments:

> Land, our land,
> there is so much land between us now.

Mahapatra's view of his country is mostly tinged with irony. In "March," he accepts his country, but not without a pinch of salt: "this country of mine/home to the home of vows." In "Another Love Poem" he is at his best in scathing his country: "This country lives, on its image." What sort of image does the country have before the world? Image of poverty, violence, and what else? The images the poet associates with his country and its people are, "in a boy's hand/the flipped coin of life's meaning," "the faces" are ominous and cruel as the moon," "a sunlit blind sky," etc. After piling up all these images which throw light on the dark face of his country, he comes out with his declaration:

> In a country drugged with its image,
> I only find my way in metaphor.
>
> (*A Whiteness of Bone* 63)

So, the ostrich of a poet buries his head again in the sands of metaphor since what the substance of the poem points is that either the poet is being torn between the horns of dilemma the kind of which he articulates in political metaphors like

> We have become stiff and cautious with each other
> as this country is with the US and the USSR

or he is growing melancholic: "Do I ask too much of my land?" which is redolent of the lamentation we had noticed earlier in "The Fifteenth of August." Not that he was not unaware of this streak of melancholy creeping of late into his poetry but he had not laid so much stress on it as he does now. In the very first poem of *A Whiteness of Bone*, "Silent in the Valleys", putting his first step, with the first line, into the world (of his poetry) he finds it is "full with toys, many of them unused" and in the line following it, he is back at his self: "Do I detect a note of melancholy in my voice?"

Mahapatra's resorting to "metaphors" certainly helps him. It is evident in a poem like "Song of the Homeless Girl." Dealing with political themes in India, perhaps there could be no better way of hinting at the prospect of a homeless girl than bringing in the bedlam in the parliament whose live telecast one watches on television:

> as a parliament groans
> under the weight of another debate

because everybody knows all these debates have hardly changed the lot of the poor.

Then, poem after poem, which are largely of identical themes, tending to be repetitive, where does the poet lead us? He seeks a bliss not to be had easily neither in life, nor in poetry, not certainly in his land, where "everything is called sacred. Even poems." Are we to accept these words on their face-value, or to read the reverse side of it: *Nothing is sacred. Not even the poems?*

These being the sociological factors before which he finds his poems cowering, Mahapatra's concern with his ageing in these two collections of poems has its due place. In "Life," he says, "when death is near/there is nothing else to see." He feels the shadow of his ageing on his eyebrows; so, an autumn casts "the shadow" of "its isolated hours." In the poem "Someone in My Room", Mahapatra is lucidly and elegantly gliding about a time "twenty years after now" when he will be no more, when a stranger will be pacing in his room, trying to construct a brief history of "pain" of a poet who despite his disclaimers left some ways "to assert (his) will" to act upon another's:

> Air has a terrible density; it has no formal laws,
> but strangely it asserts a person's will
> to act upon another's. (*Shadow Space* 79)

This essay will be incomplete if a brief reference to Jayanta Mahapata's foray into Oriya writing is not made. Mahapatra started writing poems in his mother tongue, Oriya, sporadically in late eighties and seriously in nineties. It is not surprising to find him at the end of his English writing as a bilingual poet. It is because although he writes in English, he lives among his people with whom he converses in his mother tongue, of whose cultural milieu he is a part. Usually a poet living in metropolises like Delhi and Mumbai does not have to be a bilingual, as has been the case with Adil Jussawalla and Vikram Seth. On the other hand, those bilingual poets who have made their presence felt are A.K. Ramanujan, Arun Kolatkar, Dilip Chitre, etc. And now Jayanta Mahapatra writes in his mother-tongue, Oriya.

In many of his prose pieces, Jayanta Mahapatra had reiterated that he wrote in English because of his English education from the British teachers. But then, his love for his native place and mother tongue drove him to translate Oriya poetry into English. He has translated as many as five books of Oriya poems. But the translation in itself did not give him solace. He began to feel, after a long career in English writing, that perhaps his poetry did not reach his own people. As to the cause of his turning into an Oriya poet, the impact of his Oriya poems on the Oriya readers and poets and the aesthetic as well as creative satisfaction in writing in his mother tongue, Mahapatra says this: "I think the younger readers are looking up to me and the younger poets are emulating my style. My language is not that good. My *bhasa* is not that good in Oriya. My poetry is more colloquial and uses the common idioms and it makes me very happy that I am a part of my own milieu, part of my environment, or else, at the end of my life, I wouldn't have turned to Oriya poetry. I wanted to touch the rickshaw puller in the street, the cycle mechanic who repairs my bicycle. I couldn't have done all this with an English book in my hand." (*The Hindu*)

In fact in all the three Oriya books of poems that Jayanta Mahapatra has written so far, there are a good number of poems which he could not have written in English. It's because they are more culture-specific. Perhaps, he couldn't have found proper substitutes and equivalents of the Oriya words in English. Their verve and cadence could not perhaps have been brought in successfully in a foreign language. In a way, this radical rewriting of Mahapatra of his present time as well as his past speaks of the triumph of the Indian language tradition over that of English in India. For example, Mahapatra has a poem called "Grandfather" in *Life Signs* which is quite striking and is evocative of that period in which his grandfather became a Christian. But the poem he has written now in Oriya on the same subject is no less intense. Here we have this poignant expression, that comes with his grandfather's conversion from Hinduism into Christianity: "The God's face changed in an instant."

Likewise, there is a poem "The Sprouting Grass" in his second collection, *Kahibi Gotia Katha* (I Will Tell You a Story). In this poem the poet talks of the forbearance and fate of a woman living in the rural Orissa countryside. "Her palms are hard as stone." "Long cracks furrow her feet." Her days are "like hard knots in her stomach". And finally the poet endows her with the virtues of earth:

> But then
> when the children sit down for their evening meal
> around her in the lamp's frail glow, they feel
> as if grass, green and tender,
> begins to sprout from her tired limbs.
>
> (Translated from Oriya by the poet)

Mahapatra is better with those Oriya poems of his where he deals with the sociological themes. The characters depicted in those poems are like "Raju," the sweeper boy or a cycle mechanic or a rickshaw puller. His empathy with his characters saves his poems from being didactic. As he himself admits, his diction in Oriya is lacking in felicity as he is not well conversant with the language found in contemporary Oriya writing. This is a problem with his abstract Oriya poems in which the words, appropriate ones, perhaps do not come to him naturally as they are said to come. It is ironical that his mother tongue is his second language so far as his poetry writing is concerned. Jayanta Mahapatra has translated a few of his own Oriya poems into English to see for himself and to let others see as to how they emerge in English, but the ones he rewrites in English work wonders, bring him back to his essentially immaculate, poetic self and to his sentient being. One such poem is "Silence" which he re-did from his Oriya for *The New Yorker*. A stanza from it shows how like "a garden spider", he "silently spins (his) web" of poetry:

> The saints are all silent inside their own truths.
> Moss broods silently in the cracks of the stone,
> Four-year-old Pratick is silent inside his screams.
> Nobody answers him although they surround his fears.

Works Cited

Allen, Dick. Review of *A Rain of Rites, Poetry,* CXX, V (September, 1997), 342-52.

Allen, Frank. "Crisis of Belief," *Parnassus: Poetry in Review*, 9, 1 (Spring/Summer 1981), 332-41.

Anonymous. "Some Contemporary Poets," *The Statesman*, October 24, 1971.

Barnie, John. Review of *Life Signs, Kunapipi*, 6, 3 (1984), 107-22.

Bayes, Ronald H. "World Music from a Land Often Stricken by Tragedy," *The Fayeteville Observer*, Sunday Morning, December 2, 1971.

Chitre, Dilip. "Poetry in the Enemy's Tongue," *New Quest* (March-April 14, 1979), 77-82.

Corseri, Gary. "Vision of a Reconciliator," *Fiction, Literature and the Arts Review*, 1,3 (1983) 20-21.

Cotter, James Finn. Review of *The False Start*, *The Hudson Review*, XXX, 3 (Autumn 1982), 477-78.

Cox, C.B. Review of *The False Start, Critical Quarterly*, 24.1 (1982), 90-91.

Daruwalla, Keki N. Review of *Shadow Space*, "Circular Meditations," *Biblio*, Jan-Feb, 1998, p.28.

Ellen, Hymowitz. Review of *A Rain of Rites, What is New in Scholarly Books*, Fall 1976.

E.N. Review of *Close the Sky, Ten by Ten, The Illustrated Weekly of India*, 9 April, 1972, p. 45.

Gabriel, M.C. "A Latest Arrival," *Thought*, December 25, 1971.

Gopalkrishnan. A review of *Close the Sky, Ten by Ten, The Hindustan Times*, April 6, 1972.

Grosholz, Emily. "Poetry Chronicle," *The Hudson Review*, XXXV,

2 (Summer 1981), 319-33.
Howard, Ben. Review of Jayanta Mahapatra's *Selected Poems. Poetry*, CLII, 2 (November 1988), 113-14.
Jussawalla, Adil. "Just a Poem Maker," *The Times of India*, January 15, 1973, p. 11.
Kemp, Jan. "Poet to Poet," *Kunapipi*, XI, 3 (1989), 45-49.
King, Bruce. *Modern Indian Poetry in English* (New Delhi: Oxford University Press, 1987).
——. "The Shapes of Solitude," *The Poetry of Jayanta Mahapatra*, ed. Madhusudan Prasad.
Kohli, Suresh. Review of *Close the Sky, Ten by Ten, Indian Literature*, 15, 1 (1975), 37-38
Mahapatra, Jayanta. *Close the Sky, Ten by Ten* (Calcutta: Dialogue Publication, 1971).
——. *Svayamvara and Other Poems* (Calcutta: Writers' Workshop, 1971).
——. *A Father's Hours* (Calcutta: United Writers, 1976).
——. *A Rain of Rites* (Athens: University of Georgia Press, 1976).
——. *Waiting* (New Delhi: Samkaleen Prakasan, 1979).
——. *The False Start* (Bombay: Clearing House, 1980).
——. *Relationship* (New York: The Greenfield Review Press, 1980).
——. *Life Signs* (New Delhi: Oxford University Press, 1983).
——. *Dispossessed Nests* (Jaipur: Nirla Publications, 1986).
——. *Burden of Waves and Fruit* (Washington D.C.: Three Continents Press, 1988).
——. *Selected Poems* (New Delhi: Oxford University Press, 1987).
——. *Temple* (Denmark: Dangaroo Press, 1989).
——. *A Whiteness of Bone* (New Delhi: Viking, 1992).
——. *Shadow Space* (Kottayam: DC Books, 1997).
——. *Bali* (Cuttack: Vidyapuri, 1993).
——. *Kahibi Gotia Katha* (Cuttack: Arya Prakashan, 1995).
——. *Baya Raja* (Cuttack: Vidyapuri, 1997).
——. "about HUNGER and myself," *Keynote*, No.1 March, 1982.
——. "An Orissa Journal, July to November 1972," *Queen's Quarterly*, LXXX, 1, (Spring 1973), 65-73.

——. "Face to Face with the Contemporary Poem," Indian Association for Commonwealth Literature and Language Studies Newsletter, Mysore, No. 9, April 1991, 38-43.

——. "The Door," Sunday Review of *The Times of India*, 7 April, 1991.

——. "I Can Mould English to My Private Needs" (in conversation with Konnakuzy Ittira), Express Weekend, *Indian Express*, Delhi, Saturday July 22, 1989.

——. "The Inaudible Resonance in English Poetry in India," *The Literary Criterion*, 15, 1 (1980), 27-36.

——. "Letters from India—Summer Dusts and a Scent of Mangoes," *The Hudson Review*, XXXIX, 2 (Summer 1996), 185-91.

——. "Poetry: Climate for Renewal," The David H. McAlpin and Sally Sage McAlpin Lecture, A Dhvanyaloka Publication, Mysore, 1985, 7-16.

——. "The Poet's Blues," *Youth Times*, VII, 17, Bombay (1-14 February 1980), 10-11.

——. "The Quality of Mystery," Postscript, *The Indian Post*, Bombay, Sunday June 21, 1987.

——. "Slow Swim in Dim Light: Quest for Modernity in Poetry" *The Bombay Literary Review*, No.1, 1991, 5-11.

——. Speech at Sahitya Akademi Award Winning Function held at New Delhi, 1982.

——. *Contemporary Authors Autobiography Series, Vol.9*, ed. Mark Zadrozny, Detroit, Michigan, Gale Research Company, 137-50.

——. "Silence to Poetry: Piercing the Rock," *Haritham*, Kottayam, 8, 1, 1997, p.8.

——. "Silence," *The New Yorker*, June 23 & 30, 1997, p.111.

Mcbride, Daniel. Review of *Life Signs*. *The Toronto South Asian Review*, 5, 2 (Fall-Winter 1986), 87-91.

Mohanty, Sachitananda, "The Mythic and the Modern," *The Hindu*, October 18, 1998.

Naik, M.K. "Only Connect," *The Indian Book Chronicle,* January 13, 1983, p.16.

Neruda, Pablo. *The Heights of Macchu Picchu* (London: Jonathan

Cape).

Paniker, Ayyappa K. "Peacocks Among Patriarchs," *New Quest*, 2, August, 1997, 59-78.

Parameswaran, Uma. Review of *Life Signs, Journal of South Asian Literatures*, 212, 1986, 255-57.

Parthasarathy, R., ed. *Ten Twentieth Century Indian Poets* (New Delhi: Oxford University Press, 1976).

Perry, J.O. "Neither Alien Nor Postmodern: Jayanta Mahapatra's Poetry from India," *The Kenyon Review*, VIII, 4, Fall 1986.

——. "Determinations of Poetry," *The Poetry of Jayanta Mahapatra*, ed. Madusudan Prasad. 40-73.

Prasad, Madhusudan, ed. *The Poetry of Jayanta Mahapatra* (New Delhi: Sterling, 1986).

Raina, M.L. "Interrogating Myths," *The Indian Book Chronicle*, VI.1 (October, 1 1981), 326-27.

Raghavan, N. "Inner View: N. Raghavan talks to Jayanta Mahapatra," *Tenor*, No.1 (June 1978), 59-64.

Samantaray, Dipak. "Poets Are Ordinary People," *The Sunday Observer* (May 27, 1984), p.18.

Sarang, Vilas. *Indian English Poetry since 1950: An Anthology* (Hyderabad: Disha Books, 1989).

Shahane, Vasant A. "*Relationship*: A Study in Myth," *The Poetry of Jayanta Mahapatra*, ed. Madhusudan Prasad. 168-80.

Simms, Norman. "A Poet of Many Worlds," *The Poetry of Jayanta Mahapatra*, ed. Madhusudan Prasad. 24-39.

Swain, Rabindra K, "The Sentient Being," *Verse*, New York, 1999.

Syal, Puspinder. "Two Shades of Metaphor," *New Quest*, May-June, 1981. 195-99.

——. "The Use of Language," *The Poetry of Jayanta Mahapatra*, ed. Madhusudan Prasad. 220-36.

Woodward, Kathleen. "Instant Repulsion: Decrepitude, The Mirror Stage and Literary Imagination," *The Kenyon Review*, V, 4 (1983), 43-67.

Young, Vernon. "Poetry Chronicle," *The Hudson Review*, XXX, 4 (Winter 1977).

कालिदासविरचितं

मेघदूतम्

སྤྲིན་གྱི་ཕོ་ཉ་ཞེས་བྱ་བ།།

MEGHADŪTA

मेघदूतम्

སྤྲིན་གྱི་ཕོ་ཉ་ཞེས་བྱ་བ།།

MEGHADŪTA

Critical Edition with Sanskrit and Tibetan Index

Edited & Prepared by

Lama Chimpa

Retired Head, Department of Indo-Tibetan Studies

Visva Bharati University, Shantiniketan(W.B.)

Bimalendra Kumar

Professor, Department of Pali & Buddhist studies, B.H.U. Varanasi

&

Jampa Samten

Associate Professor, Department of Social Science

Central University of Tibetan Studies, Varanasi

First edition India 2011

ISBN 978-81-7742-105-7

Rs. 750

Published in India by Aditya Prakashan, New Delhi.
www.adityaprakashan.com
contact@adityaprakashan.com

Printed at Salasar Imaging Systems, C-7/5, Lawrence Road
Indl. Area, Delhi – 110 035.

INTRODUCTION

The fame of the *Meghadūta* was so popular that it was translated into more than forty-five languages. The *Meghadūta* attracted the scholars of Tibet in early 14th century A.D. and was translated into Tibetan language. It is not possible to mention the exact date of the translation of the *Meghadūta* as it has not been mentioned in the work that when the work was translated. Only a tentative date of the translation may be suggested on the basis of the date of the translators.

The history of the translation activities in Tibet may be grouped into three separate periods on the basis of the date of the translation of the works. The first period may be identified from mid-seventh century A.D. to mid- 9th century A.D. The second period may be from eleventh century A.D. to 14th century A.D. and the last and the third phase may be from 15th century A.D. to 18th century A.D. During the second period, mainly the local chieftains provided the financial assistance for the translation of the works as there was no central rule during that period in Tibet. The Tibetan Royal Empire ended with the murder of the last king Lang Darma in the early 841 A.D.).

It is known from the colophon of the *Meghadūta (Tib. sPrin gyi pho nya)* of the great poet Kālidāsa (*Tib. Nag mo khol*) was translated into Tibetan by the joint efforts of the Indian Pandit Sụmanaśri and the Tibetan Lo tsa bạ Jangchub Tsemo (1303-1380) and Namkha Zangpo. According to Blue Annals, Bu ston Rinchen grub (1290-1364), a great Tibetan scholar and compiler of Tibetan Canonical literatures had received several tantric teachings concerning on Avalokiteśvara from the Kashmirian Pandit Sumanaśri . It clearly suggests that he lived in Tibet in the early years of 14th century and translated the *Meghadūta* during his stay in Tibet. Sumanaśri was a great Pandit from Kashmir. The colophon describes him as the great poet and Pandit of Kashmir (*Tib. Kha che'i pan ḍi ta snyan ngag mkhan chen po)*. The same source also suggests that the work was translated in the great monastery of Sakya Mahāvihara (*Tib. Dpal Sakya'i gtsug lag khang chen po*) in Tibet.

The Tibetan Lo tsa ba Jangchub Tsemo was a nephew and disciple of Pang lo tsa ba Lodro Tenpa (1276-1342). He was born in Water- Hare *(Tib.Chu mo yos)* which corresponds to 1303 A.D. in the southern La-stod of Tibet. In the childhood, he became the disciple of the great scholar and translator Pang Lodro Tenpa and mastered in Three *Pitakas*, the precious class of Tantras and the Sanskrit language. He also studied the lesser sciences and mastered them all. By the order of dpal ldan bla ma Dam pa, he became to have contributed five translations to *Bstan-`gyur*, one in tantra section, four in the sāstra section. Among the latter four, besides the two grammatical translations, there are two translations, worked by him in collaboration with his disciple Namkha Zangpo. These works are namely *Chandoratnākara* and *Meghadūta*. These two poetical works were also translated jointly with Sumanaśri.

According to the Blue Annals, the second translator of *Meghadūta, Namkha Zangpo was* equally well versed in Tantras, Grammar and Buddhist Logic. He preached extensively the Kàlachakra system not only in Kashmir, but also in other areas. The same source, further explains that Dharmasvamin phyogs-las rnam-rgyal learned the Kàlachakra and the commentary called Vimalaprabhà from our Lo-tsa-ba. Since the time of Dharmasvamiṇ was from 1306 A.D. to 1386 A.D., it may be presumed that the third translator of the work lived during this time.

The *Meghadàta* was translated into Mongolian language during the reign of Kublai Khan. The Mongolian scholars, however, consulted the Tibetan version of the *Meghadūta* and translated the work from its translation. However, some scholars opine that the translators of the Mongolian *Meghadūta* not only consulted the Tibetan translation but they also consulted the Sanskrit original of the *Meghadūta.*

As a result of Tibet's continuous cultural interactions with India, Tibetans have produced the largest number of translations of Indian literature. Tibetan *Tripitaka* collection, known as *Kagyur* and *Tangyur* preserves over five thousand titles translated from Indian languages, mainly Sanskrit, embracing treatises on grammar, poetry, rhetoric, logic (the fundamental works on Buddhist logic by Dignāga, Dharmakīrti, etc.), politics and social ethics (such as *Cāṇakyanītiśāstra*, Nagarjuna's three works on Nītiśāstra, etc.), medicine (such as *Aṣṭāṅgahṛdaya-saṁhitā* by Vāgbhaṭa and its commentary by Candranandana), astrology (such as Svarodayārtha-saṁhitā by Harivarma and *Āyurgaṇitaphalaprakāśa* by Mānapuruṣa), chemistry (such as *Rasasiddhiśāstra* by Vyāḍipada and Rasāyanaśāstroddhṛti by Ratnaśri), art and iconography (*Pratibimbamānalakṣaṇa* by Ātreya), biographies of saints (such as Asokāvadāna, Kuṇālāvadāna) and of course, Buddhism and Buddhist philosophy. Tibetans have not only preserved the translation, but maintained and nurtured the tradition of teaching through direct transmission from master to disciple that guarantees the authority and validity of the Buddhist doctrine and the correct interpretation of the above scriptures. Many of the Indian literatures lost in its original form can be reconstructed from its Tibetan translation.

The Tibetan translation of the *Meghadūta* is preserved in the *Tangyur* (the collection of the translation of commentarial works) authored by non-Tibetan scholars. There are four xylographic editions of *Tangyur*. They are as follows.

1. *Narthang Tangyur:* Miwang Phola Sonam Topgyal, the then ruler of Central Tibet, patronized the work of carving the woodblocks for the Tangyur in 1741 at Shelkar and was completed in 1742. This remarkable speed was achieved by employing about 400 men. *Narthang Tangyur* is based on the *Tangyur* written out at Chingwa Tagtse under the auspices of Desi Sangyaẏ Gyatsho in 1688 and which is consisted of 224 volumes. *Narthang Tangyur* has also 224 volumes.

2. *Derge Tangyur:* Under the patronage of Tenpa Tsering, the King of Derge, the work of carving the wood blocks for a *Derge Tangyur* began in 1737 and was completed in 1744. . The first edition of Derge *Tangyur* consisted of 209 volumes, but, like the *Kagyur*, was later expanded, four new volumes were inserted and the final volume was amended. Therefore, the present *Derge Tangyur* consists of 214 volumes. Despite being a smaller edition than some, the Derge edition remains the most accurate, in that it contains the fewest mistakes.

3. *Chone Tangyur*: The eldest son of Marzor Gonpo (1686-?), King of Chone, a province of Amdo, Tibet initiated the work of carving blocks for an edition of the Tanjur which was begun in 1753 and completed in 1772, within a period of twenty one years. It is a faithful copy of the earlier edition of *Derge Tangyur* and consisted of 209 volumes including the volume of catalogue.

4. Peking edition: the work of carving of the blocks for the *Tangyur* collection began some time in 1724 at Peking under the patronage of Emperor Khang-shi of China,. This Peking edition of *Tangyur* is a faithful copy of the *Tangyur* commissioned by Desi Sangyas Gyatsho, the ruler of Tibet in 1688. The Khang-shi edition of *Kagyur* of 1700 and *Tangyur* of 1724 were reprinted in book form in between 1958-1965 by Suzuki Research Foundation, Tokyo in 151 Volumes and was freely distributed to many Universities and Educational institutions all over the world.

The Tibetan text of the *Meghadūta* prepared for this bilingual publication is based on the Derge edition, nevertheless, the variant readings of Narthang and Peking editions are also provided in footnotes for the convenience of readers.

(Prof. Bimalendra Kumar)

कालिदासविरचितं मेघदूतम्

སྤྲིན་གྱི་ཕོ་ཉ་ཞེས་བྱ་བ།།

༄༅། །རྒྱ་གར་སྐད་དུ། མེ་གྷ་དཱུ་ཏམ། བོད་སྐད་དུ། སྤྲིན་གྱི་ཕོ་ཉ་ཞེས་བྱ་བ།
ཡང་དག་པར་རྫོགས་པའི་སངས་རྒྱས་གསུང་གི་དབང་ཕྱུག་ལ་ཕྱག་འཚལ་ལོ།

कश्चित् कान्ताविरहगुरुणा स्वाधिकारप्रमत्तः
शापेनास्तंगमितमहिमा वर्षभोग्येण भर्तुः।
यक्षश्चचक्रे जनकतनयास्नानपुण्योदकेषु
स्निग्धच्छायातरुषु वसतिं रामगिर्याश्रमेषु।।1।।

རྗེ་བོ་ཁྲིམས་པའི་[1] ཤིན་ཏུ་ལྕི་བའི་བཀའ་ལུང་དག་གིས་གཟི་བརྗིད་ཉམས་པར་བྱས་གྱུར་ཅིང་།
གནོད་སྦྱིན་འགའ་ཞིག་ལ་ནི་རང་ཉིད་བག་མེད་དབང་གྱུར་མཛེས་མ་སྤངས་[2] ལ་ལོ་ཡི་བར།
ཡིད་འོང་སྐྱེད་བྱེད་བུ་མོའི་ཁྲུས་བྱ་བསོད་ནམས་ཆེ་བ་[3] ཆུམས་དང་ཤིན་ཏུ་རབ་མཛེས་པའི།
རབ་བཟང་ལྗོན་གྲིབ་མ་དང་ལྡན་དྲ་མའི་རི་བོར་[4] སོང་ལ་སྤྱོད་པས་གནས་པར་གྱིས། ༡།

तस्मिन्नद्रौ कतिचिदबलाविप्रयुक्तः स कामी
नीत्वा मासान्कनकवलयभ्रंशरिक्तप्रकोष्ठः।
आषाढ़स्य प्रथमदिवसे मेघमाश्लिष्टसानुं
वप्रक्रीडापरिणतगजप्रेक्षणीयं ददर्श।।2।।

---

༡ པེ། སྣར། པས།
༢ པེ། སྣར། སྤོང་།
༣ པེ། སྣར། ཆུ་བོ།
༤ པེ། སྣར། རྣ་མའི་ར།

འདོད་ལྡན་དེ་ནི་མཛེས་མ་སྤངས་ཤིང་ཟླ་བ་འགའ་ཡིས་རི་བོ་དེ་ར་ནི་ཕྱིན་བྱས་པས།
ལག་པ་ཕྲ་བ་གྱུར་ནས་གསེར་གྱི་གདུ་བུ་དག་ནི་དཔུང་པའི་བར་དུ་རྒྱུ་བར་བྱེད།
ཆུ་སྟོད་ཟླ་བ་རྫོགས་པའི་ཉིན་ལ་སྤྲིན་རྣམས་རི་ཐོད་རི་སྟེང་ཉལ་བར་གྱུར་པ་ནི།
མཆོག་ཏུ་རོལ་ཅིང་མཛེས་པར་གྱུར་པའི་གླང་ཆེན་ཡིན་ནམ་སྙམ་དུ་རྟོག་ཅིང་མཐོང་བར་གྱུར། ༢།

तस्य स्थित्वा कथमपि पुरः कौतुकाधानहेतो
रन्तर्बाष्पश्चिरमनुचरो राजराजस्य दध्यौ।
मेघालोके भवति सुखिनोऽप्यन्यथावृत्ति चेतः
कण्ठाश्लेषप्रणयिनि जने किं पुनर्दूरसंस्थे।।3।।

ནོར་ཅིང་[1] རྒྱལ་པོའི་རྗེས་འབྲངས་དེ་ལྟར་གནས་དེ་མདུན་དུ་ཀེ་ཏའི་མེ་ཏོག་རྒྱས་སྟོབས་ཀྱིས།
ནང་དུ་ཡིད་ལ་རབ་ཏུ་གདུང་བའི་མཆི་མ་ཡུན་རིང་དག་ཏུ་ཅི་ཡང་བྱུང་གྱུར་ཏེ།
མགྲིན་པར་འཁྲུད་བྱ་དགའ་མ་རིང་ན་གནས་པར་གྱུར་པའི་སྐྱེ་བོའི་སེམས་ནི།
ཆུ་འཛིན་མཐོང་ན་བདེ་ལྡན་ཡང་ནི་རྣམ་པ་གཞན་དུ་གདུང་བ་ཅི་ཡང་འདུག་པར་འགྱུར། ༣།

प्रत्यासन्ने नभसि दयिताजीवितालम्बनार्थी
जीमूतेन स्वकुशलमयीं हारयिष्यन्प्रवृत्तिम्।
स प्रत्यग्रैः कुटजकुसुमैः कल्पितार्घाय तस्मै
प्रीतः प्रीतिप्रमुखवचनं स्वागतं व्याजहार।।4।।

དབྱར་དུས་ཟླ་བ་གཉིས་པ་འོངས་པར་གྱུར་ཚེ་བརྩེ་ལྡན་མ་ཡི་ཆེད་དུ་སྲོག་ཆགས་ནི་[2]།
བདེ་[3] ལ་ཆར་སྤྲིན་དག་གིས་རང་ཉིད་བདེ་འམ་ཞེས་པའི་ཚིག་འདི་ཁྱེར་ནས་འདུག་པ་བཞིན།
ཀུན་དའི་ཟླ་[4] ཡི་ཆུ་སྐྱེས་འཛུམ་པ་རྣམས་ཀྱིས་དེ་ལ་མཆོད་པའི་ཆེད་དུ་དགའ་བྱེད་བཞིན།
མཛའ་བ་མངོན་དུ་གྱུར་པའི་ཚིག་དེ་[1] ལེགས་པར་འོངས་སམ་དགའ་བཞིན་བརྗོད་པ་བཞིན། ༤ །

---

༡ པེ། སྣར། སྤྲིན།

༢ པེ།སྣར། འཆང་བ། དེ།

༣ པེ། སྣར། དེ།

༤ པེ། སྣར།> ཀུ་ཏ་ཛ།

धूमज्योतिः सलिलमरुतां सन्निपातः क्व मेघः
संदेशार्थाः क्व पटुकरणैः प्राणिभिः प्रापणीयाः।
इत्योत्सुक्यादपरिगणयन्गुह्यकस्तं ययाचे
कामार्ता हि प्रकृतिकृपणाश्चेतनाचेतनेषु।।5।।

གང་དུ་དུ་བ་གཟི་ལྡན་ཆུ་གཏེར་རླུང་འགྲོ་རྣམས་ཀྱི་ཚོར་བ་ལས་ནི་ཆར་སྤྲིན་ཏེ།
གང་དུ་མཁས་པའི་བྱེད་པ་རྣམས་དང་སྲོག་རྣམས་ཀྱིས་ནི་ལེགས་བཤད་ཚེད་དུ་ཐོབ་པར་བྱེད།
ཅེས་པ་མཆོག་ཏུ་དགའ་བའི་ [༡]གསང་བ་བ་ནི་དེ་ལས་ [༢]ཡོངས་སུ་མི་ཤེས་གང་གིས་ [༣]ནི།
འདོད་པའི་དོན་དུ་མཁས་དང་མི་མཁས་རྣམས་དང་སེམས་ལྡན་སེམས་མེད་རྣམས་ལ་ཞུ་བར་བྱེད། ༥།

जातं वंशे भुवनविदिते पुष्करावर्तकानां
जानामि त्वां प्रकृतिपुरुषं कामरूपं मघोनः।
तेनार्थित्वं त्वयि विधिवशाद् दूरबन्धुर्गतोऽहं
याच्ञा मोघा वरमधिगुणे नाधमे लब्धकामा।।6।।

ཁྱོད་ནི་རིགས་མཆོག་དང་ལྡན་མཆོད་སྤྲིན་བརྒྱ་བའི་བློན་པོ་མཆོག་སྟེ་འདོད་འཛིན་ངོ་བོ་ཉིད།
ས་གསུམ་མཐའ་དག་རིག་ཅིང་བསྐལ་པར་འཇུག་པའི་ཚེ་བའི་རྒྱུ་འཛིན་ཉིད་དུ་བདག་གིས་ཤེས།
དེས་ན་ཁྱོད་ནི་དོན་གཉིས་ [༥]ཉིད་ལ་སྐལ་བའི་དབང་གིས་དམན་མིན་འདོད་པ་ཐོབ་པ་ཉིད།
མཆོད་སྤྲིན་འབྲས་མེད་བདག་གི་རིང་གནས་གཉེན་འདུན་ [༦]དག་ཏུ་ཡོན་ཏན་མཆོག་དབང་ཁྱོད་
གཤེགས་མཛོད། ༦།

---

༡ པེ་། སྣར་།> ནི་དེ་ལ།

༢ པེ་། སྣར་།> བས།

༣ པེ་། སྣར་།> ལ།

༤ པེ་། སྣར་།> གི

༥ པེ་། སྣར་།> གཉེར།

༦ པེ་། སྣར་།> མདུན།

संतप्तानां त्वमसि शरणं तत्पयोद प्रियायाः

संदेशं मे हर धनपतिक्रोधविश्लेषितस्य।

गन्तव्या ते वसितरलका नाम यक्षेश्वराणां

बाह्योद्यानस्थितहरशिरश्चन्द्रिकाधौतहर्म्या।।7।।

ཀ་ཡི་ཆུ་ལྷན་ཁྱོད་ནི་ཤིན་ཏུ་གདུངས་གྱུར་སྐབས་ཉིད་དེ་ཕྱིར་བདག་གི་དགའ་བ་[1]ལ།
གཏམ་[2]ཀྱི་བདག་པོ་ཆེད་[3]ཆེར་ཁྲོས་པས་འབྲུམས་ཤིང་བྲལ་བ་དག་གི་ཕྲིན་ནི་མཛད་དུ་གསོལ།
ཕྱི་རོལ་སྐྱེད་མོས་[4]མཆོག་གནས་འཁྲིག་བྱེད་གཙུག་གི་ཟླ་བའི་འོད་ཀྱིས་སྣང་བྱས་ཁང་བཟངས་[5]ཅན།
གསང་བའི་བདག་པོའི་བསྟི་གནས་ཆེན་པོ་[6]ལྕང་ལོ་ཅན་ཞེས་བྱ་བའི་གནས་སུ་ཁྱོད་གཤེགས་མཛོད། ༧།

त्वामारूढं पवनपदवीमुद्गृहीतालकान्ताः

प्रेक्षिष्यन्ते पथिकवनिताः प्रत्ययादाश्वसन्त्यः।

कः संनद्धे विरहविधुरां त्वय्युपेक्षेत जायां

न स्यादन्योऽप्यहमिव जनो यः पराधीनवृत्तिः।।8।।

ཁྱོད་ནི་དྲི་ཡི་བཞོན་པ་དག་ལྷན་མཁའ་[7]ལམ་གཤེགས་པའི་དབང་གིས་ལམ་བགྲོད་མཛེས་མ་རྣམས་།
བསམ་པ་དགའ་བར་གྱུར་ཏེ་ལེན་[8]བུའི་ཅོ་མོ་རྒྱབ་ཏུ་བྱས་ནས་བལྟ་ཞིང་གུས་པ་བྱེད།

---

༡ ཕེ་། སྣར་།> དགའ་མ།

༢ ཕེ་།སྣར་།> གཏན།

༣ ཕེ་། སྣར་།> ཆེས།

༤ ཕེ་།སྣར་།> སྐྱེད་ཚལ།

༥ ཕེ་།སྣར་།> བཟང་།

༦ ཕེ་། སྣར་།> བསྟི་གནས་ཆེན་པོ། ཚད

༧ ཕེ་། སྣར་།> མཁས།

༨ ཕེ་། སྣར་།> ལན།

ཁྱོད་འོངས་ཚེ་ན་བྲེལ་[1]བས་མཆོག་ཏུ་ཉེན་ཅིང་གཡོག་བཞིན་གཞན་དབང་གྱུར་པ་དག་འདྲ་དང་།
གང་ཞིག་གཞན་ཡང་མི་ཡི་[2]སྐྱེ་བོ་སུ་ཞིག་གུས་སེང་[3]དགའ་བ་[4]རྒྱ་ཆེར་བྱེད་མི་འགྱུར། ༨།

मन्दं मन्दं नुदति पवनश्चानुकूलो यथा त्वां
वामश्चायं नदति मधुरश्चातकस्ते सगन्धः।
गर्भाधानक्षणपरिचयान्नूनमाबद्धमालाः
सेविष्यन्ते नयनसुभगं खे भवन्तं बलाकाः।।9।।

དལ་བུ་དལ་བུས་བསྐྱོད་པའི་དྲི་བཞོན་དག་གིས་ཁྱོད་ལ་མཛེས་[5]མཐུན་ཞབས་ཏོག་བྱེད་པ་བཞིན།
མྱོས་པའི་ཙ་ཏ་ཀ་འདི་འང་ཁྱོད་ལ་སྙན་པའི་བསྟོད་པའི་[6]བསྟོད་པ་གཡོན་ནས་སྒྲོགས་པ་དང་།
ཆུ་སྐྱུར་མཛེས་མ་རྣམས་ཀྱང་སྐལ་བཟང་མིག་གིས་མཁའ་ལ་ཁྱོད་མཐོང་ཕྲེང་བར་བྱས་ནས་བརྟེན་[7]།
ངེས་པར་མངལ་ཉེ་རབ་ཏུ་འཛིན་པ་ཡོངས་སུ་གསལ་བ་ཉིད་དུ་བྲ་བ་བཟོད་[8]པར་ནུས། ༩།

तां चावश्यं दिवसगणनातत्परामेकपत्नी
मव्यापन्नामविहतगतिर्द्रक्ष्यसि भ्रातृजायाम्।
आशाबन्धः कुसुमसदृशं प्रायशो ह्यङ्गनानां
सद्यपाति प्रणयि हृदयं विप्रयोगे रुणद्धि।।10।।

བདག་གིས་མཛེས་མ་དེ་ཡང་ཉིན་ཞག་གྲངས་བཞིན་བདག་པོ་གཅིག་པུ་ཡིད་ལ་འདྲི་བར་ནི།
གདོན་མི་ཟ་བར་མྱུར་དུ་གཟིགས་ཏེ་བདག་ནི་མ་ཤི་བ་ཉིད་ཁྱོད་ཀྱིས་བསྟན་པ་མཛོད།

---

༡ པེ་།སྣར་།> བྲལ།

༢ པེ་། སྣར་།> གཞ།དགའན་ཡང་མཛེས་མའི།

༣ པེ་། སྣར་།> གུས་པ།

༤ པེ་། སྣར་།> དགའ་བ་། ཆད།

༥ པེ་། སྣར་།> ཛེས།

༦ པེ་། སྣར་།> བསྟོད་པའི་། ཆད་།

༧ པེ་། སྣར་།> བརྟེན་།

༨ པེ་། སྣར་།> བཟོད།

གང་ཕྱིར་འཕྲུལ་ལ་ཆུ་སྐྱེད་[༡]ཕལ་ཆེར་ཕྲེང་བས་བཅིངས་པས་ལྷུང་བ་མེད་པར་གྱུར་པ་བཞིན།
ལྷ་མོའི་སྙིང་གི་དགའ་བ་བྲལ་ལས་ལྷུང་བ་ཕྲལ་[༢]ལ་འགོག་ཅིང་མཛའ་བས་འཆིང་བར་བྱེད། ༡༠།

कर्तुं यच्च प्रभवति महीमुच्छिलीत्घ्रामबन्धयां
तच्छ्रुत्वा ते श्रवणसुभगं गर्जितं मानसोत्काः।
आकैलासाद्बिसकिसलयच्छेदपाथेयवन्तः
संपत्स्यन्ते नभसि भवतो राजहंसाः सहायाः॥11॥

གང་ཞིག་ཁྱོད་ཀྱི་འབྲུག་སྒྲ་སྒྲོགས་པ་དེ་ནི་སྐལ་[༣]བཟང་རྣ་བས་ཐོས་བྱས་ནས།
མཚོ་རུ་རྒྱས་པའི་མེ་ཏོག་དག་གིས་ས་གཞིའི་ཆེད་དུ་གདུགས་དག་བྱས་པར་གྱུར་པ་ཉིད།
ཁྱོད་ནི་ནམ་མཁའ་དག་ལ་གཤེགས་ཚེ་དགའ་བའི་ཡིད་ཀྱིས་མཚོ་དང་གངས་ཅན་བར་ལ་ནི།
པདྨའི་རྩ་བ་ལོ་མའི་ལམ་རྒྱགས་ལྡན་པའི་ངང་པའི་རྒྱལ་པོ་རྣམས་ཀྱང་གྲོགས་སུ་འགྱུར། ༡༡།

आपृच्छस्व प्रियसखममुं तुङ्गमालिङ्ग्य शैलं
वन्द्यैः पुंसां रघुपतिपदैरङ्कितं मेखलासु।
काले काले भवति भवतो यस्य संयोगमेत्य
स्नेहव्यक्तिश्चिरविरहजं मुञ्चतो बाष्पमुष्णम्॥12॥

རགྷུའི་[༤]བདག་པོའི་ཞབས་ཀྱིས་མཚན་པའི་རི་ངོས་རྣམས་ལ་སྐྱེ་བོ་ཀུན་གྱིས་ཕྱག་བྱེད་པའི།
ཆེ་བའི་རི་བོ་འདི་ནི་ཁྱོད་ཀྱི་དགའ་བའི་གྲོགས་བཟང་ཁྱོད་ལང་[༥]འཕྲུད་པ་སྔོན་འགྲོ་བའི།
མཛའ་བ་གསལ་[༦]བྱས་ཡུན་རིང་འབྲལ་ལས་བྱུང་བའི་མཆི་མའི་དྲོ་བའང་འབྱུང་བ་ཡོངས་མཐོང་ལ།
ཁྱོད་དང་གང་དེ་དུས་དུས་དག་ཏུ་ཡང་དག་མཇལ་[༧]འགྱུར་ཞེས་ནི་བྱས་ནས་ཁམས་བདེ་མཛོད། ༡༣།

---

༡ པེ་། སྣར་།> སྐྱེས།

༢ པེ་།སྣར་།> འཕྲལ།

༣ པེ་། སྣར་།> ཀྱིས་འབྲུག་སྒྲ་བསྒྲགས་པ་དེ་ནི་བསྐལ།

༤ པེ་། སྣར་།> ར་གྷུའི།

༥ པེ་། སྣར་།> ལོང་།

༦ པེ་། སྣར་།> བསལ།

༧ པེ་། སྣར་།> འཇལ།

मार्गं तावच्छृणु कथयतस्त्वत्प्रयाणानुरूपं
सन्देशं मे तदनु जलद श्रोष्यसि श्रोत्रपेयम्।
खिन्नः खिन्नः शिखरिषु पदं न्यस्य गन्तासि यत्र
क्षीणः क्षीणः परिलघु पयः स्रोतसां चोपभुज्य।।13।।

ཀཱ་ཡི་ཆུ་འཛིན་རེ་ཞིག་ཁྱོད་ནི་ལམ་ལ་བགྲོད་པའི་ཐབས་ཀྱིས་[1] གཏམ་ནི་མཉན་པར་མཛོད།
དེ་ཡི་རྗེས་སུ་བདག་གི་འཕྲིན་ནི་རྣ་བའི་བདེ་བ་སྐྱེད་[2] ཁྱོད་རྣ་བར་[3] གཟུང་བར་མཛོད།
ཤིན་ཏུ་ངལ་ཞིང་རབ་ཏུ་ངལ་ཚེ་རི་བོའི་རྩེ་ལ་རྐང་བཀོད་ངལ་བ་[4] བསལ་ནས་གཤེགས།
གང་དུ་སྐོམ་ཤིང་ཤིན་ཏུ་སྐོམ་ན་ཉུང་ངུའི་ཆུ་དང་ཆེ་བའི་མཚོ་ལའང་བཏུང་བར་བྱ། ༡༣།

अद्रेः शृङ्गं हरति पवनः किं स्विदित्युन्मुखीभि-
र्दृष्टोत्साहश्चकितचकितं मुग्धसिद्धाङ्गनाभिः।
स्थानादस्मात्सरसनिचुलादुत्पतोदङ्मुखः खं
दिङ्नागानां पथि परिहरन्स्थूलहस्तावलेपान्।।14।।

ནེ་ཙུ་ལ་ནི་གསར་པས་གནས་འདི་ལས་ནི་ཁྱོད་ལངས་[5] མཁའ་ལ་བྱང་དུ་གདོང་ཕྱོགས་མཛོད།
ཕྱོགས་ཀྱི་གླང་པོ་རྣམས་ཀྱི་ལག་པ་ཆེ་བས་བཅིངས་པའི་ལམ་ནི་ཡོངས་སུ་དོར་བར་གྱིས།
རི་ཡི་རྩེ་མོ་ཕྲོགས་ནས་དྲི་བཞིན་འགྲོ་བའམ་ཆུ་འཛིན་ལངས་ནས་འགྲོ་བའི་[6] ཅེ་ཞེས་ཐེ་ཚོམ་དུ། །
གྲུར་ནས་གྲུབ་པའི་བུད་མེད་རྣམས་ཀྱིས་གྱེན་ཕྱོགས་བལྟས་ཏེ་འཛིགས་ཤིང་སྐྲག་པས་སྔོངས་པར་འགྱུར། ༡༤།

रत्नच्छायाव्यतिकर इव प्रेक्ष्यमेतत्पुरस्ता
द्वल्मीकाग्रात्प्रभवति धनुष्खण्डमाखण्डलस्य।

---

༡ པེ། སྣར།> ཀྱི།
༢ པེ། སྣར།> རྣ་བའི་བདེ་སྐྱེས།
༣ པེ། སྣར།> ཁྱོད་ཀྱི་རྣ་བས།
༤ པེ། སྣར།> བས།
༥ པེ། སྣར།> ལོང་།
༦ པེ། སྣར།> བའམ།

येन श्यामं वपुरतितरां कान्तिमापत्स्यते ते
बर्हेणेव स्फुरितरुचिना गोपवेशस्य विष्णोः।।15।।

རིན་ཆེན་འོད་ཀྱིས་[༡] སྣང་བ་བཞིན་དུ་རབ་མཛེས་མཆོད་སྦྱིན་བརྒྱ་པའི་གཞུ་ཡི་དུམ་བུ་ནི།
ཆེ་བའི་གྲོག་[༢] མཁར་རྩེ་ལས་བྱུང་བ་དེ་ནི་མདུན་དུ་ཡང་དག་མཐོང་བར་འགྱུར།
ཁྱབ་འཇུག་གླང་རྫིའི་ཚུལ་བཟུང་[༣] རྨ་བྱའི་སྒྲོ་ཡི་འོད་ཀྱིས་[༤] ཁྱབ་པར་གྱུར་པ་བཞིན།
ཁྱོད་སྐུ་མཆོག་ཏུ་མཛེས་པ་མཐིང་ནག་གང་གིས་ཀུན་དུ་ཁྱབ་པར་བྱེད་པ་ཐོབ་པར་འགྱུར། ༡༥།

त्वय्यायत्तं कृषिफलमिति भ्रूविकारानभिज्ञैः
प्रीतिस्निग्धैर्जनपदवधूलोचनैः पीयमानः।
सद्यः सीरोत्कषणसुरभि क्षेत्रमारुह्य मालं
किंचित्पश्चाद् व्रज लघुगतिर्भूय एवोत्तरेण।।16।।

ཁྱོད་འོངས་ཚེ་ན་གྲོང་ཁྱེར་ན་ཆུང་དགའ་ཞིང་ཆགས་པའི་མིག་རྣམས་ཀྱིས་ནི་སྨིན་མ་ཡི།
རྣམ་འགྱུར་མངོན་པར་མི་ཤེས་བཞིན་དུ་བལྟ་ཞིང་འབྲུ་རྣམས་ཀུན་ནི་འཕེལ་བར་བྱེད་པའི་ཕྱིར།
ཁྱོད་ནི་ཙུང་ཟད་ནུབ་ཏུ་བསྐྱོད་ཅིང་གནས་བྱ་འཕྲིན་ལ་སྨོན་གྱི་རོ་ལ་[༥] དགའ་བ་ཡི།
གནམ་ཆུ་སྨུག་པའི་ཞིང་ལ་གྱུ་ཆར་རྒྱུས་བྱ་སླར་ཡང་བྱང་དུ་མྱུར་བར་དལ་གྱིས་གཤེགས། ༡༦།

त्वामासारप्रशमितवनोपप्लवं साधु मूर्ध्ना
वक्ष्यत्यध्वश्रमपरिगतं सानुमानाम्रकूटः।
न क्षुद्रोऽपि प्रथमसुकृतापेक्षया संश्रयाय
प्राप्ते मित्रे भवति विमुखः किं पुनर्यस्तथोच्चैः।।17।।

---

༡ པེ་། སྣར་།> ཀྱི།

༢ པེ་། སྣར་།> གྲོགས།

༣ པེ་། སྣར་།> གཟུང་།

༤ པེ་། སྣར་།> ཀྱི།

༥ པེ་། སྣར་།> འཕྲུལ་ལ་སྨོས་ཀྱི་རོལ་གྱིས།

ལམ་དུ་ཡོངས་སུ་ངལ་བའི་ཚེ་ན་[༡]ངོས་ལྡན་ཨ་མྲ་བརྩེགས་[༢]པའི་རི་རྩེར་གནས་བྱ་སྟེ། །
ཁྱོད་ཀྱི་[༣]ནགས་ནང་ཞིང་སྐམ་རྣམས་ནི་ཆར་གྱིས་བཀླན་པར་བྱས་བཞིན་[༤]ལེགས་པར་མཛོད། །
གང་ཕྱིར་ཆེ་བའི་སྐྱེ་བོ་དང་པོར་ལེགས་བྱས་རྒྱུ་མཚན་ཐོབ་པའི་གྲོགས་བཟང་ལ། །
དེ་ལྟའི་བྱ་བས་གནས་ཆེད་ཅི་ཡང་གྱུར་ལ་ཕྱིར་ཕྱོགས་ངན་པའི་སྐྱེ་བོའང་འགྱུར་[༥]མ་ཡིན། ༡༧།

अध्वक्लान्तं प्रतिमुखगतं सानुमान् चित्रकूट
स्तुङ्गेन त्वां जलद शिरसा वक्ष्यति श्लाघमानः।
आसारेण त्वमपि शमयेस्तस्य नैदाघमग्निं
सद्भावार्द्रः फलति न चिरेणोपकारो महत्सु।।18।।

ཀཱ་ཡེ་རྒྱུ་འཛིན་ཁྱོད་ནི་ལམ་ལ་ངལ་ཚེ་སྣ་ཚོགས་བརྩེགས་པ་ཞེས་པའི་རི་བོ་ནི།
ངོས་ལྡན་རྩེ་མོ་ཡངས་ལ་བསྡད་ནས་ཕན་ཚུན་མངོན་[༦]དུ་ཕྱོགས་པའི་བསྐུན་ནི་བྱེད་བཞིན་པས།
ཁྱོད་ཀྱང་དེ་ཡི་སོ་ཀའི་མ་[༧]ནི་བདུད་རྩིས་ཞི་བྱེད་དེ་ཡང་ཕན་པའི་དངོས་པོའི་རྗེན་[༨]དུ་འགྱུར།
ཆེན་པོ་རྣམས་ལ་ཕན་བཏགས་ལན་དུ་འཕྲུལ་ལ་འབྲས་བུ་དམ་པས་བཀྲན་པ་ཉིད། ༡༨།

छन्नोपान्तः परिणतफलद्योतिभिः काननाम्रैः
स्त्वय्यारूढे शिखरमचलः स्निग्धवेणीसवर्णे।
नूनं यास्यत्यमरमिथुनप्रेक्षणीयामवस्थां
मध्ये श्यामः स्तन इव भुवः शेषविस्तारपाण्डुः।।19।।

---

༡ པེ་། སྣར་།> ངལ་བའི་ཚེ་།
༢ པེ་། སྣར་།> ཨ་མྲ་རྩེགས་།
༣ པེ་། སྣར་།> ཀྱིས།
༤ པེ་། སྣར་།> བྲན་པར་བྱས་ནས།
༥ པེ་། སྣར་།> འགྱུར་མ་ཡིན།
༦ པེ་། སྣར་།> སྔོན།
༧ པེ་། སྣར་།> སོ་ཀའི་མེ་།།
༨ པེ་། སྣར་།> བརྗེན།

ཁྱོད་ནི་གཡོ་མེད་རྩེ་མོར་གནས་ཚེ་ཨ་མྲའི་ནགས་ཀྱི་འབྲས་བུ་རྒྱས་པར་སྨིན་པ་ནི།
ཕྱོགས་ཀུན་ཁྱབ་པར་བཀྲམ་པ་དཀའ་མའི་རྣམ་མཛེས་ལེན་བུ་དག་དང་མཚུངས་པ་བཞིན་དུ་གྱུར།
ས་གཞིའི་མཛེས་མའི་ནུ་རྒྱས་ལྷག་མ་དཀར་ཞིང་ཐིག་[1] ལེ་སྔོན་པོས་མཛེས་པ་བཞིན།
འཆི་མེད་ཁྱོ་ཤུག་དག་ནི་[2] ཡ་མཚན་ངེས་པ་ཐོབ་པའི་མིག་གིས་རབ་ཏུ་ལྟ་བར་བྱེད། ༡༩།

स्थित्वा तस्मिन्वनचरवधूभुक्तकुञ्जे मुहूर्तं
तोयोत्सर्गद्रुततरगतिस्तत्परं वर्त्म तीर्णः।
रेवां द्रक्ष्यस्युपलविषमे विन्ध्यपादे विशीर्णां
भक्तिच्छेदैरिव विरचितां भूतिमङ्गे गजस्य।।20।।

དེ་ནས་རི་དྭགས་བདག་པོའི་ཆུང་མའི་ནགས་ཀྱི་ཁང་པ་དེ་ལ་ཡུད་ཙམ་གནས་བྱས་ནས། །
དེ་ཡི་ཕ་རོལ་ཆུ་ལས་ཐོན་ནས་མཆོག་ཏུ་མྱུར་བས་ལམ་གཞན་དག་ཏུ་གསེགས་ཤིང་བགྲོད་པ་ན།
ངང་སྒྲོང་བུ་མོའི་ཆུ་བོ་འབིགས་བྱེད་རི་ཡི་ཞབས་ནི་རྡུབ་པའི་རྡོ་ལ་འཁྱོག་ཏུ་འབབ་ལྡན་མ།
སོ་གཉིས་ཡན་ལག་མཆོག་ལས་དཀར་མོ་ཆོན་གྱིས་ལེགས་བྲིས་བཞིན་དུ་ཁྱོད་ཀྱིས་མཐོང་བར་འགྱུར། ༢༠།

तस्यास्तितक्तैर्वनगजमदैर्वासितं वान्तवृष्टि-
र्जम्बूकुञ्जप्रतिहतरयं तोयमादाय गच्छेः।
अन्तःसारं घन! तुलयितुं नानिलः शक्ष्यति त्वां
रिक्तः सर्वो भवति हि लघुः पूर्णता गौरवाय।।21।।

ཁྱོད་ཀྱིས་ཐོག་མར་ཆར་བ་སྐྱུག་བྱ་དེ་ཡི་ཆུ་ནི་འཐུངས་ནས་བགྲོད་པར་བྱ་སྟེ་ཕྱིན་ནས་ནི།
ནགས་ཀྱི་གླང་པོ་མྱོས་པའི་ཏིག་ཏའི་རོ་དང་འཛམ་བུའི་ཤིང་གི་ཆུ་དེ་འང་མྱུར་དུ་འགེངས།
ཀྭ་ཡེ་སྤྲིན་སྟུག་ཁྱོད་ནི་ནང་གི་སྙིང་པོ་ལྡན་ན་དྲི་བཞིན་དག་གིས་གཡོ་མི་ནུས།
གང་ཕྱིར་ཐམས་ཅད་སྟོང་ན་ཡང་བར་འགྱུར་ཞིང་ཡོངས་སུ་གང་ན་ཀུན་ཀྱང་ལྕི་[3] བ་ཉིད། ༢༡།

---

༡ པེ། སྣར།> དཀར་ཞིང་དབུས་ཀྱི་ཐིག

༢ པེ། སྣར།པེ། ཁྱོ་ཤུགས་གི

༣ པེ། སྣར།> ལྕི།

नीपं दृष्ट्वा हरितकपिशं केसरैरर्धरुढै-
राविर्भूतप्रथममुकुलाः कन्दलीश्चानुकच्छम्।
दग्धारण्येष्वधिकसुरभिं गन्धमाघ्राय चोर्व्याः
सारङ्गास्ते जललवमुचः सूचयिष्यन्ति मार्गम्।।22।।

དང་པོར་ཀཱ་ནྡ་ལི་ཡི་མེ་ཏོག་ཁ་འབུས་རྣམས་ནི་ཕྱུན་པས་བསྐྱིབས་པ་བྱུང་བ་དང་།
འདབ་མ་ལྗང་ཞིང་གེ་སར་དཀར་སེར་ཕྱེ་ལྡན་བརྟན[1] པ་རྣམས་ཀྱི་ཆུ་སྐྱེས་མེ་ཏོག་མཐོང་ནས་ཀྱང་།
འབྲོག་དགོན་རྣམས་སུ་མེས་བསྲེགས་ས་གཞི་ར་དྲི་འཛིན་མནམ་བྱ་དྲི་བཟང་མང་པོ་བྱུང་བ་ན།
ཆུ་འཛིན་དལ་བུས་ཆར་བསྐུན་ཁྱོད་ལ་སཱ་རིགས་རྣམས[2] ནི་སྟོན་པར་བྱེད་པར་འགྱུར། ༢༢།

अम्भोबिन्दुग्रहणचतुरांश्चातकान् वीक्षमाणाः
श्रोणीभूताः परिगणनया निर्दिशन्तो बलाकाः।
त्वामासाद्य स्तनितसमये मानयिष्यन्ति सिद्धाः
सोत्कम्पानि प्रियसहचरीसंभ्रमालिङ्गितानि।।23।।

ཁྱོད་ནི་ལེགས་པར་འོངས་ཚེ་སྐན་པའི་སྒྲ་བསྒྲགས་དུས་ན་གྲུབ་པ་རྣམས་ཀྱིས་མཆོད་བྱེད་ཅིང་།
ཙཱ་ཏ་ཀ་རྣམས་ཆུ་ཡི་ཐིགས་པ་བཟུང་ནས་དགའ་བས་འཕྱུང་ལ་ལྟ་བར་བྱེད་བཞིན་དང་།
ཆུ་སྐྱོགས་རྣམས་ནི་ཕྲེང་བར་བསྒྲིགས་རྣམས་ཡོངས་སུ་བསྒྲེང་ཞིང་ཅི་ཞེས་ངེས་པར་ལྟ་བཞིན་དང་།
མཆོག་ཏུ་འདར་བྱས་དགའ་བས་དགའ་མ་ལ་ནི་དམ་དུ་འཁྱུད་པ་རྣམས་ནི་བྱེད་པ་ཡིན། ༢༣།

उत्पश्यामि द्रुतमपि सखे मत्प्रियार्थं यियासोः
कालक्षेपं ककुभसुरभौ पर्वते पर्वते ते।
शुक्लापाङ्गैः सजलनयनैः स्वागतीकृत्य केकाः
प्रत्युद्यातः कथमपि भवान् गन्तुमाशु व्यवस्येत्।।24।।

ཀྱཱ་ཡེ་གྲོགས་པོ་ཁྱོད་ནི་བདག་གི་དགའ་བའི་དོན་ལ་མྱུར་དུ་འགྲོ་སྙམ་ཡོད་ན་ཡང་།
ཀ་ཀུ་བྷ་ཡི་དྲི་ལྡན་རི་བོ་རི་བོ་རྣམས་ལ་ཡུན་རིང་ཐོགས་པར་བདག་གི་སེམས།

༡ ཅེ། སྣར།> ཕྱེད་ལྡན་བརྟན།
༢ ཅེ། སྣར།> རིག་རྣམས་ལ།

གཙུག་ཕུད་ཅན་གྱི་འདྲེན་བྱེད་ཆུ་[༡]དང་བཅས་པས་ལེགས་པར་འོངས་སམ་བྲུས་ནས་ཡུན་རིང་
གནས་པར་འདོད།
དེ་སྐད་ཁྱོད་ནི་ཤིན་ཏུ་ཤིན་ཏུ་མྱུར་བ་འགྲོ་བར་འགྱུར་བ་དག་ཀྱང་ངེ་ལྟར་ཡིན། ༢༤།

पाण्डुच्छायोपवनवृतयः केतकैः सूचिभिन्नै-
नींडारम्भैर्गृहबलिभुजामाकुलग्रामचैत्याः।
त्वय्यासन्ने परिणतफलश्यामजम्बूवनान्ताः
संपत्स्यन्ते कतिपयदिनस्थायिहंसा दशार्णाः।।25।।

ཁྱོད་འོངས་ཚེ་ན་ངང་པ་རྣམས་ནི་དེ་ཉིད་ཙུང་ཟད་གནས་ནས་འགྲོ་ཞིང་འབྲས་བུ་ནི།
ཡོངས་སུ་སྨིན་པ་ལྗང་སྔོན་དང་ལྡན་འཛམ་བུའི་ནགས་ཀྱིས་བསྐོར་དབུས་དཀར་པོའི་འོད་ལྡན་ཆེ་བ་ཡི།
ནགས་ཀྱི་འཁྲི་ཤིང་ཀེ་ཏ་ཀའི་ཆུ་སྐྱེས་གེ་སར་གསལ་བར་རྒྱས་ཤིང་གྲོང་དང་མཆོད་རྟེན་གྱིས།
བསྐོར་བའི་ཁང་པར་གཏོར་ལེན་ཚང་སྐྱེད་[༢]ཇོམ་པའི་གྲོང་ཁྱེར་དམ་[༣]ཤ་ཞེས་པས་མཆོད་པར་འགྱུར། ༢༥།

तेषां दिक्षु प्रथितविदिशालक्षणां राजधानीं
गत्वा सद्यः फलमतिमहत्कामुकत्वस्य लब्धा।
तीरोपान्तस्तनितसुभगं पास्यसि स्वादु यस्मात्
सभ्रूभङ्गं मुखमिव पयो वेत्रवत्याश्चलोर्मि।।26।।

དེ་ཡི་བྱང་ཕྱོགས་གཞི་ལ་བེ་དེ་ཤ་ཞེས་མཆོད་ཆ་[༤]རྒྱལ་པོའི་ཁབ་ཏུ་མྱུར་སོང་ནས།
དེ་ར་ནི་ཁྱོད་ཀྱིས་ཤིན་ཏུ་ཆེ་བའི་འབྲས་བུ་ཐོབ་མཆོག་[༥]གོ་འཕང་འཕྲུལ་ལ་ཐོབ་འགྱུར་ཞིང་།

---

༡ པེ་། སྣར་།> གྱིས་འདྲེན་བྱེད་མཆུ།

༢ པེ་། སྣར་།> ཚུངས་སྐྱེས།

༣ པེ་། སྣར་།> ཏ།

༤ པེ་། སྣར་།> མཆོན་པ་།

༥ པེ་། སྣར་།> འབྲས་ཐོབ་མཆོག་གི།

ཆེ་བའི་ཁ་ཞིང་དག་ལྡན་མཐའ་ནས་ལྷུང་ལྷུང་སྐད་སྐན་སྒྲོགས་ཤིང་དང་ཞིང་བསིལ་[༡]ལྡན་པ།
གཡོ་བའི་རླབས་ཕྲེང་གདོང་ཁ་[༢]སྨིན་མ་གཡོ་བཞིན་པ་འདྲའི་[༣]མཚོ་དེའང་སྐལ་བཟང་ཁྱོད་འཐུང་འགྱུར། ༢༦།

नीचैराख्यं गिरिमधिवसेस्तत्र विश्रामहेतो-
स्त्वत्संपर्कात्पुलकितमिव प्रौढपुष्पैः कदम्बैः।
यः पण्यस्त्रीरतिपरिमलोद्गारिभिर्नागराणा-
मुद्दामानि प्रथयति शिलावेश्मभिर्यौवनानि।।27।।

གང་ཞིག་ནི་ཙ་ཞེས་གྲགས་རི་བོར་ཁྱོད་འོངས་ཐོབ་ལས་དེ་ར་ནི་ངལ་བསོའི་[༤]ཆེད་དུ་གནས།
ཀ་དམ་པ་ཡི་མེ་ཏོག་དགའ་བས་སྤུ་ལོང་རྒྱས་ཤིང་གི་སར་འཛུམ་པར་བྱེད་པ་བཞིན།
གྲོང་ཁྱེར་རྣམས་ནི་སྨན་[༥]འཚོང་མ་རྣམས་དགའ་བར་བྱེད་པའི་དྲི་བཟངས་དག་གིས་གང་བ་རྣམས་།
རྡོ་ཡི་ཕྲག་ཕུག་རྣམས་ཀྱི་[༦]མཆོག་ཏུ་མཛེས་པའི་ལང་ཚོ་མ་རྣམས་སྒྲ་རུ་འདུག་པ་བཞིན། ༢༧།

विश्रान्तः सन् व्रज वनदीतीरजातानि सिञ्चन्
नुद्यानानां नवजलकणैर्यूथिकाजालकानि।
गण्डस्वेदापनयनरुजाक्लान्तकर्णोत्पलानां
छायादानात्क्षणपरिचितः पुष्पलावीमुखानाम्।।28।।

ངལ་སོས་གྱུར་ན་བགྲོད་བྱ་གསར་སྐྱེས་རྣམས་ཀྱི་མེ་ཏོག་གསར་པའི་[༧]དྲ་བ་མཛེས་པ་རྣམས།
ཆུ་བོ་ཆུ་ངོགས་སྐྱེས་པ་རྣམས་ནི་ཆུ་ཐིགས་རྣམས་ཀྱིས་བྲན་པ་འཕྲུལ་དུ་འོངས་འགྱུར་ཞིང་།

---

༡ པེ་། སྣར་།> སྒྲོག་དང་རྩེ་ཞིམ་དང་།

༢ པེ་། སྣར་། གདོང་ལ་།

༣ པེ་། སྣར་།>བཞིན་པི་ཏའི།

༤ པེ་། སྣར་།> གསོའི།

༥ པེ་། སྣར་།> སྨད།

༦ པེ་། སྣར་།> རྡོ་ཡི་བྲག་ཕུག་རྣམས་ཀྱིས།

༧ པེ་། སྣར་།> ཀྱིས་མེ་ཏོག་སེར་པོའི།

ཆུ་སྐྱེས་ཐོག་མའི་གདོང་གི་འགྲམ་པའི་ཧུ་ལ་ཐིགས་སེར་[1]ལ་རྣ་བའི་ཨུཏྤལ་ངལ་བ་དང་།
རྐེ་ངས་ཀྱུར་ལ་ནི་ཉིད་ཀྱིས་སྐད་ཅིག་བདེ་བའི་གྲིབ་བསིལ་ཡོངས་སུ་གནང་བར་མཛོད་ཅིག་གི། ༢༨།

वक्रः पन्था यदपि भवतः प्रस्थितस्योत्तराशां
सौधोत्सङ्गप्रणयविमुखो मा स्म भूरुज्जयिन्याः।
विद्युद्दामस्फुरितचकितैस्तत्र पौराङ्गानानां
लोलापाङ्गैर्यदि न रमसे लोचनैर्वञ्चितोऽसि।।29।।

ཡང་ནི་བྱང་གི་ཕྱོགས་སུ་བགྲོད་ཅིང་གང་ཞིག་ཁྱེད་ནི་འཁྱོག་པོའི་ལམ་ལ་ཞུགས་པའི་ཚེ།
གྲོང་ཁྱེར་ཨུཛྫ་ཡ་ནའི་རྒྱལ་པོའི་ཕོ་བྲང་ནང་དུ་ཕྱིར་ཕྱོགས་མིན་པར་གནས་པར་མཛོད།
དེ་ན་གྲོང་གི་དགའ་མ་རྣམས་ཀྱི་རོལ་སྣེག་ཟུར་མིག་གློག་གི་ཐག་པ་གཡོ་བ་ནི།
སྐྱོང་བྱེད་མིག་གིས་གལ་ཏེ་ཁྱོད་ནི་མ་མཐོང་འབྲས་བུ་མེད་ཅིང་བསླུས་པ་ཉིད་དུ་འང་འགྱུར། ༢༩།

वीचिक्षोभस्तनितविहगश्रेणिकाञ्चीगुणायाः
संसर्पन्त्याः स्खलितसुभगं दर्शितावर्तनाभेः।
निर्विन्ध्यायाः पथि भव रसाभ्यन्तरः सन्निपत्य
स्त्रीणामाद्यं प्रणयवचनं विभ्रमो हि प्रियेषु।।30।।

རླབས་ཕྲེང་གཡོ་ལྡན་སྐྱན་པར་སྒྲོགས་ཤིང་འདབ་ཆགས་ཕྲེང་བའི་སྐེད་རྒྱན་སྐ་རགས་སིལ་སིལ་ཅན།
དལ་གྱིས་དལ་གྱིས་འགྲོ་ཞིང་ལང་ལིང་མཛེས་པའི་སྐལ་བཟང་འཁོར་ལོའི་ལྟེ་བ་དང་ལྡན་པ།
རོ་མཆོག་དང་ལྡན་ཆུ་བོའི་ན་ཆུང་ནི་ར་བི་ནྡྷ་[2] ནི་ཁྱོད་ནི་ལམ་ན་མངོན་བཞུགས་ནས།
དགའ་མ་རྣམས་ཀྱིས་མཛའ་བོ་རྣམས་ལ་རོལ་སྣེག་ཐོག་མར་སྟོན་ཅིང་སྐེད་རྒྱན་འགྲོལ་འདྲ་མཐོང་། ༣༠།

वेणीभूतप्रतनुसलिला तामतीतस्य सिन्धुः
पाण्डुच्छाया तटरुहतरुभ्रंशिभिर्जीर्णपर्णैः।
सौभाग्यं ते सुभग विरहावस्थया व्यञ्जयन्ती
कार्श्यं येन त्यजति विधिना स त्वयैवोपपाद्यः।।31।।

---

༡ པེ། སྣར།> ཐིགས་སེལ།

པེ། སྣར།> བི་ཏེན་རྡྷ།

དེ་ནལ་སིནྡྷའི་ཆུ་ནི་ལེན་བུ་བཞིན་དུ་ལུས་ནི་རབ་ཏུ་ཕྲ་བར་གྱུར་པ་ཅན།

དགོས་སུ་གྱུར[༡]་པའི་ཞིང་ནི་སྐྱེ་ངས་པའི་འདབ་མ་ལྷུང་བ་རྣམས་ཀྱིས་ཁྱབ་པར་བགྲམ[༢]་པས་དཀར།

ཀྱཻ་ཡེ་སྐལ་བཟང་ཁྱོད་དང་བྲལ་བར་གནས་པས་ལུས་ཀྱི་གནས་སྐབས་འདི་འདྲར་འགྱུར།

གང་གི་ཆུང་མ་སྤངས་ནས་ཆེ་བའི་གནས་སྐབས་མཛད་དམ་ཁྱོད་མཁྱེན་དེ་ནི་རྗོད་པར་བྱེད། ༣༡།

प्राप्यावन्तीनुदयनकथाकोविदग्रामवृद्धान्
पूर्वोद्दिष्टामुपसर पुरीं श्रीविशालां विशालाम्।
स्वल्पीभूते सुचरितफले स्वर्गिणां गां गतानां
शेषैः पुण्यैर्हृतमिव दिवः कान्तिमत्खण्डमेकम्।।32।।

ཨ་ཝནྟཱའི་ཡུལ་གྲོག་ན[༣]་ཨུད་ཡ་ནའི་གཏམ་ནི་གྲོང་གི་རྒན་མོས་ཤེས་པ་ཡོད།

དེ་རྗེས་གྲོང་ཁྱེར་སྔར་བསྟན་ཁང་པ[༤]་ཡངས་ཞིང་དཔལ་དང་ཕུན་ཚོགས་ཆེ་ལྡན་ཡངས་པ་ཅན།

འཛམ་གླིང་ས་གཞིར་མཐོ་རིས་མཛེས་ལྡན་དུམ་བུ་བསོད་ནམས་ལྷག་མ་རྣམས་ཀྱི་སྐབས་གསུམ་པའི།

ལེགས་བཤད་འབྲས་བུར་གྱུར་པ་ཉུང་ཤས་འགའ་ཞིག་དག་ནི་ཕྱོགས་ནས་འོངས་པར་གྱུར་པ་བཞིན། ༣༢།

दीर्घीकुर्वन् पटु मदकलं कूजितं सारसानां
प्रत्यूषेषु स्फुटितकमलामोदमैत्रीकषायः।
यत्र स्त्रीणां हरति सुरतग्लानिमङ्गानुकूलः
शिप्रावातः प्रियतम इव प्रार्थनाचाटुकारः।।33।।

གང་དུ་བཞད་རྣམས་སྨོས་པའི་གདངས་སྙན་ཆེ་བར་སྒྲོགས་ཞིང་ཡིད་འོང་སྒྲ་ནི་གསལ་བར་བྱེད།

ཉི་གཞོན་གྱིས་རྒྱས་ཆུ་སྐྱེས་དྲི་བཟངས་དགའ་སྐྱེད་བསྐྱ་བའི་རོ་ལྡན་ཡིད་དུ་འོང་གྱུར་ཅིང་།

---

༡ པེ། སྣར།> ངོམས་སུ་སྐྱེས་པའི།

༢ པེ། སྣར།> བསྒྲིབས།

༣ པེ། སྣར།> གྲོབ་ན།

༤ པེ། སྣར།> ཁྲང་བཟང་།

ཆུ་ཐིགས་ཀྱིས་བྲན་དྲི་བཞོན་བུད་མེད་ཆགས་གཟིར་གདུང་བ་ཕྱོག་བྱེད་ལུས་ཀྱི་རྗེས་མཐུན་པ།
བདག་པོ་མཆོག་ནི་འདོད་དོན་གཉེར་བར་བྱེད་ལ་སྣན་པར་སྦྲོགས་ཤིང་དགའ་བར་བྱེད་པ་བཞིན། ༣༣།

जालोद्गीर्णैरुपचितवपुः केशसंस्कारधूपै-
बन्धुप्रीत्या भवनशिखिभिर्दत्तनृत्तोपहारः।
हर्म्येष्वस्याः कुसुमसुरभिष्वध्वखेदं नयेथा
लक्ष्मीं पश्यँललितवनितापादरागाङ्कितेषु॥34॥

དེ་ཡི་ནོར་ལྡན་ཁང་པ་རྣམས་ན་ལེན་བུ་སྤོས་ཀྱིས་བདུགས་པའི་དྲི་བཟངས་དྲ་བ་ནས། །
འཐོན་པས་ཁྱོད་ལུས་ཆེར་འགྱུར་ཁྱིམ་གྱི་གཙུག་ཕུད་ཅན་ནི་དགའ་བས་གཉེན་མཐོང་གར་གྱིས་ནི།
མཆོད་འབུལ་ཆུ་སྐྱེས་དྲི་བཟངས་ལྡན་པ་བུད་མེད་རོལ་སྙེག་ལྡན་པའི་རྐང་པའི་ཚོན་རྣམས་ཀྱིས།
མཚན་པ་རྣམས་ཀྱི་དབུས་སུ་[༡]དུབ་པར་གྱུར་པའི་རང་ཉིད་སྡུག་བསྔལ་བསལ་བར་བྱ། ༣༤།

भर्तुः कण्ठच्छविरिति गणैः सादरं वीक्ष्यमाणः
पुण्यं यायास्त्रिभुवनगुरोर्धाम चण्डीश्वरस्य।
धूतोद्यानं कुवलयरजोगन्धिभिर्गन्धवत्या-
स्तोयक्रीडानिरतयुवतिस्नानतिक्तैर्मरुद्भिः॥35॥

ཡང་ནི་སྲིད་པ་གསུམ་གྱི་བླ་མ་དཔལ་མགྲིན་གནས་སུ་བསོད་ནམས་ལྡན་ཁྱོད་བགྲོད་པར་བྱ།
འཁོར་ཚོགས་ཚོས་ཀྱི་[༢]ཁྱབ་བདག་མགྲིན་འདྲ་མཚུངས་བཞིན་ཞེ་ས་[༣]གུས་དང་བཅས་པས་ལྟ་བར་བྱེད་[༤]།
ཡིད་འོང་དྲི་ལྡན་ཆུ་ལ་ཡང་ཚོ་མ་རྣམས་རོལ་སྙེག་ཁྲུས་ནི་བྱེད་པའི་དྲི་ལྡན་ཞིང་།
ཨུཏ྄པལ་གེ་སར་ལྡན་པའི་དྲི་རྣམས་ཀྱིས་བསྒོས་རླུང་གི་[༥]སྐྱེད་ཚལ་གཡོ་བར་བྱེད་པ་ཡོད། ༣༥།

---

༡ པེ། སྣར།> སུ་རྣམས་སུ་ལམ་གྱི–དབུས་སུ།

༢ པེ། སྣར།> འཁོར་གྱི་ཚོགས་ཀྱིས།

༣ པེ། སྣར།> ཞེས་ནི།།

༤ པེ། སྣར།> ལྟ་བྱེད་དེ།

༥ པེ། སྣར།> གེས།

अप्यन्यस्मिञ्जलधर महाकालमासाद्य काले
स्थातव्यं ते नयनविषयं यावदत्येति भानुः।
कुर्वन्संध्याबलिपटहतां शूलिनः श्लाघनीया-
मामन्द्राणां फलमविकलं लप्स्यसे गर्जितानाम्।।36।।

ཀྱཻ་ཡེ་ཆུ་འཛིན་ནག་པོ་ཆེན་པོའི་གནས་བགྲོད་ནས་ཉིན་ཞག་གཞན་པའི་དུས་ལ་ཡང་།
ཉིན་མོར་བྱེད་པ་འདྲེན་བྱེད་ཡུལ་དུ་འོངས་པར་གྱུར་གྱི་བར་དུ་ཁྱོད་ནི་གནས་པར་མཛོད།
ཅི་གསུམ་ཅན་ལ་ཐུན་མཚམས་ལ་ནི་གཏོར་མ་རྔ་ཆེན་བསྒྲགས་ཤིང་བསྔོད་དབྱངས་བྱེད་པ་བཞིན།
ཁྱོད་ཀྱིས་འབྲུག་དབྱངས་བསྒྲགས་ཚེ་མ་ཚང་མེད་པའི་འབྲས་བུ་ཐོབ་པས་ཀུན་གྱི་དོན་ཡང་བྱེད། ༣༦།

पादन्यासक्वणितरशनास्तत्र लीलावधूतैः
रत्नच्छायाखचितवलिभिश्चामरैः क्लान्तहस्ताः।
वेश्यास्त्वत्तो नखपदसुखान्प्राप्य वर्षाग्रबिन्दू-
नामोक्ष्यन्ते त्वयि मधुकरश्रेणिदीर्घान्कटाक्षान्।।37।।

དེ་ནས་རྐང་པ་བཀོད་པར་གྱུར་ཚེ་འོག་པག་དག་ལས་སིལ་སིལ་སྙན་པའི་སྒྲ་འབྱུང་ཞིང་།
རོལ་སྙེག་གཡོ་བའི་རིན་ཆེན་འོད་འཕྲོས་ལུས་མཛེས་རྔ་ཡབ་འཛིན་པས་ངལ་བའི་ལག་པ་ཅན།
ཚོགས་ཀྱི་མཛེས་མ་སེན་རྗེས་གསར་པས་གདུངས་ལ་ཁྱོད་ལས་ཆར་ཐིགས་ཐོབ་ན་ཚིམ་བྱེད་པ།
ཁྱོད་ལ་སྦྲང་རྩི་བྱེད་པའི་ཕྲེང་བ་བཞིན་དུ་གཡོ་བའི་ཟུར་མིག་རིང་བ་དག་གིས་བལྟ་བར་འགྱུར། ༣༧།

पश्चादुच्चैर्भुजतरुवनं मण्डलेनाभिनीलः
सान्ध्यं तेजः प्रतिनवजपापुष्परक्तं दधानः।
नृत्तारम्भे हर पशुपतेरार्द्रनागाजिनेच्छां
शान्तोद्वेगस्तिमितनयनं दृष्टभक्तिर्भवान्या।।38।।

ཕྱུགས་བདག་གླང་ཆེན་ལྤགས་རློན་འདོད་བཞིན་གྲོན་ནས་གར་ནི་རྩོམ་པ་འཕྲོགས་པར་གྱུར་པ་བཞིན།
ཁྱོད་འོངས་སྤྱི་དོའི་ཐུན་མཚམས་ཉི་གཞོན་དམར་བའི་འོད་ཀྱིས་དམར་བའི་ཆུ་སྐྱེས་འཛིན་བྱེད་ཅིང་།

རྒྱབ་ནས་མཐོ་བའི་ལག་པ་ཟླུམ་པོ་ནགས་ཀྱི་ཤིང་ཚེན་དག་གིས་བརྒྱངས་ནས་འཛིན་ཅིང་གནས།
ཞི་བའི་ཆར་རྒྱུན་འབབ་[༡] ཚེ་རི་ཡི་སྲས་མོས་གཡོ་མེད་མིག་གིས་གུས་པས་ལྟ་བར་བྱེད། ༣༨།

गच्छन्तीनां रमणवसतिं योषितां तत्र नक्तं
रुद्धालोके नरपतिपथे सूचिभेद्यैस्तमोभिः।
सौदामन्या कनकनिकषस्निग्धया दर्शयोर्वीं
तोयोत्सर्गस्तनितमुखरो मा स्म भूर्विक्लवास्ताः।।39।।

དེ་ས་ན་བདག་པོའི་གནས་སུ་མཆོག་གི་བཙུན་མོ་རྣམས་ནི་རབ་དགས་སྙེག་[༢] པར་བྱེད་པ་ན། །
མཚན་མོའི་མུན་པ་སྟུག་པོ་རྣམས་ཀྱིས་མི་ཡི་བདག་པོའི་ལམ་གྱི་སྣང་བ་འགོག་བྱེད་པས། །
ཁྱོད་ཀྱི་གློག་འོད་གསེར་མཚུངས་འོད་ཀྱི་སྣང་བས་ས་གཞིའི་ལམ་ནི་ཀུན་ནས་བསྟན་པར་མཛོད།
ཆུ་ཆར་འབྱུག་དབྱངས་སྒྲ་ཆེན་མང་པོ་མ་བྱེད་མཛེས་པ་དེ་རྣམས་སྐྲག་ཅིང་འཆི་བར་འགྱུར། ༣༩།

तां कस्यांचिद्भवनवलभौ सुप्तपारावतायां
नीत्वा रात्रिं चिरविलसनात्खिन्नविद्युत्कलत्रः।
दृष्टे सूर्ये पुनरपि भवान्वाहयेदध्वशेषं
मन्दायन्ते न खलु सुहृदामभ्युपेतार्थकृत्याः।।40।।

དེ་རྣམས་ཀྱིས་ནི་ཁང་བཟངས་ཕུག་རོན་[༣] ཉལ་ས་སྟེང་གི་རྒྱ་ཕུབས་འགའ་ཞིག་དག་ཏུ་ནི།
ཡུན་རིང་འོངས་ལས་དུབ་པའི་རང་གི་དགའ་མ་གློག་མའི་དོན་དུ་མཚན་མོ་གནས་བྱས་ནས།
ཉི་མ་མཐོང་ཚེ་ཁྱོད་ནི་སླར་ཡང་ལྷག་མའི་ལམ་དག་ཤིན་ཏུ་མགྱོགས་པས་བགྲོད་པར་བྱ།
གང་ཕྱིར་སྙིང་གྲོགས་དག་གི་དོན་དུ་འབད་པ་བྱས་པ་ངེས་པར་བྱ་བ་བྱས་ཉིད། ༤༠།

तस्मिन्काले नयनसलिलं योषितां खण्डितानां
शान्तिं नेयं प्रणयिभिरतो वर्त्म भानोस्त्यजाशु।

---

༡ པེ་། སྣར་།> ཕབ་།

༢ པེ་། སྣར་།> དགའ་སྙེག་།

༣ པེ་། སྣར་།> དེ་རྣམས་ཀྱི་ནི་ཁང་བཟང་ཕུག་རོན་།

प्रालेयास्रं कमलवदनात्सोऽपि हर्तुं नलिन्याः
प्रत्यावृत्तस्त्वयि कररुधि स्यादनल्पाभ्यसूयः।।41।।

དེ་ཡི་དུས་སུ་ཉིན་མོར་བྱེད་པས་ལམ་ནི་དོར་ནས་མྱུར་དུ་འགྲོ་བར་བྱ།
འོད་ཟེར་རབ་ཏུ་འཕྲོ་བ་བསྒྲུགས[1]ན་ཁྲོ་བ་ཆུང་བ་མིན་པ་ཁྱོད་ལ་བྱེད་པར་འགྱུར།
མཚན་མོ་བདག་པོ་སོང་བའི་བུད་མེད་མིག་གི་མཆི་མ་སེལ་ལ་བདག་པོ་འོང་བ་བཞིན།
པདྨོའི་ཡུམ་གྱི་ཆུ་སྐྱེས་གདོང་གི་མིག་ཆུ་དེ་ཡང་རབ་ཏུ་སེལ་བ་བྱེད་པར་འགྱུར། ༤༡།

गम्भीरायाः पयसि सरितश्चेतसीव प्रसन्ने
छायात्माऽपि प्रकृतिसुभगो लप्स्यते ते प्रवेशम्।
तस्मादस्याः कुमुदविशदान्यर्हसि त्वं न धैर्यान्
मोघीकर्तुं चटुलशफरोद्वर्तनप्रेक्षितानि।।42।।

རབ་ཏུ་དང་བའི་སེམས་བཞིན་ཤིན་ཏུ་ཟབ་མོ་དང་ལྡན་མཚོ་ཡི་ཆུ་ཡི་ནང་དུ་ནི།
ཁྱོད་ཀྱི་གཟུགས་བརྙན་ཡང་ནི་རང་བཞིན་སྐལ་བ་བཟང་པོ་བདག་ཉིད་འཆར་བ་ཐོབ་པར་འགྱུར།
དེ་སླད་དེ་ཡི་ཀུ་མུ་ཏ་ནི་དཀར་པོ་རྣམས་ཀྱིས་ཁྱོད་ལ་བཀུར་བསྟི་བསྙེན་བཀུར་བྱེད།
བརྟགས་པས[2]དོན་ཡོད་བྱ་བའི་ཆེད་དུ་གཡོ་ལྡན་ཉ་རྣམས་གྱེན་དུ་འཕར་ཞིང་ལྟ་བར་བྱེད། ༤༢།

तस्याः किंचित्करधृतमिव प्राप्तवानीरशाखं
हृत्वा नीलं सलिलवसनं मुक्तरोधोनितम्बम्।
प्रस्थानं ते कथमपि सखे लम्बमानस्य भावि
ज्ञातास्वादो विवृतजघनां को विहातुं समर्थः।।43।।

དེ་ཡི་ཆུ་གོས་སྔོན་པོས་ཆུ་ཡི་དོགས་ཀྱི་ཆིང་ར་འཁྲིགས[3]པར་བྱས་ནས་སྤྲངས་པ་ན།
མ་འཁྲིག་ཅེས་ནི་ཤིང་ཆེན་ཡལ་གའི་ལག་པ་དག་གིས་དབུས་སུ་ཅུང་ཟད་འཛིན་པ་བཞིན།

---

༡ པེ་། སྣར་།> བསྒྲིབས།

༢ པེ་། སྣར་།> བརྟག་པ་།

༣ པེ་། སྣར་།> ཚང་ར་འཁྲིགས་།

ཀྱཱ་ཡེ་གྲོགས་པོ་ཆུ་འཕྲུངས་ཧྨོ་ཁྱིངས་ལྷི་ནས་ལམ་དུ་འགྲོ་བ་[1] ཡང་ནི་ཧི་ལྟར་ཡིན།
མཛེས་མའི་སྨིན་མ་[2] མཛེས་པའི་བྲོ་བ་[3] ཤེས་ན་ཧི་ལྟར་འདོར་བའི་ནུས་པ་ཡོད་པ་ཡིན། ༤༣།

त्वन्निंष्यन्दोच्छ्वसितवसुधागन्धसंपर्करम्यः
स्रोतोरन्ध्रध्वनितसुभगं दन्तिभिः पीयमानः।
नीचैर्वास्यत्युपजिगमिषोर्देवपूर्वं गिरिं ते
शीतो वायुः परिणमयिता काननोदुम्बराणाम्।।44।।

ཁྱོད་ནི་དེ་པའི་རི་ལས་ཉེ་བར་འགྲོ་ཚེ་དལ་བུ་དལ་བུའི་རླུང་ནི་ལྡང་འགྱུར་ཞིང་།
བསིལ་བའི་རླུང་གིས་བསྐོས་པའི་ཨུ་དུམྦཱ་རའི་ནགས་ཀྱི་འབྲས་བུ་འཚང་ཞིང་རོ་ལ་རྩེད་བྱེད།
ཁྱོད་ཀྱི་ཆར་ཆེན་ཕབ་པས་ནོར་འཛིན་མ་ཡི་དྲི་དང་རླངས་པ་གཙང་མ་ཚོགས་པ་ནི།
སོ་ལྡན་རྣམས་ཀྱི་སྣ་ཡིས་ཧྲུབ་ཅིང་བུ་གའི་ནང་དུ་སྐལ་བཟང་སྒྲ་དབྱངས་སྒྲོགས་པར་བྱེད། ༤༤།

तत्र स्कन्दं नियतवसतिं पुष्पमेघीकृतात्मा
पुष्पासारैः स्नपयतु भवान्वयोमगङ्गाजलार्द्रैः।
रक्षाहेतोर्नवशशिभृता वासवीनां चमूना-
मत्यादित्यं हुतवहमुखे संभृतं तद्धि तेजः।।45।।

དེ་ར་ནི་སྐྱེ་མཆེད་ཉི་མ་ལས་ལྷག་གཟི་ལྡན་སྲེག་ཟླ་ལས་སྐྱེས་སོན་དུ་ཕྱོགས་པ་ཅན།
གཙུག་ན་ཟླ་བ་རིན་ཆེན་མང་གི་དམག་ཚོགས་བསྲུང་པའི་དོན་དུ་བསྐོས་པ་དེ་ནི་གནས།
ཁྱོད་ཀྱི་མཁའ་ཡི་གནྡའི་ཆུ་ལས་སྤྲིན་གྱི་མེ་ཏོག་གསེར་བ་མང་པོ་རྣམས་ཀྱིས་ནི།
མེ་ཏོག་གྲུ་ཆར་བདག་ཉིད་ཕབ་པ་རྣམས་ཀྱིས་གང་ཞིག་དེ་ནི་ཁྲུས་ནི་བྱེད་པར་འགྱུར། ༤༥།

ज्योतिर्लेखावलयि गलितं यस्य बर्हं भवानी
पुत्रप्रेम्णा कुवलयदलप्रापि कर्णे करोति।

---

༡ པེ་། སྣར་།> ཧྨོ་འཕྲུང་ཧི་ན་འགྲོ་བར་ནུས་པ།

༢ པེ་། སྣར་།> མདུན་སྨྲིམ།

༣ པེ་། སྣར་།> བྲོ་གར།

धौतापाङ्गं हरशशिरुचा पावकेस्तं मयूरं
पश्चादद्रिग्रहणगुरुभिर्गर्जितैनर्तयेथाः।।46।।

གཙུག་ཕུད་ལྡན་དེ་ཆུ་འབྱུངས་དགའ་བས་ཕྱིན་ནས་རི་གཟུང་སྐན་པའི་སྨྲ་སྒྲོགས་གར་དག་བྱེད།
མིག་ཟུར་དཀར་བའི་ཟེར་གྱིས་འཁྱིལ་བྱེད་གཙུག་གི་ཟླ་བའི་འོད་ཀྱི་ཟེར་ནི་སྐྱེངས་བྱེད་ཀྱང་།
གང་གི་ཆེ་བའི་མདུག་སྒྲོ་མདངས་འོད་ཚོན་རྩེས་བྲིས་བཞིན་མཛེས་པ་[1] འོད་གྱུར་པ།
ཨུ་མའི་སྲས་ནི་དགའ་བར་བྱེད་པ་ཆུ་སྐྱེས་འདབ་མ་བཞིན་དུ་རྣ་བར་བྱེད་པ་ཡོད། ༤༦།

आराध्यैनं शरवणभवं देवमुल्लङ्घिताध्वा
सिद्धद्वन्द्वैर्जलकणभयाद्वीणिभिर्मुक्तमार्गः।
व्यालम्वेथाः सुरभितनयालम्भजां मानयिष्यन्
स्रोतोमूर्त्या भुवि परिणतां रन्तिदेवस्य कीर्तिम्।।47।।

སྐྱེག་མའི་ཚལ་ན་སྐྱེས་པའི་ལྷ་དེ་ཡང་དག་མཆོད་ནས་སླར་ཡང་ལམ་ནི་བགྲལ་བར་མཛོད།
གྲུབ་པའི་ཁྲོ་ཤུག་དག་གི་ལག་པའི་པི་ཝང་ཆུ་ཐིགས་བརླན་ལ་འཇིགས་པས་ལམ་ནི་སྤེ་ར།
ཁྱོད་ཀྱིས་མཐོང་བར་འགྱུར་བའི་ས་བདག་དགའ་བའི་ལྷ་ཡི་སྲས་པོ་ཆུ་གཏེར་གཟུགས་འཛིན་ནི།
ས་ཡི་གཞི་ལ་བྱུང་ཞིང་ལྷུན་པོ་[2] འདོད་འཛོའི་བུ་མོས་འོངས་ནས་མཆོད་པ་བྱེད་པར་འགྱུར། ༤༧།

त्वय्यादातुं जलमवनते शार्ङ्गिणो वर्णचौरे
तस्याः सिन्धोः पृथुमपि तनुं दूरभावात्प्रवाहम्।
प्रेक्षिष्यन्ते गगनगतयो नूनमावर्ज्य दृष्टी-
रेकं मुक्तागुणमिव भुवः स्थूलमध्येन्द्रनीलम्।।48।।

ཁྱོད་ཀྱི་[3] དེ་ཡི་རླབས་ལྡན་མཚོ་ཡི་ཆུ་འབྱུངས་འོངས་པའི་ཚེ་ན་ཐག་རིང་མཐུ་ལས་ནི།
ཆེན་པོ་ཡིན་ཡང་ཕྲ་མོ་དང་ནི་སྤྲང་རྩེའི་བུ་ཡི་ཁ་དོག་བསྒྲུས་པར་གྱུར་པ་དང་།

---

༡ པེ།སྣར།> མཛེས་པ་ལྷུང་བ།

༢ པེ། སྣར།> ལྷུང་བ།

༣ པེ། སྣར།> ཀྱིས།

ཆེན་པོའི་[1]ས་ལ་ཨིནྡྲ་ནཱི་ལ་མུ་ཏི་ག་དོ་ཤལ་དག་ནི་གཅིག་ཏུ་བགོད་པ་བཞིན།
མཁའ་ལ་བགྲོད་པ་རྣམས་ཀྱི་མིག་རྣམས་དག་གིས་འོག་ཏུ་བལྟ་ཞིང་ངེས་པར་མཐོང་བར་འགྱུར། ༤༨།

तामुत्तीर्य व्रज परिचितभ्रूलताविभ्रमाणाम्
पक्ष्मोत्क्षेपादुपरिविलसत्कृष्णशारप्रभाणाम्।
कुन्दक्षेपानुगमधुकरश्रीमुषामात्मबिम्बं
पात्रीकुर्वन्दशपुरवधूनेत्रकौतूहलानाम्।।49।।

དེ་རྣམས་བཀལ་ནས་བགྲོད་ཚེ་སྨིན་མ་འཁྲི་ཤིང་གཞོན་ནུ་རོལ་པ་རྣམས་ཀྱིས་མཛེས་པ་ཅན།
དཀར་ནག་འོད་ཟེར་དང་ལྡན་རྣམས་ཀྱི་རྫི་མ་སྟེང་དུ་བསྐྱོད་པར་གྱུར་པའི་མཛེས་པ་དག
ཀུན་དའི་མེ་ཏོག་གཡོ་བའི་རྗེས་འགྲོ་སྦྲང་རྩི་བྱེད་པའི་དཔལ་གྱི་མཛེས་པ་བཞིན་དུ་ནི།
མཛེས་ལྡན་ད་ཤ་ཞེས་བྱའི་གྲོང་ཁྱེར་ན་ཆུང་མིག་གིས་བལྟ་འདོད་ལ་ནི་རང་ལུས་བསྟན་པར་མཛོད། ༤༩།

ब्रह्मावर्तं जनपदमथच्छायया गाहमानः
क्षेत्रं क्षत्रप्रधनपिशुनं कौरवं तद्भजेथाः।
राजन्यानां शितशरशतैर्यत्र गाण्डीवधन्वा
धारापातैस्त्वमिव कमलान्यभ्यवर्षन्मुखानि।।50।।

དང་པོར་ཚངས་པ་འཇུག་ཞེས་བྱའི་ལྗོངས་ལ་ཁྱོད་ནི་བགྲོད་བྱ་འོག་ཏུ་གྲིབ་[2]བསིལ་བྱ།
དེ་ནས་རྒྱལ་རིགས་བཅོམ་པའི་དུར་ལྡན་ཀུ་རུ་བ་ཡི་བཞིན་[3]ནི་ཁྱོད་ཀྱིས་བསྟན་པར་བྱ།
གང་དུ་སྲིད་སྒྲུབ་མདའ་རྣོན་[4]བརྒྱ་ཕྲག་དག་གིས་རྒྱལ་རིགས་མིང་པོའི་མགོ་བོ་བཅད་པ་ནི།
ཁྱོད་ཀྱི་གྲུ་ཆར་ཆེན་པོ་རབ་ཏུ་མང་པོ་ཕབ་པས་པདྨ་རྣམས་ནི་ཆད་པ་བཞིན། ༥༠།

हित्वा हालामभिमतरसां रेवतीलोचनाङ्कां
बन्धुप्रीत्या समरविमुखो लाङ्गली याः सिषेवे।

---

༡ པེ་། སྣར་།> ཆེ་བའི།

༢ པེ་། སྣར་།> སྲིབ།

༣ པེ་། སྣར་།> ཀུ་རུ་པའི་ཞིང་།

༤ པེ་། སྣར་།> རྣོ།

कृत्वा तासामभिगममपां सौम्य सारस्वतीना-
मन्तःशुद्धस्त्वमपि भविता वर्णमात्रेण कृष्णः।।51।।

སྒྲོས་པར་བྱེད་པའི་རོ་ལྡན་དགའ་མ་སྣར་མའི་ཚིག་གིས་མཚན་པའི་ཆང་ནི་སྤང་བྱས་ནས།
རང་གི་གཉེན་ལ་དགའ་བར་འགྱུར་བས་ཡུལ་ལས་ཕྱིར་ཕྱོགས་སྟོབས་བཟང་གང་དེ་བཏྲ་བར་བྱ།
ཀུ་ཡི་ཞི་ལྡན་སྨྲ་ར་སྭ་ཏིའི་ཆུ་ལ་མངོན་པར་ཕྱོགས་ཚེ་ཁྱོད་ཀྱིས་འཐུངས་བྱས་ནས།
ལུས་ཀྱི་ཁ་དོག་དག་ནི་ནག་པོར་འགྱུར་ཞིང་ནང་གི་བསམ་པ་ཡང་ནི་དཀར་བ་ཉིད། ༥༡།

तस्माद्गच्छेरनुकनखलं शैलराजावतीर्णां
जह्नोः कन्यां सगरतनयस्वर्गसोपानपंक्तिम्।
गौरीवक्त्रभ्रुकुटिरचनां या विहस्येव फेनैः
शंभोः केशग्रहणमकरोदिन्दुलग्नोर्मिहस्ता।।52।।

དེ་ནས་བགྲོད་པའི་ཕྱི་ནས་ཀན་ཁ་ལ་ཡི་གྲོང་ཡོད་ཛ་ཧྣུའི་[1] བུ་མོ་རི་རྒྱལ་གྱི།
ངོས་ལ་བགྲོད་པ་དུག་ཅན་རྒྱལ་པོའི་བུ་ནི་མཐོ་རིས་དེ་ཡི་[2] ཐེམ་སྐས་བགྲོད་པ་བཞིན།
གང་གི་དབུ་བའི་ཕྲེང་བ་རྣམས་ཀྱིས་གཽ་རཱི་འི་ཞལ་གྱི་ཁྲོ་གཉེར་རྣམས་ལ་དགོད་[3] པ་བཞིན།
བདེ་འབྱུང་སྐྲ་ནས་ཆླབས་ཀྱི་[4] ལག་པ་དག་གིས་བཟུང་ནས་ཟླ་ཕྱེད་འཁྲིག་པར་བྱེད་པ་བཞིན། ༥༢།

तस्याः पातुं सुरगज इव व्योम्नि पश्चार्धलम्बी
त्वं चेदच्छस्फटिकविशदं तर्कयेस्तिर्यगम्भः।
संसर्पन्त्या सपदि भवतः स्रोतसिच्छाययाऽसौ
स्यादस्थानोपगतयमुनासंगमेवाभिरामा।।53।।

ཁྱོད་ནི་གལ་ཏེ་དེ་ཡི་ཆུ་འཐུངས་བསམས་ནས་ལུས་ཕྱེད་སྟེ་མ་མཁར་ལས་འཕྱང་བ་ནི།
ལྷ་ཡི་གླང་པོ་བཞིན་ཏེ་ཆུ་དེའི་ཞིང་ནི་དྲི་མེད་དཀར་བའི་ཤེལ་བཞིན་སྣང་བ་ཉིད།

---

༡ པེ། སྣར།> ཛྷུའི།

༢ པེ། སྣར།> ཏོ་ཡི།

༣ པེ། སྣར།> ཀོད།

༤ པེ། སྣར།> ཀྱིས།

ཆུ་བོ་དེ་ལ་ཁྱོད་ཀྱི་སླག་མ་བསམ་པས་[༡] འཕྲུལ་ལ་ཡང་དག་འབྱུང་འགྱུར་མཛེས་པ་ནི།
ཡ་མུ་ན་ཡི་ཆུ་དང་གཙྭ་འགྲོགས་པའི་མཛེས་པ་ལས་འོངས་གྱུར་ལ་གནས་མ་ཡིན། ༥༣།

आसीनानां सुरभितशिलं नाभिगन्धैर्मृगाणां
तस्या एव प्रभवमचलं प्राप्य गौरं तुषारैः।
वक्ष्यस्यध्वश्रमविनयने तस्य शृङ्गे निषण्णः
शोभां शुभ्रां त्रिनयनवृषोत्खातपङ्कोपमेयाम्।।54।।

རྡོ་ལེབ་སྟེང་དུ་རི་དྭགས་གནས་པས་རི་དྭགས་ལྟེ་བའི་དྲི་བཟང་འཛིན་པའི་རྡོ་ལྡན་ཞིང་།
གཙྭ་ཉིད་ཀྱི་ཡབ་གྱུར་ཁ་བར་[༢] དཀར་བའི་གཡོ་མེད་གངས་ལྡན་དེ་ཉིད་ཐོབ་བྱས་ནས།
ལམ་གྱིས་དལ་[༣] བ་རྣམ་པར་འདུལ་བའི་ཆེད་དུ་དེ་ཡི་རྩེ་ལ་སླེབས་ནས་འདུག་པ་ཡི།
མཛེས་པ་མིག་གསུམ་པ་ཡི་བཞིན་[༤] པ་དཀར་བའི་ཁྲུ་མཆོག་རྭ་ཡིས་འདམ་ནི་བླངས་པ་བཞིན། ༥༤།

तं चेद्वायौ सरति सरलस्कंधसंघट्टजन्मा
बाधेतोल्काक्षपितचमरीबालभारो दवाग्निः।
अर्हस्येनं शमयितुमलं वारिधारा सहस्रै-
रापन्नार्तिप्रशमनफलाः संपदो ह्युत्तमानाम्।।55।।

དེ་ལ་གལ་ཏེ་རླུང་གིས་རབ་བསྐྱོད་ཐང་ཤིང་ལག་པ་ཀུན་དུ་འཐབས་པ་ལས་བྱུང་བའི།
མེ་ཡི་དུག་དང་མེ་སྟེག་དག་གིས་འབྲོང་གི་དགའ་མའི་སྤུ་ཚོགས་མང་པོ་སྲེག་བྱེད་ན།
ཁྱོད་ཀྱིས་དེ་རྣམས་ཞི་བའི་ཆེད་དུ་ཆུ་འཛིན་སྟོང་ཕྲག་མང་པོའི་ཆར་ནི་བྱ་བར་འོས།
གང་ཕྱིར་ཆེན་པོ་རྣམས་ཀྱི་ཕུན་ཚོགས་འབྲས་བུ་མང་པོའི་སྡུག་བསྔལ་ཞི་བར་བྱེད་པ་ཉིད། ༥༥།

ये त्वां मुक्तध्वनिमसहनाः स्वाङ्गभङ्गाय तस्मिन्
दर्पोत्सेकादुपरि शरभा लङ्घयिष्यन्त्यलङ्घयम्।

---

༡ པེ་། སྣར་།> ཁྱོད་ཀྱིས་གྲིབ་མ་བབས་པས།

༢ པེ་། སྣར་།> ཁ་བས།

༣ པེ་། སྣར་།> གྱི་ངལ།

༤ པེ་། སྣར་།> མཛེས་པའི་བཞིན།

तान्कुर्वीथास्तुमुलकरकावृष्टिपातावकीर्णान्
के वा न स्युः परिभवपदं निष्फलारम्भयत्नाः।।56।।

དེ་ར་ནི་ཁྱོད་ཀྱིས་སྒྲ་ཆེན་བསྒྲགས་ལ་མ་བཟོད་ཆེ་བའི་དྲེགས་པ་ཀུན་དུ་ལྡན་པའི་ཤ༹ང་བརྒྱད་པ།
ཁྱོད་ཀྱི་སྟེང་དུ་མཆོང་བར་བྱའོ་སྙམ་ནས་མ་མཚངས[༡] རང་གི་ཡན་ལག་ཀུན་དུ་རྨས།
དེ་རྣམས་དག་ལ་རབ་ཏུ་བཞད་ལྡན་ཐོག་སེར་ཆར་པ་དྲག་ཕབ་མང་པོས་གཞོམ་པར་མཛོད།
རང་བཞིན་ངན་པའི་གནས་པ་དག་གི་འབྲས་མེད་རྩོམ་པའི་འབད་པ་རྣམས་ནི་ཅི་ཡང་མེད[༢]། ༥༦།

तत्र व्यक्तं दृषदि चरणन्यासमर्धेन्दुमौलेः
शश्वत्सिद्धैरुपहृतबलिं भक्तिनम्रः परीयाः।
यस्मिन्दृष्टे करणविगमादूर्ध्वमुद्धूतपापाः
कल्पन्तेऽस्य स्थिरगणपदप्राप्तये श्रद्धधानाः।।57।।

དེ་ར་ནི་ཆེ་ཞིང་གསལ་བའི་རྡོ་ལ་གཙུག་ན་ཟླ་ཕྱེད་འཛིན་པའི་ཤ༹ང་བཀོད་རྗེས་ལ་ནི།
རྟག་ཏུ་གྲུབ་པ་རྣམས་ཀྱིས་གཏོར་མ་མཆོད་ཀྱིས[༣] གུས་པས་ཕྱག་དང་བསྐོར་བ་མཛོད།
གང་ཞིག་མཐོང་ན་བྱེད་པས་བྱས་པའི་སྡིག་པ་རྣམས་ནི་ཤིན་ཏུ་རིང་པོར་འདོར་བྱེད་ཅིང་།
གུས་པ་འཛིན་པ་རྣམས་ནི་དེ་ཡི་འཁོར་དུ་གནས་པ་ཐོབ་བྱེད་བརྟན་པ་ཐོབ་པར་འགྱུར། ༥༧།

शब्दायन्ते मधुरमलिनैः कीचकाः पूर्यमाणाः
संसक्ताभिस्त्रिपुरविजयो गीयते किन्नरीभिः।
निर्ह्लादी ते मुरज इव चेत्कन्दरेषु ध्वनिः स्यात्
सगीतार्थो ननु पशुपतेस्तत्र भावी समस्तः।।58।।

---

༡ པེ་། སྣར་།> ཚངས།

༢ པེ་། སྣར་།> ཅི་ཡང་མིན།

༣ པེ་། སྣར་།> མཆོད་དོ་ཁྱོད་ཀྱིས།

དྲི་ཞིམ་རྣམས་ཀྱིས་[1] ཁེངས་པར་གྱུར་པའི་ཁང་[2] པ་ནང་[3] ནས་སྙན་པའི་ཡིད་འོང་སྒྲ་འབྱུང་ཞིང་།
མིའམ་ཅི་མོ་རྣམས་ཀྱིས་གྲོང་ཁྱེར་གསུམ་རྒྱལ་འགྱུར་ལས་ཡང་དག་དགའ་བས་གླུ་དབྱངས་སྒྲོགས་[4]།
ཛ་ཀླུམ་སྙན་པའི་སྒྲ་བཞིན་གཡལ་ཏེ་ཁྱོད་ཀྱིས་རྔ་ཡི་གཅུག་ལག་ཁང་དེ་ར་སྒྲ་སྙན་[5] ནི།
བསྒྲགས་པར་གྱུར་ན་ངེས་པར་ཕྱུགས་[6] བདག་དུང་དུ་གསུམ་འདུས་དབྱངས་སྙན་དོན་གྱི་ཚོགས་པ་འབྱུང་། ༥༨།

प्रालेयाद्रेरुपतटमतिक्रम्य तास्तान्विशेषान्
हंसद्वारं भृगुपतियशोवर्त्म यत्क्रौञ्चरन्ध्रम्।
तेनोदीचीं दिशमनुसरेस्तिर्यगायामशोभी
श्यामः पादो बलिनियमनाभ्युद्यतस्येव विष्णोः।।59।।

གངས་ཀྱི་རི་ལ་ཉེ་བའི་ཐང་ལ་ཀྲང་པ་བསྐྱོད་ཚེ་དེ་དང་དེ་ཡི་ཁྱད་པར་ལ།
ཀྲཽཉྩའི་རི་ཡི་ལམ་ལ་རབ་གྲགས་བྷྲྀ་གུའི་བདག་པོའི་མདའ་ཕུག་དང་པའི་སྒོ་[7] ཅན་ཡོད།
དེ་ནས་ནོར་སྦྱིན་ཕྱོགས་སུ་ཁྱོད་ནི་རྗེས་སུ་འགྲོ་ཚེ་འཁྱོག་པོར་འགྲོ་བའི་མཛེས་པ་ནི།
སྟོབས་ལྡན་སླུ་བའི་ཚེད་དུ་ཁྱབ་འཇུག་ས་འཛལ་ཀྲང་པ་སྤོ་བསངས་ཡང་དག་བཀོད་པ་བཞིན། ༥༩།

गत्वा चोर्ध्वं दशमुखभुजोच्छ्वासितप्रस्थसन्धेः
कैलासस्य त्रिदशवनितादर्पणस्यातिथिः स्याः।
शृङ्गोच्छ्रायैः कुमुदविशदैर्यो वितत्य स्थितः खं
राशीभूतः प्रतिदिशमिव त्र्यम्बकस्याट्टहासः।।60।।

---

༡ པེ། སྣར།> བཞོན་རྣམས་ཀྱི།

༢ པེ། སྣར།> གྱུར།

༣ པེ། སྣར།> པའི་སྐྱིག་སྒྲོམ་ནང་།

༤ པེ། སྣར།> ཀྱིས།སྒྲོག

༥ པེ། སྣར།> བརྙན།

༦ པེ། སྣར།> ཕྱུག

༧ པེ། སྣར།> མདའ་ཕུགས་དང་པའི་སྒྲོ།

མགྲིན་བཅུའི་ལག་པས་བསྐྱོད་བྱ་རི་ངོས་ཡངས་པ་དང་ལྡན་ཤེལ་གྱི་ཀཻ་ལ་ཤ་ཡི་རི།
སྐབས་གསམ་མཛེས་མའི་གདོང་གི་མེ་ལོང་[1] བསྟན་བྱའི་སྙེང་དུ་འདང་སོང་སྟེ་ཚུང་ཟད་གནས་པར་བྱ།
གང་གི་རྩེ་མོ་ཤིན་ཏུ་མཐོ་བ་ཀུ་མུ་ཏ་ལྟར་མཁའ་ལ་ཁྱབ་པར་གནས་པ་ནི།
མིག་གསུམ་པ་ཡིས་རབ་ཏུ་བཤད་[2] པ་ཕྱོགས་བཅུ་དག་ནས་གཅིག་ཏུ་སྤུངས་པར་གྱུར་པ་བཞིན། ༦༠།

उत्पश्यामि त्वयि तटगते स्निग्धभिन्नाञ्जनाभे
सद्यः कृत्तद्विरददशनच्छेदगौरस्य तस्य।
लीलामद्रेः स्तिमितनयनप्रेक्षणीयां भवित्रीमम्
अंसन्यस्ते सति हलभृतो मेचके वाससीव॥61॥

དེ་ཡི་རི་ངོས་དག་ལ་ཁྱོད་ནི་འགྲོ་ཚེ་སྨུམ་པའི་སྨན་མཆོག་[3] དག་དང་མཚུངས་དང་།
དེ་ནི་གཉིས་འཐུང་སོ་ནི་འཕྲུལ་ལ་བཅད་པར་བྱས་པ་ལྟ་བུར་དཀར་ཞིང་མཛེས་པ་དེ།
མཛེས་པའི་རི་བོ་ལ་ནི་གཡོ་བ་མེད་པའི་མིག་གིས་[4] བལྟ་བྱ་ཉིད་དུ་འགྱུར་བ་དང་།
སྟོབས་ལྡན་དཀར་པོའི་དཔུང་པ་དག་ལ་གོས་སྔོན་བཀོད་པར་གྱུར་བཞིན་འབྱུང་བ་བདག་གིས་སེམས། ༦༡།

हित्वा तस्मिन्भुजगवलयं शम्भुना दत्तहस्ता
क्रीड़ाशैले यदि च विहरेत्पादचारेण गौरी।
भङ्गीभक्त्या विरचितवपुः स्तम्भितान्तर्जलौघः
सोपानत्वं व्रज पदसुखस्पर्शमारोहणेषु॥62॥

དེ་ར་ནི་བདེ་འབྱུང་སྦྲུལ་གྱི་གདུ་བུ་དོར་ནས་གཽ་རཱའི་ལག་པ་དག་ལ་འཛིན་[5] བྱེད་ཅིང་།
གལ་ཏེ་ཡང་ནི་རོལ་རྩེད་ཆེད་དུ་ཞབས་ཀྱིས་འགྲོ་བས་རི་ལ་དེ་དག་དལ་འགྲོ་ན།

---

༡ པེ། སྣར།> མཛེས་མའི་གདོང་གི་མེ་ལོང་།

༢ པེ། སྣར།> རྗོད།

༣ པེ། སྣར།> སྨུམ་པའི་མིག་སྨན།

༤ པེ། སྣར།> གི།

༥ པེ། སྣར།> རིའི་ལག་པ་འཛིན།

ཁྱོད་བསྒྲོད་ལུས་ནི་འཁྱོག་པོར་འགྲོ་ཞིང་ནང་ན་གནས་པའི་ཆུ་ཆེན་དག་ནི་སྲུང་བྱ་ཞིང་།
བཀབ་[༡]པར་བྱས་ནས་སྟེང་དུ་འགྲོ་བ་རྣམས་ལ་རྐང་པའི་བདེ་བ་རེག་པར་བྱ་བ་མཛོད། ༦༢།

तत्रावश्यं वलयकुलिशोद्धट्टनोद्गीर्णतोयं
नेष्यन्ति त्वां सुरयुवतयो यन्त्रधारागृहत्वम्।
ताभ्यो मोक्षस्तव यदि सखे धर्मलब्धस्य न स्यात्
क्रीडालोलाः श्रवणपरुषैर्गर्जितैर्भाययेस्ताः।।63।।

རིགས་གནས་དེ་རུ་ནི་ཁྱོད་ཀྱིས་ཆུ་རྣམས་སྐྱུགས་པར་བྱས་པས་ངེས་པར་ནང་ན་མེད་པ་ན།
ལྷ་ཡི་ན་ཆུང་རྣམས་ཀྱིས་ཁྱོད་ནི་འཁྲུལ་འཁོར་གྱིས་བཟུང་ཁང་བཟངས་ནང་དུ་འཁྱེར་བར་བྱེད།
ཀྱཻ་ཡེ་གྲོགས་བཟང་ཚ་བས་གདུངས་པ་དེ་རྣམས་ཆེད་དུ་གལ་ཏེ་ཁྱོད་ནི་མི་གཏོང་ན།
རོལ་སྙེག་གཡོ་བའི་མཛེས་མ་དེ་རྣམས་རྣ་བར་རྩུབ་པའི་སྒྲ་ཆེན་བསྒྲགས་པས་འཇིགས་པར་བྱ། ༦༣།

हेमाम्भोजप्रसवि सलिलं मानसस्याददानः
कुर्वन्कामात्क्षणमुखपटप्रीतिमैरावतस्य।
धुन्वन्वातैः सजलपृषतैः कल्पवृक्षांशुकानि
च्छायाभिन्नः स्फटिकविशदं निर्विशेस्तं नगेन्द्रम्।।64।।

ཆུ་ཐིགས་དག་གིས་བྲན་པ་དང་ལྡན་དྲི་བཞོན་གྱིས་བསྐྱོད་དཔག་བསམ་ཤིང་[༢]ལ་གཡོ་བཞིན་དུ།
ཁྱོད་ཀྱི་གྲིབ་འོད་ཤེལ་ལྟར་དཀར་བའི་གོས་[༣]ཀྱིས་རི་དབང་དེ་ནི་ཡོངས་སུ་གཡོགས་[༤]བྱ་ཞིང་།
ཡིད་འོང་ཆུ་བོ་བཞི་ཡི་རྒྱུན་ནི་གསེར་[༥]གྱི་ཆུ་སྐྱེས་གསར་པ་ལྟར་དེ་འདང་[༦]འབྱུང་བ་དང་།
ས་སྲུང་བུ་ཡི་གདོང་པའི་གོས་ནི་ཅི་འདོད་སྤྱོད་ཅིང་དགའ་བའང་སྐད་ཅིག་བྱ་བར་མཛོད། ༦༤།

---

༡ པེ་། སྣར་།> སྐམས།

༢ པེ་། སྣར་།> ཞིང་།

༣ པེ་། སྣར་།> འོད།

༤ པེ་། སྣར་།> རི་དབང་དེ་ནི་གཡོགས།

༥ པེ་། སྣར་།> ཡིད་འོང་མཚོ་ནི་གསེར།

༦ པེ་། སྣར་།> ཆུ་སྐྱེས་གེ་སར་ལྡན་དེ་འདང་།

तस्योत्सङ्गे प्रणयिन इव स्रस्तगङ्गादुकूलां
न त्वं दृष्ट्वा न पुनरलकां ज्ञास्यसे कामचारिन्।
या वः काले वहति सलिलोद्गारमुच्चैर्विमाना
मुक्ताजालग्रथितमलकं कामिनीवाभ्रवृन्दम्।।65।।

ཀྭ་ཡེ་འདོད་བཞིན་རྒྱུ་བྱེད་ཁྱོད་ནི་དེས[༡] ལས་ཀལ་ཆེ་ལྷུང་བོ་ལྡན་མ་ཤེས་པར་འགྱུར།
སླར་ཡང་རི་དེ་གཡོ་ལྡན་གངྒཱའི་རྒྱུ་གོས་ལྡན་མའི་བདག་པོ་བཞིན་དུ་མི་མཐོང་མིན།
མཐོང་[༢] བའི་གཞལ་མེད་ཁང་སྟེང་ཆར་སྤྲིན་ཆེ་ལས་ཁྱོད་ཀྱི་ཆུ་བྱུས་སྐྱུགས་བྱས་དུས་སུ་ནི།[༣]
གང་ཞིག་འདོད་ལྡན་མ་ནི་ལེན་བུ་མུ་ཏིག་དྲ་བས་བསྒྲིགས་པའི་ཕྲེང་བ་ལྡན་པ་བཞིན། ༦༥།

विद्युत्वन्तं ललितवनिताः सेन्द्रचापं सचित्राः
संगीताय प्रहतमुरजाः स्निग्धगम्भीरघोषम्।
अन्तस्तोयं मणिमयभुवस्तुङ्गमभ्रंलिहाग्राः
प्रासादास्त्वां तुलियतुमलं यत्र तैस्तैर्विशेषैः।।66।।

ཁྱོད་ལ་གློག་འོད་ལྡན་བཞིན་སྣེག་པའི་མཛེས་མ་དང་ལྡན་དབང་པོའི་གཞུ་བཞིན་བཀྲ་བར་ལྡན།
སྙན་པའི་དབྱངས་ནི་ཟབ་པ་བཞིན་དུ་སླུ་དབྱངས་དག་དང་རོ་ལ་མོའི་དབྱངས་སྙན་རྣམས་དང་ལྡན།
ཆུ་ཡི་སྙིང་པོ་ཅན་བཞིན་ས་གཞི་ནོར་བུའི་རང་བཞིན་མཐོ་བཞིན་རྩེ་མོ་མཁའ་ལ་རེག
གང་དུ་ཁྱད་པར་དེ་རྣམས་ཀྱིས་ནི་ཁྱོད་དང་ཁང་བཟངས་མཚུངས་པའི་ཆེད་དུ་ནོར་བུར[༤] ལྡན། ༦༦།

हस्ते लीलाकमलमलकं बालकुन्दानुविद्धं
नीता लोध्रप्रसवरजसा पाण्डुतामाननश्रीः।
चूडापाशे नवकुरवकं चारु कर्णे शिरीषं
सीमन्ते च त्वदुपगमजं यत्र नीपं वधूनाम्।।67।।

---

༡ པེ་། སྣར་།> །དེ།

༢ པེ་། སྣར་།> མཐོ།

༣ པེ་། སྣར་།> ཁྱོད་ཀྱིས་ཆུ་སྐྱུག་བྱས་དུས་ནི།

༤ པེ་། སྣར་།> ནུས་པར།

གང་དུ་ན་ཆུང་རྣམས་ནི་ལག་པད་མཛེས་ཤིང་ལན་བུའི་ཀུན་ད་གཞོན་ནུའི་སྐྲ་ནི་འཆིང་།
གདོང་གི་ཆུ་སྐྱེས་འཛུམ་ཞིང་དཀར་བའི་གེ་སར་དཔལ་ནི་གསར་པ་དག་གིས་མཛེས་བྱས་ཤིང་།
གཙུག་ཕུད་ཀུ་རུ་བ་ཀའི་མེ་ཏོག་ཞགས་པས་བཅིངས་པ་མཛེས་ཤིང་རྣ་བར་ཨུ་ཏ྄པལ་ཅན།
སྐྲ་མཚམས་བཀྲ་བའི་མེ་ཏོག་དག་དང་ལྡན་པའང་ཁྱོད་ནི་ཉེ་བར་འོངས་ལས་སྐྱེས་པ་[1]ཡིན། ༦༧།

यस्यां यक्षाः सितमणिमयान्येत्य हर्म्यस्थलानि
ज्योतिश्छायाकुसुमरचनान्युत्तमस्त्रीसहायाः।
आसेवन्ते मधु रतिफलं कल्पवृक्षप्रसूतं
त्वद्गम्भीरध्वनिषु शनकैः पुष्करेष्वाहतेषु।।68।।

གང་གི་དཀར་པོའི་ནོར་བུ་དང་ལྡན་རིན་ཆེན་འོད་ཀྱིས་ཁྱབ་པ་ཆུ་སྐྱེས་ལྟར་མཛེས་པའི།
ཡང་ཐོག་གཞི་ལ་གནོད་སྦྱིན་རྣམས་ནི་མཆོག་གིས་དགའ་མ་དང་བཅས་ཡང་དག་གནས་བྱས་ནས།
དཔག་བསམ་ཤིང་ལས་རབ་ཏུ་འབྱུངས་པའི་དགའ་མའི་རོ་ལྡན་ཆང་ནི་ཀུན་དུ་འཐུང་བྱེད་ཅིང་།
དལ་བུ་རྣམས་ཀྱིས་ཛ་[2]རྣམས་ལ་ནི་བརྡུངས་པ་ཁྱོད་ཀྱི་འབྲུག་སྒྲ་ཟབ་པའི་དབྱངས་སྙན་བཞིན།༦༨།

गत्युत्कम्पादलकपतितैर्यत्र मन्दारपुष्पैः
पत्रच्छेदैः कनककमलैः कर्णविभ्रंशिभिश्च।
मुक्ताजालैः स्तनपरिचितच्छिन्नसूत्रैश्च हारैः
नैशो मार्गः सवितुरुदये सूच्यते कामिनीनाम्।।69।।

གང་དུ་རབ་བགྲོད་ཚེས་ཚེར་འདར་བས་ལེན་བུ་ལྷུང་ཞིང་མནྡ་ར་བའི་མེ་ཏོག་ནི།
མཚར་བར་འགྱུར་ཅིང་རྣ་བའི་རྒྱན་གྱུར་རབ་མཛེས་གསེར་གྱི་མེ་ཏོག་ལྷུང་བ་གྱུར་པ་དང་།
ནུ་རྒྱུས་མུ་ཏིག་དྲ་བ་མཚར་བ་གྱུར་ཅིང་དོ་ཤལ་སྲད་བུ་ཆད་པར་གྱུར་པ་ཡི[3]།
འདོད་ལྡན་མ་རྣམས་མཚན་མོ་ལམ་དུ་འགྲོ་ལ་བྱུང་བ་འོད་ལྡན་ཤར་ཚེ་གསལ་བར་བྱེད། ༦༩།

---

༡ པེ་། སྣར་།> སྐྱེ་བ།

༢ པེ་། སྣར་།> ཀྱིས་རབ་ཏུ་ཛ་།

༣ པེ་། སྣར་།> ཡིས།

नीवीबन्धोच्छ्वसितशिथिलं यत्र यक्षाङ्गनानां
वासः कामादनिभृतकरेष्वाक्षिपत्सु प्रियेषु।
अर्चिस्तुङ्गानभिमुखमपि प्राप्य रत्नप्रदीपान्
ह्रीमूढानां भवति विफलप्रेरणा चूर्णमुष्टिः।।70।।

གང་ཆེད་ཆགས་[1]པས་གནོད་སྦྱིན་བུད་མེད་རྣམས་ཀྱི་འོག་པག་བཅིངས་པ་འགྲོལ་ཞིང་གོས་དག་ནི།
བསལ་ལ་མཛའ་བོ་རྣམས་ལ་འདོད་མས་འདར་བར་གྱུར་ཅིང་གཡོ་བའི་ལག་པ་འཕེན་པ་ན།
མཆོག་ཏུ་ཆེ་བའི་འོད་ཟེར་དང་ལྡན་རིན་ཆེན་མར་མེ་མདོན་དུ་མཐོང་བར་བྱེད་པ་ནི།[2]
ངོ་ཚས་རྨོངས་པ་རྣམས་ཀྱི་ལག་པ་དག་གིས་ཕྱེ་མ་གཏོར་བར་གྱུར་པ་འབྲས་མེད་འགྱུར། ༧༠།

नेत्रा नीताः सततगतिना यद्विमानाग्रभूमीः
आलेख्यानां सलिलकणिकादोषमुत्पाद्य सद्यः।
शङ्कास्पृष्टा इव जलमुचस्त्वादृशा यत्र जालै-
र्धूमोद्गारानुकृतिनिपुणा जर्जरा निष्पतन्ति।।71।।

གང་དུ་རྒྱུ་འཛིན་ནས་སྟེང་གནས་རྣམས་འདྲེན་བྱེད་རྟག་འགྲོས་གཞལ་མེད་ཁང་ནང་དེད་པ་ན།
གང་ཞིག་རང་གི་རྒྱུ་ཐིགས་དག་གིས་བཀྲ་བའི་རི་མོ་རྣམས་ལ་འཕྲུལ་དུ་སྐྱོན་བྱུང་ནས།
ངོ་ཚ་[3]རིག་པ་བཞིན་དུ་ཁྱོད་འདྲ་དུམ་བུ་དུམ་བུ་དག་ཏུ་[4]འཐོན་པར་བྱེད་པ་ནི།
དྲི་མིག་རྣམས་ཀྱི་ནང་ནས་དུ་བ་ཞུགས་པ་འཐོན་པ་རྣམས་ཀྱི་རྗེས་སུ་བྱེད་པ་བཞིན། ༧༡།

यत्र स्त्रीणां प्रियतमभुजोच्छ्वासितालिङ्गितानाम्
अङ्गग्लानिं सुरतजनितां तन्तुजालावलम्बाः।
त्वत्संरोधापगमविशदैश्च्योतिताश्चन्द्रपादैः
व्यालुम्पन्ति स्फुटजललवस्यन्दिनश्चन्द्रकान्ताः।।72।।

---

༡ པེ་། སྣར་།> གང་དུ་ཆགས།

༢ པེ་། སྣར་།> མངོན་དུ་གནས་པ་མཐོང་བྱས་ནས།

༣ པེ་། སྣར་།> ངོ་ཚས།

༤ པེ་། སྣར་།> དུམ་བུ་དག་དུ།

གང་དུ་བུད་མེད་མཆོག་རྣམས་བདག་པོས་[1] མཆོག་གིས་[2] ཀུན་ནས་འཁྲུད་པ་རྣམས་ནི་བཏང་བ་ན།
ལུས་ནི་ཀུན་ནས་གདུང་བར་བྱེད་ལ་ཟླ་བ་ཆུ་ཤེལ་སྲུད་བུའི་དྲ་བ་འཕྱང་བ་ཅན།
ཁྱོད་ཀྱིས་བསྒྲིབས་པ་མེད་ཅིང་དཀར་བའི་ཟླ་བའི་འོད་རྣམས་གསལ་བར་མཐོང་བར་གྱུར་པ་ན།
ཆུ་ཐིགས་འབབ་པ་ཀུན་ནས་བྲུགས་པས་ཞི་བར་བྱེད་ཅིང་མཆོག་ཏུ་དགའ་བ་སྐྱེད་པ་ཉིད། ༧༢།

मत्वा देवं धनपतिसखं यत्र साक्षाद्वसन्तं
प्रायश्चापं न वहति भयान्मन्मथः षट्पदज्यम्।
सभ्रूभङ्गप्रहितनयनैः कामिलक्ष्येष्वमोघैः
तस्यारम्भश्चतुरवनिताविभ्रमैरेव सिद्धः॥73॥

གང་དུ་གནོད་སྦྱིན་བདག་པོའི་གྲོགས་བཟང་ལྷ་ཉིད་མངོན་སུམ་ཉིད་དུ་གནས་པ་ཤེས་བྱས་ནས།
འཇིགས་པ་མང་ལས་ཡིད་སྨུབས་གཞུ་ནི་རྐང་དྲུག་པ་ཡི་གཞུ་རྒྱུད་ཅན་དེ་དོར་བས་ཆོག །
བདག་པོའི་འཕེན་ལ་མཛེས་མའི་སྨིན་མ་འཁྱོག་པོའི་གཞུ་ལ་ཟུར་མིག་གཡོ་བ་དག་གི་མདའ།
རོལ་སྙེག་གཡོ་བ་བརྩོམ་པར་བྱེད་པ་ཉིད་ཀྱིས་དེ་ཡི་འབྲས་བུ་ངེས་པར་གྲུབ་པ་ཉིད། ༧༣།

तत्रागारं धनपतिगृहादुत्तरेणास्मदीयं
दूराल्लक्ष्यं तदमरधनुश्चारुणा तोरणेन।
यस्योद्याने कृतकतनयः कान्तया वर्धितो मे
हस्तप्राप्यस्तबकनमितो बालमन्दारवृक्षः॥74॥

དེ་ན་ནོར་གྱི་བདག་པོའི་ཁང་བཟངས་ལས་ནི་བྱང་གི་ཕྱོགས་ན་བདག་གི་གྲོང་ཁྱེར་ནི།
མཐོ་རིས་བདག་པོའི་གཞུ་དང་འདྲ་བའི་རྟ་བབས་མཛེས་པས་རིང་ནས་འཚམ་[3] པར་བྱས་པ་སྟེ།

---

༡ པེ་། སྣར་།> བུད་མེད་རྣམས་ཀྱི་བདག་པོ།

༢ པེ་། སྣར་།> གི།

༣ པེ་། སྣར་།> མཚན།

གང་གི་སྐྱེད་ཚལ་མཛ་ར་[༡] དང་ལྡོན་ཤིང་གཞོན་ནུ་བདག་གི་མཛེས་མའི་བུ་ལྟ་ར་ནི།
བསྐྱངས་པའི་མཐུ་ལས་འཕེལ་[༢] ངའི་མེ་ཏོག་ཆུན་འཕྱང་ཕྱུར་དུ་འཕྱང་བ་ལག་པས་ཐོབ་བྱ་ཡོད། ༧༤།

वापी चास्मिन्मरकतशिलाबद्धसोपानमार्गा
हैमैः स्यूता कमलमुकुलैः स्निग्धवैदूर्यनालैः।
यस्यास्तोये कृतवसतयो मानसं सन्निकृष्टं
नाध्यास्यन्ति व्यपगतशुचस्त्वामपि प्रेक्ष्य हंसाः।।75।।

བཀོད་མ་བཟང་མོའི་ཆུ་ནི་མ་ར་ཀ་ཏའི་རྡོ་ཡི་ཕྲེང་བ་བསྒྲིགས་པའི་ལམ་སྐས་ཅན།
འདི་ནས་[༣] མཛེས་པའི་གསེར་གྱི་པདྨ་རྒྱས་པ་རིན་ཆེན་ཅཻ་ཌཱུན་རྣམས་ཀྱིས་ཁྱབ་པ་སྟེ།
གདུང་བ་དང་བྲལ་ངང་པའི་ཚོགས་རྣམས་དག་ནི་གནྡྷའི་ཆུ་ལ་གནས་པར་བྱས་པའི་ཚེ།
ཁྱོད་ཉིད་ཡང་དག་མཐོང་བར་གྱུར་ཀྱང་ཉེ་བར་གནས་པའི་ཡིད་འོང་མཚོ་ལས་འགྲོ་མི་འགྱུར། ༧༥།

तस्यास्तीरे रचितशिखरः पेशलैरिन्द्रनीलैः
क्रीडाशैलः कनककदलीवेष्टनप्रेक्षणीयः।
मद्गेहिन्याः प्रिय इति सखे चेतसा कातरेण
प्रेक्ष्योपान्तस्फुरिततडितं त्वां तमेव स्मरामि।।76।।

ཀྲ་ཡི་ཁྲིགས་བཟང་ཁྱོད་ནི་སློག་གི་དགའ་མ་གཡོ་བཞིན་ཉེ་བར་མཐོང་བར་གྱུར་པ་ན།
མཚོ་དེའི་ངོགས་ན་མཛེས་པའི་རི་བོ་ཡིད་འོང་མཆོག་གི་ཨིན་དྲ་ནཱི་ལ་རྣམས་ཀྱིས་ནི།
རྩེ་མོ་མཛེས་པར་བྱས་པར་གསེར་གྱི་བསྐོར་བ་རྣམས་[༤] ཀྱིས་བསྐོར་བ་ཁྱོད་ཀྱིས་བལྟ་བྱ་བ།
བདག་གི་དགའ་མ་དགའ་བྱེད་དང་བཅས་དེ་ཉིད་སེམས་གདུངས་བདག་ནི་ཤིན་ཏུ་དྲན་པར་གྱུར། ༧༦།

---

༡ པེ་། སྣར་།> གང་གི་སྐྱེད་མོས་ཚལ་ནས་མཛ་ར།

༢ པེ་། སྣར་།> བསྐྱངས་པའི་འཕེལ།

༣ པེ་། སྣར་།> འདི་ན།

༤ པེ་། སྣར་།> མཛེས་པར་བྱས་པ་གསེར་གྱི་ལྡོན་པ་རྣམས།

रक्ताशोकश्चलकिसलयः केसरश्चात्र कान्तः
प्रत्यासन्नौ कुरबककवृतेर्माधवीमण्डपस्य।
एकः सख्यास्तव सह मया वामपादाभिलाषी
काङ्क्षत्यन्यो वदनमदिरां दोहदच्छद्मनाऽस्याः।।77।।

དེ་ལ་ཀུ་རུ་བ་ཀའི་ཤིང་གིས་བསྐོར་བའི་ཡལ་གའི་ཁང་བཟངས་དང་ལྡན་ཉེ་བ་ན།
སྐྱ་ངན་མེད་ཤིང་དམར་དང་གེ་སར་ཡི་ཤིང་ཆེན་ཡལ་འདབ་གཡོ་བ་མཛེས་པ་ཡོད།
གཅིག་ལ་ཁྱོད་ཀྱི་གྲོགས་སུ་གྱུར་པའི་དགའ་མ་བདག[1] དང་བཅས་པའི་གཡོན་པས་བསྣུན་འདོད་ ཅིང་།
གཞན་ལ་གདོང་གི་ཆང་འཐུངས་མེ་ཏོག་འབྱུང་བའི་དོན་དུ་དགའ་མ་དེ་ནི་བདག་འདོད་གྱུར། ༧༧།

तन्मध्ये च स्फटिकफलका काञ्चनी वासयष्टिः
मूलं बद्धा मणिभिरनतिप्रौढवंशप्रकाशैः।
तालैः शिञ्जद्वलयसुभगैर्नतितिर्तः कान्तया मे
यामध्यास्ते दिसविगमे नीलकण्ठः सुहृद् वः।।78।।

དེ་ཡི་དབུས་ན་རབ་དཀར་ཤེལ་གྱི་གཞི་ལ་གསེར་གྱི་སྡོང་པོ་ཆེ་ཞིང་མཐོང་བར་གནས།
རྩ་བ་རིན་ཆེན་ཕྲེང་བས་བཅིངས་པ་རྡོ་རྗེ་ཕ་ལམ་ཆེ་བ་མིན་པ་འོད་འཕྲོ་བ།
གང་ལ་ཁྱོད་ཀྱི་གྲོགས་བཟང་མགྲིན་སྔོན་གནས་ནས་ཉིན་ཕྱེད་སོང་ཚེ་རོ་ལ་སྙེག་གར་བྱེད་ཅིང་།
བདག་གི་མཛེས་མ་རིན་ཆེན་གདུ་བུ་འཐབ་པའི་དབྱངས་སྙན་སྐལ་བཟང་མཆོག་ཏུ་མཛེས་པ་ཡོད། ༧༨།

एभिः साधो हृदयनिहितैर्लक्षणैर्लक्षयेथा
द्वारोपान्ते लिखितवपुषौ शंखपद्मौ च दृष्ट्वा।
क्षामच्छायं भवनमधुना मद्वियोगेन नूनं
सूर्यापाये न खलु कमलं पुष्यति स्वामभिख्याम्।।79।।

དེ་རྣམས་ཀྱིས་ནི་ལེགས་པར་མཚན་པ་ཀྱཱ་ཡེ་ལེགས་པའི་ཐུགས་འཛིན་ཁྱོད་ཀྱིས་བལྟ་བར་བྱ།
སྒོ་ཡི་མཐའ་དང་ཉེ་བ་དག་ན་དུང་དང་པདྨའི་གཟུགས་བྲིས་མཐོང་བར་བྱས་པ་ན།

---

༡ པེ། སྣར།> གྲོགས་སུ་གྱུར་མ་བདག

༢ པེ། སྣར།> གཡོན་པའི་རྐང་པས་བསྣུན།

ད་ལྟ་བདག་དང་བྲལ་བར་གྱུར་པས་ངེས་པར་མཛེས་པ་དམན་པ་ཉིད་དུ་གནས་པར་ངེས།
ཉི་མ་ནུབ་པར་གྱུར་པས་ངེས་པར་པདྨ་དག་གིས་མཛེས་པ་ཉམས་པར་གྱུར་པ་ཉིད། ༧༩།

गत्वा सद्यः कलभतनुतां शीघ्रसंपातहेतोः
क्रीडाशैले प्रथमकथिते रम्यसानौ निषण्णः।
अर्हस्यन्तर्भवनपतितां कर्तुमल्पाल्पभासं
खद्योतालीविलसितनिभां विद्युदुन्मेषदृष्टिम्।।80।।

མཛེས་མ་དེ་ནི་ཡོངས་སུ་བསྐྱངས་ཆེད་མྱུར་དུ་གཤེགས་ནས་གླང་ཕྲུག་ལུས་བཞིན་ཆུང་བ་ཡིས།
མཛེས་པའི་རི་བོ་དེ་ཡི་ངོས་ལ་གནས་ནས་དང་པོར་ལེགས་བཤད་སྣན་པའི་གསུང་གླེང་མཛོད།
བདག་གི་ཁང་ནང་འཇུག་ཚེ་མེ་ཁྱེར་ཕྲེང་བ་ལྟ་བུའི་སྣང་བ་ཆུང་ཤིང་ཆུང་བ་ནི།
མཛེས་ཤིང་རོལ་པའི་སྨིན་མ་གཡོ་[༡]བའི་གློག་གི་མིག་ནི་ཕྱས་ནས་ཁྱོད་ཀྱིས་བལྟ་བར་འོས། ༨༠།

तन्वी श्यामा शिखरिदशना पक्वबिम्बाधरोष्ठी
मध्ये क्षामा चकितहरिणीप्रेक्षणा निम्ननाभिः।
श्रोणीभारादलसगमना स्तोकनम्रा स्तनाभ्यां
या तत्र स्याद् युवतिविषये सृष्टिराद्येव धातुः।।81।।

དེ་ན་བདག་གི་དགའ་མ་ལུས་ཕྲ་མདོག་མཛེས་གཉིས་སྐྱེས་བགྲ་བའི་ཕྲ་ལམ་མཆུ་དག་ནི།
ཐེ་ལ་མ་[༢]སྨིན་པ་བསྐྱེད་པ་[༣]ཕྲ་ཞིང་འདྲེན་བྱེད་གཡོ་བའི་རི་དྭགས་མིག་ཅན་ལྟེ་བ་དམའ།
རོ་སྨད་སྦོམ་ཞིང་དལ་གྱིས་འགྲོ་མཁས་འོ་མ་འཛིན་པ་དག་གི་བར་དག་མཆོག་ཏུ་མཛེས།
ན་ཆུང་དག་གི་ཡུལ་ལ་མངོན་དུ་ཞེན་པར་[༤]བྱེད་པོ་ཚངས་པས་དང་པོ་ཉིད་དུ་གྱུར་[༥]། ༨༡།

---

༡ པེ་། སྣར་།> རོལ་བའི་གཡོ།

༢ པེ་། སྣར་།> ཐེམབ།།

༣ པེ་། སྣར་།> སྐྱེས་པ།

༤ པེ་། སྣར་།> མངོན་དུ་ཞེན་པར། ཆད།

༥ པེ་། སྣར་།> ཚངས་པས་དང་པོ་ཉིད་དུ་སྤྲོས་པ་ཉིད་དུ་འགྱུར།

तां जानीयाः परिमितकथां जीवितं मे द्वितीयं
दूरीभूते मयि सहचरे चक्रवाकीमिवैकाम्।
गाढोत्कण्ठां गुरुषु दिवसेष्वेषु गच्छत्सु बालां
जातां मन्ये शिशिरमथितां पद्मिनीं वान्यरूपाम्।।82।।

གཞོན་མ་དེ་ནི་བདག་གི་སྲོག་ནི་གཉིས་པར་ཤེས་པར་མཛོད་ཅེས་[༡] དལ་གྱིས་སྨྲ་བར་བྱ།
བདག་དང་ལྷན་ཅིག་སྤྱོད་ལ་ཤིན་ཏུ་རིང་བར་གྱུར་ཏེ་ངང་མོ་གཅིག་པར་གྱུར་པ་བཞིན།
འདི་ལ་ཉིན་ཞག་མང་པོ་འོང་བ་རྣམས་སུ་ཡིད་ལ་གཅུགས་[༢] པ་མེད་པ་ཉིད་དུ་གྱུར།
དགུན་སྨད་པད་མ་ཅན་ནི་ཁ་བས་ཉམས་པ་བཞིན་དུ་གཟུགས་གཞན་ཐོབ་[༣] པར་བདག་གིས་ཤེས། ༨༢།

नूनं तस्याः प्रबलरुदितोच्छूननेत्रं बहूनां
निःश्वासानामशिशिरतया भिन्नवर्णाधरोष्ठम्।
हस्तन्यस्तं मुखमसकलव्यक्ति लम्बालकत्वाद्
इन्दोर्दैन्यं त्वदुपसरणक्लिष्टकान्तेर्बिभर्ति।।83।।

དགའ་མ་དེ་ནི་ངེས་པར་མཆི་མ་མང་པོ་བབས་ལས་མིག་འཕྱུར་[༤] ཆེ་བ་དག་ཏུ་གྱུར།
སྙིང་འོག་ཆུ་[༥] ཡི་པགས་པ་དག་ནི་ཤུགས་རིང་ཤིན་ཏུ་དྲོ་བའི་དབུགས་ནི་དུ་མ་བྱུས[༦]།
གདོང་ནི་ལེགས་པར་བཀོད་ལ་ལེན་བུ་འཕྱང་བས་བསྒྲིབས་པས་མཐའ་དག་གསལ་བ་མིན་པ་ནི།
ཟླ་བའི་འོད་ཀྱིས་[༧] མཛེས་པ་ཁྱོད་ནི་འོངས་པས་བསྒྲིབས་ལས་སྣང་མིན་སྣན་པ་འཛིན་པ་བཞིན། ༨༣།

---

༡ པེ། སྣར།> ཅིག

༢ པེ། སྣར།> བཅུགས།

༣ སྣར།> ཐོབས།

༤ པེ། སྣར།> བཅུགས།འཕྱུར།

༥ པེ། སྣར།> མཆུ།

༦ པེ། སྣར།> དབུགས་དེ་ཡིས་ནི་དུམ་བུར་བྱུས།

༧ པེ། སྣར།> ཀྱི།

आलोके ते निपतति पुरा सा बलिव्याकुला वा
मत्सादृश्यं विरहतनु वा भावगम्यं लिखन्ती।
पृच्छन्ती वा मधुरवचनां सारिकां पञ्जरस्थां
कच्चिद्भर्तुः स्मरसि रसिके त्वं हि तस्य प्रियेति।।84।।

གཏོར་མ་བྱེད་པའང་བྲལ་བས་བཏུད་[༡]པར་གྱུར་པ་བདག་འདྲ་ཡིད་[༢]ཀྱིས་རྟོགས་བྱ་འདྲི་བའམ།
སྙན་པའི་ཚིག་གིས་སྨྲ་བའི་ཤ་རི་ཀ་ནི་གུར་གྱི་ནང་ན་གནས་ཤིང་གནས་པ་ལ་[༣]།
ཀཱ་ཡེ་གྲོགས་མོ་དེ་[༤]ཡི་དགའ་བ་དྲན་ནམ་ཞེས་པའི་དྲི་བ་བྱེད་པ་བདག་ཀྱང་[༥]ནི།
ཁྱོད་ནི་མཐོང་བར་གྱུར་པ་ན་ནི་ཅིང་[༦]ནི་མདུན་དུ་འོངས་ཤིང་དགའ་བར་བྱེད་པར་འགྱུར། ༨༤།

उत्सङ्गे वा मलिनवसने सौम्य निक्षिप्य वीणां
मद्गोत्राङ्कं विरचितपदं गेयमुद्गातुकामा।
तन्त्रीमार्द्रां नयनसलिलैः सारयित्वा कथंचिद्
भूयो भूयः स्वयमपि कृतां मूर्च्छनां विस्मरन्ती।।85।।

ཀཱ་ཡེ་གྲོགས་བཟང་དྲི་མའི་གོས་དང་བཅས་པའི་རང་གི་པང་པར་པི་ཝང་བཞག་བྱས་ནས།
བདག་གི་མིང་ནས་བོད་[༧]པས་མཚན་ཅིང་འདོད་པའི་དབྱངས་སྙན་ཆེར་སྒྲོགས་སྙན་པར་གྱུར་པའི་ཚེ་[༨]།
རང་གིས་བྱས་པར་གྱུར་ཀྱང་དབྱངས་སྙན་དུམ་བུ་དུམ་བུར་བཅས་ནས་[༩]སེམས་ཞིང་ཡང་ཡང་ནི།
མིག་ཆུས་བརླན་པའི་རྒྱུད་མངས་ཅུང་ཟད་ཕྱི་བར་བྱས་ནས་ཀྱང་ནི་དེ་ནི་འོང་བར་འགྱུར། ༨༥།

---

༡ པེ་། སྣར་།> རྡུད།
༢ པེ་། སྣར་།> ཡིས།
༣ པེ་།> གུར་གྱི་ནང་གནས་པ་ལ། སྣར་།> གུར་གྱི་ནང་ན་གནས་པ་ལ།
༤ པེ་། སྣར་།> གྲོགས་མོ་ཧཻ་བོ་དེ།
༥ པེ་། སྣར་།> དགའ་མ་དྲན་ནམ་ཞེས་པའི་དྲི་བ་བྱེད་ཀྱང་ནི།
༦ པེ་། སྣར་།> དེ།
༧ པེ་།> འབོད།
༨ པེ་། སྣར་།> ཚིག
༩ པེ་། སྣར་།> དབྱངས་སྙན་དུམ་བུར་བཅད་ནས།

शेषान् मासान् विरहदिवसस्थापितस्यावधेर्वा
विन्यस्यन्ती भुवि गणनया देहलीमुक्तादत्तपुष्पैः।
संयोगं (मत्सङ्गं) वा हृदयनिहितारम्भमास्वादयन्ती
प्रायेणैते रमणविरहेष्वङ्गनानां विनोदाः॥86॥

བདག་ནི་འོངས་པའི་ཉིན་ནས་བརྩམས་ཏེ་ཉིན་ཞག་དང་ནི་ཟླ་བ་སོང་བའི་ལྷག་མ་རྣམས།
ས་ལ་རྣམ་པར་འགོད་ཅིང་སྒོ་ཡི་ནང་དུ་གངས་ཀྱི་མེ་ཏོག་རྣམས་ནི་སྤྲུར་བར་བྱེད།
བདག་ཅན་[༡] ནམ་ནི་ཕྲད་པར་འགྱུར་རམ་སྙམ་པ་སྙིང་ལ་སེམས་པའི་རྩོམ་པ་མང་པོ་བྱེད།
ཕལ་ཆེར་བུད་མེད་རྣམས་ནི་བདག་པོ་བྲལ་བས་ཡིད་ཀྱི་ལས་ཀྱི་[༢] གདུང་བ་མང་པོ་ཉིད། ༨༦

सव्यापारामहनि न तथा पीडयेद्विप्रयोगः
शङ्के रात्रौ गुरुतरशुचं निर्विनोदां सखीं ते।
मत्संदेशैः सुखयितुमतः पश्य साध्वीं निशीथे
तामुन्निद्रामवनिशयनासन्नवातायनस्थः॥87॥

ཉིན་མོའི་བར་ལ་བྱ་བ་དང་ལྡན་བདག་དང་བྲལ་ལས་དེ་ལྟར་ཤིན་ཏུ་མིན་[༣] ན་ཡང་།
མཚན་མོ་ཤིན་ཏུ་རིང་ལས་ཁྱོད་ཀྱི་གྲོགས་མོ་བྱ་མེད་གདུང་བ་ཆེ་བར་བདག་གིས་ཤེས།
ལེགས་མ་མཚན་རིང་རྣམས་ལ་གཉིད་བྲལ་སྟན་མེད་ས་ལ་ཉལ་ཚེ་དྲ་མིག་ཉེ་བར་ནི།
གནས་ནས་བལྟ་བྱ་བདག་གི་ཕྲིན་རྣམས་བརྗོས་པ་རྣམས་ནི་བདེ་བའི་ཆེད་དུ་ཉུས་པ་ཉིད། ༨༧

आधिक्षामां विरहशयने सन्निषण्णैकपार्श्वां
प्राचीमूले तनुमिव कलामात्रशेषां हिमांशोः।
नीता रात्रिः क्षण इव मया सार्धमिच्छारतैर्या
तामेवोष्णैर्विरहमहतीमश्रुभिर्यापयन्तीम्॥88॥

---

༡ པེ་། སྣར་།> བདག་ཅག

༢ སྣར་།> ཀྱིས།

༣ པེ་། སྣར་།> ཤིན་ཏུ་གདུང་མིན།

བྲལ་བས་ལྷག་པར་གདུངས་པས་ས་ཡི་གཞི་ལ་གཞོགས་གཅིག་བརྟེན་[༡] དེ་ཉལ་བར་གྱུར་པ་ནི།
ཆེས་གཅིག་ཟླ་བ་ཤར་བ་ཆ་གཅིག་ལྷག་མ་རྩ་བར་གནས་པའི་ལུས་བཞིན་དུ་ནི་གྱུར།
བདག་དང་ལྷན་ཅིག་གནས་ཚེ་འདོད་པའི་དགའ་མ་རྣམས་ཀྱི་[༢] མཚན་མོ་སྐད་ཅིག་བཞིན་དུ་སོང་།
གང་དེ་ད་ལྟར་བྲལ་བ་ལས་སྐྱེས་མཆི་མ་དྲོན་མོ་རྣམས་བཅས་ཤིན་ཏུ་རིང་བ་ཉིད། ༨༨།

निःश्वासेनाधरकिसलयक्लेशिना विक्षिपन्तीं
शुद्धस्नानात्परुषकमलं नूनमागण्डलम्बम्।
मत्संयोगः कथमुपनमेत्स्वप्नजोऽपीति निद्राम्
आकाङ्क्षन्तीं नयनसलिलोत्पीडरुद्धावकाशाम्।।89।।

བུས་ཀྱིས་དག་[༣] ཅིང་ཡངས་ཤིང་རྩུབ་པའི་སྐྲ་ཡི་ལེན་བུ་འགྲམ་པ་དག་ལས་འཕྱང་བ་རྣམས།
དབུགས་ཀྱི་རླུང་གིས་སེལ་བར་བྱེད་པ་རྣམས་ལ་མཆུ་ཡི་འདབ་མ་དག་ནི་དལ་བར་ངེས།
གཉིད་ནི་འདོད་པ་མེད་ཅིང་བདག་དང་ཕྲད་པ་ལས་བྱུང་གཉིད་ནི་ཅུང་ཟད་འབྱུང་འགྱུར་ཞེས།
དགའ་མ་དེ་ནི་འདྲེན་བྱེད་མཆི་མ་དང་བཅས་ཤིན་ཏུ་གདུངས་པ་མཐོང་བས་[༤] འགོག་པར་བྱེད། ༨༩།

आद्ये बद्धा विरहदिवसे या शिखा दाम हित्वा
शापस्यान्ते विगलितशुचा तां मयोद्वेष्टनीयाम्।
स्पर्शक्लिष्टामयमितनखेनासकृत्सारयन्तीं
गण्डाभोगात्कठिनविषमामेकवेणीं करेण।।90।।

དག་གིས་བཅིངས་པའི་སྤྱི་གཙུག་ལེན་བུ་བྲལ་བའི་ཉི་མ་དང་པོ་ཉིད་ལ་དོར་བྱས་ནས།
ན་བུ་རྣམས་ནི་གཅིག་གྱུར་རེག་པ་རྩུབ་པ་མི་བཟད་འགྲམ་པ་དག་ལ་གནས་པ་ལས།

---

༡ པེ། སྣར། > བསྟེན།

༢ པེ། སྣར། > ཀྱིས།

༣ སྣར། > བདག

༤ པེ། སྣར། > གདུངས་པས་མཐོང་བ།

སེན་མོ་རིང་བའི་ལག་པས་རེག་པའི་ཉོན་མོངས་ལྡན་པས་ལན་ཅིག་མིན་པར་སྐྱུར་[༡]བྱེད་མ།
རྗེ་བོ་བྲིས་པའི་བཀའ་ལུང་རྫོགས་པ་[༢]གདུང་བྲལ་གྱུར་པ་བདག་གིས་གང་བདེ་དགྲོལ་[༣]བར་བྱ། ༩༠།

पादानिन्दोरमृतशिशिराञ्जालमार्गप्रविष्टान्
पूर्वप्रीत्या गतमभिमुखं सन्निवृत्तं तथैव।
चक्षुः खेदात्सलिलगुरुभिः पक्ष्मभिश्छादयन्तीं
साभ्रेऽह्नीव स्थलकमलिनीं न प्रबुद्धां न सुप्ताम्।।91।।

མིག་ནི་མཆི་མ་མང་པོ་རྣམས་ཀྱིས་གདུངས་ལ་[༤]རྫི་མ་རྣམས་ཀྱིས་བཀབ་པར་བྱས་ནས་ནི།
ཟླ་བའི་ཀྲང་པའི་འོད་ཟེར་བདུད་རྩི་སིལ་[༥]མ་རྣམས་ནི་དྲ་མིག་ནང་ནས་ཞུགས་པ་ན།
བཀབ་པ་བསལ་ཏེ་མངོན་དུ་འོངས་ནས་དང་པོར་དགའ་འགྱུར་ལྡོག་པ་ན་ནི་དེ་བཞིན་ཉིད།
སྤྲིན་དང་བཅས་པའི་ཉིན་མོ་ས་ལ་གནས་པའི་པདྨ་རྒྱས་མིན་ཟུམ་པ་མ་ཡིན་བཞིན། ༩༡།

स्निग्धाः सख्यः कथमपि दिवा तां न मोक्ष्यन्ति तन्वीम्
एकप्रख्या भवति हि जगत्यङ्गनानां प्रवृत्तिः।
स त्वं रात्रौ जलद शयनासन्नवातायनस्थः
कान्तां सुप्ते सति परिजने वीतनिद्रामुपेयाः।।92।।

དགའ་མ་དེ་ནི་ཉིན་པར་མཛའ་བོའི་གྲོགས་མོ་རྣམས་ཀྱིས་སྐད་ཅིག་ཀྱང་ནི་གཏོང་མིན་བཞིན་[༦]།
ལུས་ཕྲ་མ་ལ་གཅིག་ནི་བལྟ་ཚེ་ཀུན་གྱི་[༧]རྨད་བྱུང་བལྟ་བས་འདུག་པར་འགྱུར་བ་ཉིད།

---

༡ པེ་། སྣར་།> སྐྱུར།

༢ པེ་། སྣར་།> རྫོགས་ཚེ།

༣ པེ་།དེ་འགྲོལ། སྣར་།> དེ་བགྲོལ།

༤ པེ་། སྣར་།> གདུངས་ལས།

༥ པེ་།བདུད་རྩི་བསིལ། སྣར་།> བདུས་བརྩི་བསིལ།

༦ པེ་། སྣར་།> ཞིང་།

༧ པེ་། སྣར་།> ལྟ་ཚེ་ཀུན་གྱིས།

མཚན་མོ་སྐྱེ་བོ་རྣམས་ནི་ཉལ་བར་གྱུར་ལ་མཛེས་མ་གཉིད་བྲལ་ཀྱ་ཡི་ཆུ་འཛིན་ཁྱོད།
ད་མིག་དང་ནི་ཉེ་བར་གནས་ནས་ཉལ་སར་ཉེ་བར་འོངས་ཏེ་དེ་ནི་དགའ་བར་མཛོད། ༩༢།

अन्वेष्टव्यामवनिशयने सन्निकीर्णैकपार्श्वां
तत्पर्यङ्क(न्त)प्रगलितलवैश्छिन्नहारैरिवास्रैः।
भूयो भूयः कठिनविषमां सारयन्तीं कपोलाद्
आमोक्तव्यामयमितनखेनैकवेणीं करेण।।93।।

ལེན་བུ་གཅིག་ཏུ་གྱུར་ལ་རེག་[༡] པ་འགྲམ་པ་ལ་གནས་སེན་མོ་མཐོ་བའི་ལག་པ་ཡིས།
ཡང་དང་ཡང་དུ་སེལ་བར་བྱེད་ཅིང་[༢] ས་ཡི་གཞི་ཡི་མལ་གྱི་སྟེང་དུ་གཞོགས་གཅིག་ནི།
ལྷུང་བར་གྱུར་ཅིང་དེ་ཡི་མཐའ་ན་མཆི་མ་རྣམས་ནི་འབབ་པ་དོ་ཤལ་ཆད་པ་དག
གཡོ་ཞིང་ལྷུང་བར་གྱུར་པ་བཞིན་དུ་གནས་པ་དེ་མཐོང་ཉིད་ཀྱིས་དལ་གྱིས་བརྗོད་པར་བྱ། ༩༣།

सा संन्यस्ताभरणमबला पेलवं धारयन्ती
शय्योत्सङ्गे निहितमसकृद्दुःखदुःखेन गात्रम्।
त्वामप्यस्त्रं नवजलमयं मोचयिष्यत्यवश्यं
प्रायः सर्वो भवति करुणावृत्तिरार्द्रान्तरात्मा।।94।।

མཛེས་མ་དེ་ནི་རྒྱན་རྣམས་ཡང་དག་གཞག་ཅིང་ལུས་ནི་ཤིན་ཏུ་ཕྲ་ལ་[༣] འཛིན་བྱེད་ཅིང་།
གདུང་བའི་སྡུག་བསྔལ་དག་གིས་[༤] མལ་སྟན་སྟེང་ན་ཡང་དང་ཡང་དུ་འདྲེ་ལྡོག་བྱེད་པ་ན།
ཁྱོད་ཀྱང་འཕྲུལ་ལ་ཆུ་ཡི་རང་བཞིན་མཆི་མ་འཛག་པ་ཉིད་དུ་འགྱུར་བ་གདོན་མི་ཟ།
ཕལ་ཆོས་[༥] ཐམས་ཅད་ནང་གི་བདག་ཉིད་བརླན་པས་[༡] སྙིང་རྗེ་ཅི་ཡང་འདུག་པར་འགྱུར་བ་ཉིད། ༩༤།

---

༡ ཕེ་། སྣར་།> ལན་བུ་གཅིག་གྱུར་རེག

༢ ཕེ་། སྣར་།> བྱེད་ཀྱང་།

༣ ཕེ་། སྣར་།> ཕྲ་བ།

༤ ཕེ་། སྣར་།> གི།

༥ ཕེ་། སྣར་།> ཕལ་ཆེར།

जाने सख्यास्तव मयि मनः संभृतस्नेहमस्माद्
इत्थंभूतां प्रथमविरहे तामहं तर्कयामि।
वाचालं मां न खलु सुभगमन्यभावः करोति
प्रत्यक्षं ते निखिलमचिराद्भ्रातरुक्तं मया यत्।।95।।

ཀྱེ་ཡེ་གྲོགས་པོ་ཁྱོད་ཀྱི་གྲོགས་མོ་བདག་ལ་མཛའ་བ་མང་དུ་འཛིན་པ་བདག་གིས་ཤེས།
དེ་ཕྱིར་དེ་ལྟར་གྱུར་པ་རྣམས་ནི་དང་པར་བྲལ་ལ་དེ་ནི་བདག་ལ་སེམས་པར་བྱེད།
སྐལ་བཟང་ནང་གི་བསམ་པ་དག་གིས་བརྗོད་པ་ངེས་པར་བརྩུན་མིན་བདེན་པར་ཤེས་པ་ནི།
བདག་གིས་གང་གང་བརྗོད་པ་མ་ལུས་ཡུན་རིང་མིན་པར་ཁྱོད་ལ་མངོན་སུམ་ཉིད་དུ་འགྱུར། ༩༥།

रुद्धापाङ्गप्रसरमलकैरञ्जनस्नेहशून्यं
प्रत्यादेशादपि च मधुनो विस्मृतभ्रूविलासम्।
त्वय्यासन्ने नयनमुपरिस्पन्दि शङ्के मृगाक्ष्या
मीनक्षोभाच्चलकुवलयश्रीतुलामेष्यतीति।।96।।

ལེན་བུ་རྣམས་ཀྱིས་མིག་ཟུར་གཉིས་པོ་གཡོ་བ་འགོག་ཅིང་མིག་སྨན་བྱུག་པས་གཏོར་བ་དང་།
ཉེས་པར་བྱེད་པ་ནམ་ཡང་མེད་པར་གྱུར་ལས་སྨིན་མའི་རྣམ་འགྱུར་བརྗེད་པར་འགྱུར་ན་ཡང་།
ཁྱོད་ནི་ཡང་[2]ལ་རི་དྭགས་མིག་ཅན་འདྲེན་བྱེད་སྙིང་ནི་གཡོ་བར་བྱེད་པར་བདག་གིས་ཤེས།
གང་ཞིག་ཉ་ཡིས་བསྐྱོད་ལས་ཆུ་སྐྱེས་གཡོ་བའི་དཔལ་ནི་འཛིན་པར་བྱེད་པ་ཉིད་དང་མཚུངས། ༩༦།

वामश्चास्याः कररुहपदैर्मुच्यमानो मदीयैः
मुक्ताजालं चिरपरिचितं त्याजितो दैवगत्या।
संभोगान्ते मम समुचितो हस्तसंवाहनानां
यास्यत्यूरुः सरसकदलीस्तम्भगौरश्चलत्वम्।।97।।

༡ པེ་།བཀྲན་པ། སྣར་།> བཀྲན་པས།

༢ པེ་། སྣར་།> ཡོངས།

དེ་ཡི་བདག་གི་ལག་པའི་སེན་མོའི་རྗེས་ནི་མེད་ཅིང་མུ་ཏིག་རྣམས་ཀྱི་དྲ་བ་ནི།
ཡུན་རིང་ཉིད་ནས་འདོར་བར་བྱས་པར་གྱུར་ཅིང་ལོངས་སྤྱོད་ཉིད་ཀྱིས་[1] རྫོགས་པའི་མཐའ་རུ་ནི།
བདག་གིས་[2] ལག་པ་རྣམས་ཀྱིས་མཉེས་པར་བྱས་པ་མེད་ཀྱང་ཁྱོད་འོངས་སྐལ་བཟང་དབང་གིས་ནི།
དེ་ཡི་རྒྱུ་ཤིང་གསར་པའི་སྡོང་པོ་[3] བརྒྱ་ཡང་གཡོན་པ་གཡོ་བ་ཉིད་ནི་ཐོབ་པར་གྱུར། ༼༩༧༽

तस्मिन् काले जलद यदि सा लब्धनिद्रासुखा स्याद्
अन्वास्यैनां स्तनितविमुखो याममात्रं सहस्व।
मा भूदस्याः प्रणयिनि मयि स्वप्नलब्धे कथंचित्
सद्यः कण्ठच्युतभुजलताग्रन्थि गाढोपगूढम्।।98।।

ཀྱཻ་ཡེ་ཆུ་འཛིན་དེ་ལ་དེ་ཡི་དུས་སུ་གལ་ཏེ་བདེ་བའི་གཉིད་ནི་ཐོབ་གྱུར་ན།
དེ་ཚེ་ཁྱོད་ནི་ཐུན་ཚོད་བར་དུ་སྒྲ་སྒྲོགས་མིན་པར་ལྷན་ཅིག་དག་ཏུ་གནས་པར་མཛོད།
དེ་ཡི་བདག་པོར་གྱུར་པ་བདག་ལ་དཀའ་ཚེགས་ཆེན་པོས་ཐོབ་པར་འགྱུར་བའི་རྨི་ལམ་ནི།
མགྲིན་པར་ལག་པའི་འཁྲི་ཤིང་དག་གིས་ཆེ་བར་འཁྱུད་པའི་མདུད་པ་འཕྲལ་ལ་གཏོང་བར་བྱེད། ༼༩༨༽

तामुत्थाप्य स्वजलकणिकाशीतलेनानिलेन
प्रत्याश्वास्तां सममभिनवैर्जालकैर्मालतीनाम्।
विद्युद्गर्भे स्तिमितनयनां त्वत्सनाथे गवाक्षे
वक्तुं धीरस्तनितवचनैर्मानिनीं प्रक्रमेथाः।।99।।

རང་གི་ཆུ་ཡི་ཐིགས་པ་བསིལ་བས་བསྐོས་པའི་རླུང་གི་མཱ་ལ་ཏ་ཡ་རྣམས་ཀྱིས་[4] ནི།
ཤིན་ཏུ་གཞོན་པའི་མེ་ཏོག་བཅས་པ་དེ་ནི་བསླད་[5] ནས་ཀྱང་ནི་དེ་ཡི་དབུགས་དབྱུང་མཛོད།

---

༡ པེ།། སྣར།> ཀྱི།

༢ པེ།། སྣར།> གི།

༣ པེ།། སྣར།> སྡོང་པོ་དཀར་བའི།

༤ པེ།། སྣར།> རླུང་གིས་མ་ལ་ཏི་ཡི་རྣམས་ཀྱིས།

༥ པེ།། སྣར།> བླད།

ཁྱོད་ནི་གློག་གི་འདྲེན་བྱེད་གཡོ་ཞིང་གཡོ་[1] བ་ཁྱོད་མདོག་དང་མཚུངས་གནས་སུ་གནས་བྱས་ནས།
ཁྱེངས་ལྡན་མ་ལ་འབྲུག་དབྱངས་ཚིག་ནི་སྙན་པའི་བརྗོད་པ་ཁྱོད་ཀྱིས་ཡང་ཡང་རྗོམ་པར་མཛོད། ༩༩

भर्तुर्मित्रं प्रियमविधवे विद्धि मामम्बुवाहं
तत्संदेशान्मनसि निहितादागतं त्वत्समीपम्।
यो वृन्दानि त्वरयति पथि श्राम्यतां प्रोषितानां
मन्द्रस्निग्धैर्ध्वनिभिरबलावेणिमोक्षोत्सुकानि॥100॥

ཀ་ཡེ་ཁྱོད་ལྡན་ཆུ་གཞོན་མིང་ཅན་བདག་ནི་རྗེ་ཡི་གྲོགས་བཟང་ཡིན་པར་ཤེས་པར་མཛོད།
དེ་ཡི་འཕྲིན་སྙན་ཡིད་ལ་བཟུང་ནས་ཁྱོད་ཀྱི་དྲུང་དུ་ཉེ་བར་འོངས་པར་གྱུར་པ་ཉིད།
བདག་གིས་སྒྲ་ནི་བསྒྲགས་ཚེ་ལམ་བགྲོད་དུབ་པའི་ཚོགས་རྣམས་སྒོ་ཡི་ནང་དུ་འགྲོས་པར་བྱེད།
སྙན་པའི་སྒྲ་དབྱངས་རྣམས་ཀྱིས་བུད་མེད་ལེན་བུ་འགྲོལ་ཞིང་འདོད་པས་གཟིར་བར་མཚན་པར་བྱེད། ༡༠༠

इत्याख्याते पवनतनयं मैथिलीवोन्मुखी सा
त्वामुत्कण्ठोच्छ्वसितहृदया वीक्ष्य संभाव्य चैवम्।
श्रोष्यत्यस्मात् परमवहिता सौम्य! सीमन्तिनीनां
कान्तोदन्तः सुहृदुपनतः संगमात् किञ्चिदूनः॥101॥

ཅེས་པ་དེ་སྐད་བཤད་ཚེ་དྲི་བཞོན་བུ་ནི་མི་ཐི་ལ་ཡི་བུ་མོས་མཐོང་བ་བཞིན།
དེ་ནི་དགའ་བདེའི་སྙིང་གིས་ཁྱོད་ལ་མངོན་ཕྱོགས་བལྟ་ཞིང་བདེན་པ་ཉིད་དུ་འང་ངེས་པ་ཉིད།
ཀ་ཡེ་གྲོགས་བཟང་དེ་ནས་ལེགས་པར་གནས་ལ་གཞན་ཡང་ཉན་འདོད་སྒྲ་ལྡན་མ་རྣམས་ནི།
བདག་པོའི་ཚིག་ནི་སྙིང་གྲོགས་བདག་གིས་ཁྱེར་འོངས་གྱུར་ལས་ཕྲད་ལྟར་[2] ལྷག་མར་ལུས་པ་ཉིད། ༡༠༡

तामायुष्मन् मम च वचनादात्मनश्चोपकर्तुं
ब्रूया एवं तव सहचरो रामगिर्याश्रमस्थः।
अव्यापन्नः कुशलमबले पृच्छति त्वां वियुक्तः
पूर्वाशाम्यं सुलभविपदां प्राणिनामेतदेव॥102॥

---

༡ པེ་། གློག་འདྲེན་ངན་སྤྱོད་གཡོ། སྣར་། > གློག་གི་འདྲེན་གཡོ།

༢ པེ་། སྣར་། > ཕྲད་པ།

ཀཱ་ཡེ་ཚེ་ལྷན་བདག་གི་ཚིག་དང་ཉིད་ཀྱིས་ཀྱང་ནི་དེ་ལ་ཕན་པའི་ཚེད་དུ་ནི།
ཁྱོད་ཀྱི་རྒྱལ་པོ་མཆོག་ནི་རྒྱལ་པོར་མ་ཡི་རི་[1] ཡི་གནས་ན་གནས་ཤིང་འཚོ་བ་ཉིད།
ཁྱོད་ནི་སྤངས་པར་གྱུར་ལ་ཀཱ་ཡེ་མཛེས་མ་དགེ་འམ་དྲི་ཞེས་དེ་ལྟར་སྨྲ་བར་མཛོད།
གང་ཕྱིར་སྐྱེ་བོ་རྣམས་ནི་བྱེད་པ་ཉམས་ལ་དང་པོར་དེ་འདྲའི་དབུགས་དབྱུང་བྱེད་པ་ཉིད། ༡༠༢།

अङ्गेनाङ्गं प्रतनु तनुना गाढतप्तेन तप्तं
साश्रेणाश्रुद्रवमविरतोत्कण्ठमुत्कण्ठितेन।
उष्णोच्छ्वासं समधिकतरोच्छ्वासिना दूरवर्ती
संकल्पैस्तैर्विशति विधिना वैरिणा रुद्धमार्गः॥103॥

ལུས་ཀྱི་ནང་ནས་ཤེད་དུ་ཕྲ་བས་ཕྲ་གྱུར་དང་ནི་ཤིན་ཏུ་གདུང་བས་གདུངས་གྱུར་དང་།
མཆི་མ་འཛགས་པས་མཆི་མ་འཛག་གྱུར་ཆེ་བར་ཕྲད་འདོད་ཉིད་ཀྱི་[2] ཕྲད་འདོད་མཆོག་ཏུ་གྱུར།
དབུགས་དྲོན་ཕུགས་རིངས་ལྷགས་པས་དབུགས་དྲོན་ཕུགས་རིངས་མཆོག་ཏུ་ལྷགས་གྱུར་རིང་ནས་
འདུག་པ་ཅན། བསོད་ནམས་ཆོམ་རྐུན་དག་གིས་ལམ་བཀག་གྱུར་ཅིང་དེ་རྣམས་ཡིད་ལ་སེམ་ཞིང་
འདུག་པ་ཡིན། ༡༠༣།

शब्दाख्येयं यदपि किल ते यः सखीनां पुरस्तात्
कर्णे लोलः कथयितुमभूदाननस्पर्शलोभात्।
सोऽतिक्रान्तः श्रवणविषयं लोचनाभ्यामदृष्टः
त्वामुत्कण्ठाविरचितपदं मन्मुखेनेदमाह॥104॥

གྲོགས་མོའི་མདུན་དུ་དེ་ཡི་རྣ་བ་ལ་ནི་ཁྱོད་ཀྱི་གདོང་ནི་རེག་པར་ཐོབ་གྱུར་པས།
ཁྱོད་ཀྱི་[3] གང་ཡང་གསུས་པའི་གཏམ་གྱི་[1] ཆེད་དུ་གྱུར་པའི་ཆེ་བའི་སྒྲ་འདི་བརྗོད་པར་འོས།

---

༡ པེ་།རྒྱལ་པོ་ནྟ་མའི་རི། སྣར་།> རྒྱལ་པོ་ནྟ་མའི།

༢ པེ་། སྣར་།> ཀྱིས།

༣ པེ་། སྣར་།> ཀྱིས།

གང་དེ་རྣ་བའི་ཡུལ་ལས་ཤིན་ཏུ་གང་ཡང་འདས་ཤིང་མིག་དག་གིས་ནི་མཐོང་བྱ་མིན།
ཁྱོད་དང་དགའ་བས་འཕྲད་འདོད་གྱུར་ཞེས་བདག་གིས་[1] ཁ་ཡི་ཚིག་འདི་ཟེར་ཞེས་སླ་བར་མཛོད། ༡༠༤

श्यामास्वङ्गं चकितहरिणीप्रेक्षिते दृष्टिपातं
वक्त्रच्छायां शशिनि शिखिनां बर्हभारेषु केशान्।
उत्पश्यामि प्रतनुषु नदीवीचिषु भ्रूविलासान्
हन्तैकस्थं क्वचिदपि न ते चण्डि! सादृश्यमस्ति॥105॥

འཁྲི་ཤིང་འགའ་ལ་ཡན་[2]ལག་མཛེས་པ་འཇིགས་བཅས་རི་དྭགས་མོ་ལ་མིག་མཛེས་གཡོ་བ་མཐོང་།
འགྲམ་པའི་མཛེས་འོད་རི་བོང་ཅན་ལ་སྐྲ་རྣམས་གཙུག་ཕུད་ཅན་གྱི་མདུག་སྒྲོའི་ཚོགས་ལ་མཐོང་།
སྨིན་མའི་རོ་ལ་སྒེག་མཛེས་མ་རྣམས་ནི་ཆུ་ཀླུང་རྦབས་ཕྲེང་ཕྲ་མོ་རྣམས་ལ་རབ་ཏུ་མཐོང་།
ཨེ་མ་གཅིག་ཏུ་ཚོགས་པ་དང་ལྡན་གཡོན་མིག་ཁྱོད་དང་མཚུངས་པ་འགའ་ཡང་ཡོད་མ་ཡིན། ༡༠༥

धारासिक्तस्तलसुरभिणस्त्वन्मुखस्यास्य बाले
दूरीभूतं प्रतनुमपि मां पञ्चबाणः क्षिणेति।
धर्मान्तेऽस्मिन्विगणय कथं वासराणि व्रजेयुः
दिक्संसक्तप्रविततधनव्यस्तसूर्यातपानि॥106॥

ཆར་གྱིས་བརླན་ལས་དྲི་མེད་སྤྲང་རྩེ་ཅན་བཞིན་[3] ཁྱོད་ཀྱི་གདོང་འདི་མཛེས་སོ་ལུས་ཕྲ་མ།
ཁྱོད་ནི་རིང་གྱུར་བདག་ནི་ཕྲ་བའི་ལུས་གྱུར་མདའ་ལྔ་པ་ཡི་གདུང་བ་ཡང་ཡང་བྱེན།
སོ་ཀ་རྫོགས་པའི་མཐའ་རུ་ཕྱོགས་ཀུན་ཆེ་བའི་ཆུ་འཛིན་སྟུག་པོས་བསྒྲིབས་པས་ཉི་མ་ཡི།
སྣང་བ་རྣམས་ནི་ཉམས་ཤིང་རྒྱུན་དུ་ཆར་འོང་བདག་གིས་ཞག་གིས་གྲངས་ཇི་ལྟ་བ་ཡིན་[4] ། ༡༠༦

त्वामालिख्य प्रणयकुपितां धातुरागैः शिलायाम्
आत्मानं ते चरणपतितं यावदिच्छामि कर्तुम्।

---

༡ པེ། སྣར།> ཀྱིས།

༢ པེ། སྣར།> གི།

༣ པེ། སྣར།> ལས་དྲི་བཟང་ཅན་གྱིས་བཞིན།

༤ པེ། སྣར།> ཆར་འོངས་བདག་གི་ཞག་གི་གྲངས་ཀྱང་ཇི་ལྟར་ཡིན།

अस्त्रैस्तावन्मुहुरुपचितैर्दृष्टिरालुप्यते मे
क्रूरस्तस्मिन्नपि न सहते संगमं नौ कृतान्तः।।107।।

ཁྱོད་ནི་ཧོ་ལེབ་གཞི་ལ་ཁམས་ཀྱི་ཚོན་རྣམས་ཀྱིས་ནི་དགའ་དང་ཁྲོ་བས་ལེགས་བྲིས་ཏེ།
དེ་རྐེད་རྫོགས་ནས་འདོད་པ་བྱ་བའི་ཆེད་དུ་ཁྱོད་ཀྱི་ཞབས་དྲུང་ལྷུང་བར་གྱུར་པ་ན།
ཚིག་ལན་མ་བྱུང་བདག་ལ་མཆི་མ་མང་པོ་ཡང་ཡང་བྱུང་བས་ཟུགས་པས་མིག་ལ་ཁྲོ།
དེ་ར་ཡང་བདག་ཅག་གཉིས་ནི་ལྷན་ཅིག་འགྲོགས་པའི་སྐལ་བ་མེད་པས་[1] ཉིད་དུ་གྱུར་པ་ཞིག ༡༠༧།

मामाकाशप्रणिहितभुजं निर्दयाश्लेषहेतोः
लब्धायास्ते कथमपि मया स्वप्नसंदर्शनेषु।
पश्यन्तीनां न खलु बहुशो न स्थलीदेवतानां
मुक्तास्थूलास्तरुकिसलयेष्वश्रुलेशाः पतन्ति।।108।।

ཁྱོད་ནི་བདག་གི་རྨི་ལམ་དག་ཏུ་འོངས་ཤིང་ཐོབ་པ་ཅི་ཡང་མཐོང་བར་གྱུར་པ་ན།
ཁོ་བོས་དམ་དུ་འཁྱུད་པར་བྱ་བའི་ཆེད་དུ་ནམ་མཁའ་དག་ལ་ལག་ཡུག་བྱ་བ་[2] ནི།
ས་ལ་གནས་པའི་ནགས་ཀྱི་ལྷ་རྣམས་ཀྱིས་ནི་ངེས་པར་མ་མཐོང་མ་ཡིན་མང་པོ་རུ།
མུ་ཏིག་བརྒྱུད་[3] པ་བཞིན་དུ་ཤིང་གི་ཡལ་ག་རྣམས་ལ་མཆི་མའི་དུམ་བུ་ལྷུང་བར་འགྱུར་[4]། ༡༠༨།

भित्वा सद्यः किसलयपुटान् देवदारुद्रुमाणां
ये तत्क्षीरस्रुतिसुरभयो दक्षिणेन प्रवृत्ताः।
आलिङ्ग्यन्ते गुणवति! मया ते तुषाराद्रिवाताः
पूर्वं स्पृष्टं यदि किल भवेदङ्गमेभिस्तवेति।।109।।

---

༡ པེ། སྣར།> མེད་པ།

༢ པེ། སྣར།> ལག་ཡུགས་བྱས་པ།

༣ པེ། སྣར།> བརྒྱུས།

༤ པེ། སྣར།> གྱུར།

དེ་ཨ་ནྡ་རུའི་ལྗོན་པ་རྣམས་ཀྱི་ཡལ་ག་རྣམས་ཀྱི་ཡལ་གའི་འདབ་མ་རྣམས་ནི་འཕྲུལ་དུ་བཅད་བྱས་ནས།
དེ་རྣམས་ཀྱི་ནི་འོ་མ་ཟགས་[1]པའི་དྲི་བཟང་དང་ལྡན་ལྷོ་ཕྱོགས་[2]ཞུགས་པའི་དྲི་བཞོན་རྣམས།
གང་ཞིག་བདག་ལ་[3]དང་པོར་རབ་ཏུ་འབྱུང་དོ་ཀྱཱ་ཡེ་ཡོན་ཏན་མ་ལུས་[4]དེ་རྣམས་ནི།
གངས་ཀྱི་རི་ལ་གལ་ཏེ་སོང་ན་ཁྱོད་ཀྱི་ལུས་ལ་རེག་པ་ངེས་པ་གྱུར་རོ་ཅེའོ། ༡༠༩།

संक्षिप्येत क्षण इव कथं दीर्घयामा त्रियामा
सर्वावस्थास्वहरपि कथं मन्दमन्दातपं स्यात्।
इत्थं चेतश्चटुलनयने! दुर्लभप्रार्थनं मे
गाढोष्माभिः कृतमशरणं त्वद्वियोगव्यथाभिः॥110॥

ཐུན་གསུམ་མུན་པ་ཅན་[5]མ་ཡུན་[6]རིང་གྱུར་པ་སྐད་ཅིག་བཞིན་དུ་བསྡུས་[7]པ་ཅི་ལྟར་ཡི།
ཉིན་པར་ཡང་ནི་གནས་སྐབས་ཀུན་དུ་ཚུང་ཟད་[8]གདུང་བའང་ཇི་ལྟར་གྱུར་པ་ཡིན།
ཀྱཱ་ཡེ་འདྲེན་བྱེད་གཡོ་བ་དེ་ལྟར་གྱུར་པས་བདག་སེམས་[9]དོན་གཉེར་སྐལ་བ་དམན་པར་གྱུར། །
ཁྱོད་དང་བྲལ་བའི་གདུང་བ་རྣམས་[10]དང་ཚ་བའི་སྡུག་བསྔལ་རྣམས་ཀྱིས་བརྟན་པར་མིན་པར་བྱས། ༡༡༠།

नन्वात्मानं बहु विगणयन्नात्मना नावलम्बे
तत्कल्याणि त्वमपि सुतरां मां गमः कातरत्वम्।

---

༡ པེ་། སྣར་།> འཛགས།

༢ པེ་། སྣར་།> ལྷོ་ནས།

༣ པེ་། སྣར་།> བདག་གིས

༤ པེ་། སྣར་།> ཡོན་ཏན་ལྡན་མ།

༥ པེ་། སྣར་།> ཐུན་གསུམ་ཅན།

༦ པེ་། སྣར་།> མཐུན།

༧ པེ་། སྣར་།> སྡུད།

༨ པེ་། སྣར་།> ཚུང་ཟད་ཚུང་ཟད།

༩ པེ་། སྣར་།> བདག་གི་སེམས་ནི།

༡༠ པེ་། སྣར་།> གདུང་བ་མང་པོ་རྣམས།

कस्यात्यन्तं सुखमुपनतं दुःखमेकान्ततो वा
नीचैर्गच्छत्युपरि च दशा चक्रनेमिक्रमेण।।111।।

བདག་ནི་ཞག་གྲངས་མང་པོའི་བདག་ཉིད་བགྲང་ཞིང་ནང་གི་བསམ་པས་མི་འཆི་བར་ནི་ཤེས།
ཀྱེ་ཡེ་དགེ་ལེགས་ལྡན་མ་ཁྱོད་ཀྱང་སྐྱ་ངན་མང་པོ་ཤིན་ཏུ་བྱ་བ་མ་ཡིན་ཏེ།
བདེ་བ་མཐའ་གཅིག་ལྡན་པས་[1] སུ་ཡིན་ཧག་ཏུ་སྡུག་བསྔལ་མཐའ་གཅིག་པ་ཡང་སུ་ཞིག་ཡིན།
དེ་དག་འཁོར་ལོ་[2] ཙེངས་ནི་ཅུང་ཟད་འོག་ཏུ་འགྲོ་ཞིང་སྟེང་དུ་འང་རིམ་གྱིས་བསྐོར་[3] བ་བཞིན། ༡༡༡།

शापान्तो मे भुजगशयनादुत्थिते शाङ्गर्पाणौ
मासान्यान्गमय चतुरो लोचने मीलयित्वा।
पश्चादावां विरहगुणितं तं तमात्माभिलाषं
निर्वेक्ष्यावः परिणतशरच्चन्द्रिकासु क्षपासु।।112।।

ཁྱབ་འཇུག་ལག་འགྲོའི་གནས་ན་གཉིད་ལས་ལངས་ཚེ་རྡེ་པོ་ཁྲིམས་པའི་བཀའ་ལུང་རྫོགས་པ་ཉིད།
དེ་ལ་ཟླ་བཞིན་[4] ཡོད་དེ་བར་མིག་ནི་ཟུམ་པར་བྱས་ནས་ཁྱོད་ནི་གནས་པར་མཛོད།
ཕྱི་ནས་བདག་ཅག་གཉིས་ནི་ཡུན་རིང་བྲལ་བར་[5] ལས་བྱུང་འདོད་པའི་ལོངས་སྤྱོད་དེ་ཐོབ་སྟེ་[6]།
སྟོན་ཀའི་ཟླ་བ་རྫོགས་པའི་མཚན་མ་[7] རྣམས་ལ་འདོད་པའི་ལོངས་སྤྱོད་དེ་དག་ལྡན་པར་འགྱུར། ༡༡༢།

भूयश्चाह त्वमसि शयने कण्ठलग्ना पुरा मे
निद्रां गत्वा किमपि रुदती सस्वरं विप्रबुद्धा।
मान्तर्हासं कथितमसकृत् पृच्छतश्च त्वया मे
दृष्टः स्वप्ने कितव! रमयन् कामपि त्वं मयेति।।113।।

---

༡ པེ། སྣར།> པ།

༢ པེ། སྣར།> ལོའི།

༣ པེ། སྣར།> འཁོར།

༤ པེ། སྣར།> ཟླ་བ་བཞི།

༥ པེ། སྣར།> བ།

༦ པེ། སྣར།> སྤྱོད་དེ་དེ་ཐོབ།

༧ པེ། སྣར།> མཚན་མོ།

ཡང་ནི་བརྗོད་པ་སྔོན་ནི་བདག་དང་ཁྱོད་ནི་མལ་སྟན་གནས་ན་མགྲིན་འཁྱུད་གཉིད་སོང་བས།
བདག་ནི་ཐྲལ་ལ་རབ་ཏུ་སད་པར་གྱུར་ནས་ཅི་ཡང་ངུ་བར་བྱས་པར་གྱུར་པ་ན[༡]།
ནང་ནས་ཀྱོད་པ་དང་བཅས་ལན་ཅིག་མིན་པར་ཁྱོད་ཀྱིས་བདག་ལ་དྲི་བ་བརྗོད་པ་ན།
ཀྭ་ཡེ་གཡོ་མ་འགའ་ཞིག་དང་ཡང་དགའ་བྱེད་ཀྱི་ལམ་མཐོང་ཞེས[༢]་བདག་གིས་ཁྱོད་ལའོ། ༡༡༣།

एतस्मान्मां कुशलिनमभिज्ञानदानाद्विदित्वा
मा कौलीनादसितनयने! मय्यविश्वासिनी भूः।
स्नेहानाहुः किमपि विरहे ह्रासिनस्ते ह्यभोगाद्
इष्टे वस्तुन्युपचितरसाः प्रेमराशीभवन्ति।।114।।

དེ་ལ་བདག་ནི་ཁྱོད་ལ་མཚན་མ་བཟང་པོ་སྦྱིན་པར་བྱེད་པ་ཡིན་པར་རིག་བྱས་ན[༣]།
ཀྭ་ཡེ་འདྲེན་བྱེད་དཀར་མིན་སྐྱེ་བོ་ངན་པའི་ཚིག་ལས་བདག་ལ་མི་གུས་འོས་མ་ཡིན།
གང་ཕྱིར་བྲལ་བས་གདུངས་པ་ལོངས་སྤྱོད་བྲལ་ལ་དེ་རྣམས་མཛའ་བོའི་བརྗོད་པ་ཅི་ཞིག་ཡིན།
དངོས་པོ་རྣམས་ནི་མཐོང་ཚེ་མཆོག་ཏུ་དགའ་བའི་རོ་ནི་མང་པོའི[༤]་ཕུང་པོ་ཉིད་དུ་འགྱུར། ༡༡༤།

आश्वास्यैवं प्रथमविरहोदग्रशोकां सखीं ते
शैलादाशु त्रिनयनवृषोत्खातकूटान्निवृत्तः।
साभिज्ञानप्रहितकुशलैस्तद्वचोभिर्ममापि प्रातः
कुन्दप्रसवशिथिलं जीवितं धारयेथाः।।115।।

འདི་རྣམས་ཀྱིས་ནི་དང་པོར་བྲལ་བས་གདུངས་པར་གྱུར་པའི་གྲོགས་མོ་དེ་ནི་དབུགས་དབྱུང་མཛོད།
མིག་གསུམ་པ་ཡི་ཁྱུ་མཆོག་ལྷ་བུར་དཀར་བའི་ཀཻ་ལཱ་ཤ་ཡི་རི་ལས་སླར་ལྡོག་བྱ།

---

༡ པེ་། སྣར་།> ནི།

༢ པེ་། སྣར་།> ཀྱི་ལམ་དུ་མཐོང་ཞེས་པ།

༣ པེ་། སྣར་།> ནས།

༤ པེ་། སྣར་།> རོ་ནི་མང་བའི།

དེ་ལའང་རང་གི་དགེ་བའི་མཚན་མ་ཁྱེར་འོངས་དེ་དང་དེ་ནི་བདག་ལ་བཤད་པར་བྱ།
ཁྱོད་ནི་ཀུན་དའི་གེ་སར་གཡོ་ལྡན་སྨུར་འགྲོ་རྣམས་ཀྱིས་བསྐུ་ལ་བྱུས་སྨུར་བར་འོང་བར་བྱ། ༡༡༥།

कच्चित् सौम्य व्यवसितमिदं बन्धुकृत्यं त्वया मे
प्रत्यादेशान्न खलु भवतो धीरतां कल्पयामि।
निःशब्दोऽपि प्रदिशसि जलं याचितश्चातकेभ्यः
प्रत्युक्तं हि प्रणयिषु सतामीप्सितार्थक्रियेव।।116।।

ཀྱཻ་ཡེ་གྲོགས་བཟང་ཁྱོད་ཀྱིས་བདག་གི་[1] གཉེན་འདུན་དག་ཏུ་ཚུང་ཟད་གནས་པ་འདི་བྱས་ནས།
སྐར་ཡང་འཕྲིན་རྣམས་བརྟན་པ་ཁྱོད་ལས་ངེས་པར་བདག་ལ་འོང་བར་འགྱུར་ཞེས་བདག་སེམས་སོ།
ཙུ་ཏ་ཀ་རྣམས་སྒྲ་མེད་པར་ཡང་ཆུ་ནི་སྦྱིན་པར་མཛོད་ཅེས་ཁྱོད་ལ་ཞུ་བར་སེམས།
གང་ཕྱིར་སྐྱེ་བོ་རྣམས་འདོད་པར་གྱུར་པ་རྣམས་ཀྱི་བྱ་བའི་དོན་ཉིད་ལན་གྱི་ཚིག ༡༡༦།

एतत्कृत्वा प्रियमनुचितप्रार्थनावर्त्मनो मे
सौहार्दाद्वा विधुर इति वा मय्यनुक्रोशबुद्ध्या।
इष्टान् देशान् विचर जलद! प्रावृषा संभृतश्रीः
मा भूदेवं क्षणमपि च ते विद्युता विप्रयोगः।।117।।

ཀྱཻ་ཡེ་ཆུ་འཛིན་གདུང་ལྡན་བདག་གི་བརྗོད་པ་བདག་གི་སེམས་ལ་དོན་གཉེར་དཀའ་བ་ཡི།
ཚོགས་འདི་བྱམས་པར་གྱུར་པའམ་རྗེས་སུ་རབ་ཏུ་[2] བརྩེ་བའི་བློས་ནི་འདི་རྣམས་ཀུན་བྱས་ནས།
ཁྱོད་ཀྱང་འདོད་པའི་ཡུལ་ནི་ཐོབ་ཅིང་མཛེས་པའི་ཆར་སྤྲིན་ཚོགས་འཛིན་དཔལ་དང་ལྡན་པ་དང་།
གློག་མ་དང་ཡང་ནམ་ཡང་མི་འབྲལ་གྱུར་ཅིག་དེ་བཞིན་ཀུན་ཀྱང་དགེ་ཞིང་ཤིས་གྱུར་ཅིག ༡༡༧།

इति कालिदासविरचितं मेघदूतं समाप्तम्।

སྙན་ངག་མཁན་ཆེན་པོ་ནག་མོའི་ཁོལ་གྱིས་མཛད་པའི་སྤྲིན་གྱི་ཕོ་ཉ་རྫོགས་སོ།།

---

༡ པེ་། སྣར་།> གིས།

༢ པེ་། སྣར་།> རབ་ཏུ། ཆད།

བློ་གྲོས་དང་སྙིང་རྗེ་དང་། བརྟུལ་བ་དང་དེས་པ་དང་། གཏོང་བ་ལ་སོགས་པའི་ཡོན་ཏན་ཕུལ་དུ་ཕྱུང་[1] བ་དཔག་ཏུ་མེད་པས་སྤྲས་པའི་དཔོན་[2] ཆེན་ནམ་མཁའ་བརྟན་པའི་བཀའ་ལུང་གིས། ཁ་ཆེའི་པཎྜི་ཏ་སྨན་ངག་མཁན་ཆེན་པོ་སུ་མ་ན་ཤྲི་དང་། ཞུ་ཆེན་གྱི་ལོ་ཙཱ་བ་མང་དུ་ཐོས་པའི་དགེ་སློང་བྱང་ཆུབ་རྩེ་མོ་དང་། ལོ་ཙཱ་བར་གཏོགས་པ་ལུང་རིགས་སྨྲ་བ་ནམ་མཁའ་བཟང་པོས་དཔལ་ས་སྐྱའི་གཙུག་ལག་ཁང་ཆེན་པོར་བསྒྱུར་ཅིང་ཞུས་ཏེ་གཏན་ལ་ཕབ་པ།

གང་ཞིག་ཐུགས་དགོངས་རྣམ་པར་དག་པ་ཡིས། འདི་ལ་བསྐུལ་ཞིང་མཐུན་[3] རྐྱེན་བསྒྲུབས་དང་། །བདག་ཅག་འབད་ལས་བསོད་ནམས་གང་བསྒྲུབས་པས། །འཁོར་བ་ལས་ཀུལ་[4] སྐུ་གསུམ་ཐོབ་པར་ཤོག །བྱང་གི་བདག་པོའི་གསུང་བཟང་ལས། །སྨན་ངག་འདི་ནི་བོད་སྐད་དུ། །ཁ་ཆེ་པཎ་ཆེན་དང་ལྷན་ཅིག །དགེ་སློབ་བྱང་ཆུབ་རྩེ་མོས་བསྒྱུར། །འདིས་འགྲོ་བ་དཔག་ཏུ་མེད་པ་ལ་ཕན་ཐོགས་ནས་བཀྲ་ཤིས་ཤིང་བདེ་ལེགས་སུ་གྱུར་ཅིག།

---

༡ པེ། སྣར།> བྱུང།

༢ སྣར།> དགོན།

༣ པེ། སྣར།> འཐུན།

༤ པེ། སྣར།> བཀུལ།

संस्कृत-तिब्बती सन्दर्भ सूची

अच्छ	དྲི་མེད་	53
अजिन	ལྤགས་པ་	38
अञ्जन	མིག་སྨན་	96,61
अट्टहास	རབ་ཏུ་རྒོད་པ་	60
अतिक्रम्य	རྐང་པ་བསྐྱོད་ཚེ་	59
अतिक्रान्त	ཤིན་ཏུ་གང་ཡང་འདས་	104
अतितरा	མཆོག་ཏུ་	15
अतिथि	(འགྲུལ་བ་) "བསྟན་བྱ་"	60
अतीत	རྒལ་	31
अत्यति	འོངས་གྱུར་	36
अत्यन्तम्	མཐའ་གཅིག་ལྷུན་	111
अदृष्टः	མཐོང་བྱ་མིན་	104
अद्रिग्रहण	རི་གཟུང་	46
अद्रेः	རི་, རི་ཡི་	59,14
अद्रे	རི་བོ་ལ་	61
अद्रौ	རི་བོ་	2
अधः	འོག་ཏུ་	50
अधर	མཆུ་	89
अधरोष्ठम्	སྟེང་འོག་མཆུ་	83
अधरोष्ठी	མཆུ་དག་	8
अधिक	མང་པོ་	22
अधिकार	དབང་གྱུར་	1

अन्तर	ནང་, ནང་དུ་	80,3
अन्तरात्मा	ནང་གི་བདག་ཉིད་	94
अन्तस्तोयम्	ཆུ་ཡི་སྙིང་པོ་ཅན་	66
अन्ता	དཔུས་	25
अन्ते	རྫོགས་ཚེ་	90
अन्यथा	རྣམ་པ་གཞན་དུ་	3
अन्यरूपाम्	གཟུགས་གཞན་	82
अन्यस्मिन्	གཞན་པའི་	36
अन्यो	གཞན་ལ་	77
अन्योऽपि	གཞན་ཡང་	8
अन्वास्येनाम	གནས་པར་མཛོད་	98
अपगम	མེད་ཅིང་	72
अपनयन	སེལ་ལ་	28
अपरिगणयन्	ཡོངས་སུ་མི་ཤེས་	5
अपां	ཆུ་	51
अपाङ्ग	མིག་ཟུར, ཟུར་མིག་	96,46,29
अपि	ཅིང་, ཡིན་ཡང་, ཡང་, ཡང་ ཏེ་	89,48,24
अपेक्षया	''རྒྱུ་མཚན་''	17
अबन्ध्याम्	(འཆིང་མེད་)	11
अबला	མཛེས་མ་	94
अभिख्याम्	མཛེས་པ་	79

अम्	འབྱུང་བ་	61
अम्बुवाहम्	ཆུ་འཛིན་	100
अम्भः	ཆུ་	53
अम्भोज	ཆུ་སྐྱེས་	64
अम्रैः	ཨ་མྲའི་	19
अयं	(འགྲོ་) ''ཞབས་ཏོག་བྱེད་པ་''	9
अरण्येषु	འབྲོག་དགོན་རྣམས་ (ལ་)	22
अर्घाय	མཆོད་པའི་ཆེད་དུ་	4
अर्चिं	འོད་ཟེར་	70
अर्थ	དོན་	116,40,
अर्थित्व	དོན་གཉེར་ཉིད་	6
अर्थी	ཆེད་དུ་	4
अर्द्रः	བརླན་པ་ཉིད་	18
अर्ध	ཕྱེད་	53
अर्धरूढ	ཕྱེད་ལྡན་	22
अर्धेन्दु	ཟླ་ཕྱེད་	57
अर्हसि	བཀུར་སྟི་བསྙེན་བཀུར་བྱེད་,	42
	བྱ་བར་འོས་	55
अलंघ्यम्	མ་ཚོངས་	56
अलः	ནུས་པ་	87
अलक	ལན་བུ་	83,69
अलकम्	སྐྲ་ཡི་ལན་བུ་, ལན་བུ་	89,67,65

अविरतो-त्कण्ठम्	ཕྲད་འདོད་མཆོག་ཏུ་གྱུར་	103
अविश्वा-सिनी	མི་གུས་འོས་	114
अविहतगतिः	མྱུར་དུ་གཤེགས་	10
अव्यापन्न	མ་ཤི་བ་ཉིད, འཚོ་བ་ཉིད་	10,102
अश	བགྲོད་	29
अशरणम्	བརྟེན་པར་མིན་ཡི་	110
अशिशिर	དྲོ་བ་	83
अशोक	མྱ་ངན་མེད་	77
अश्रु	མཆི་མ་	108
अश्रुभिः	མཆི་མ་རྣམས་	88
असकल	མཐའཞིན་	83
असकृत्	ལན་ཅིག་མིན་པར་,	90,113,
	ཡང་དང་ཡང་དུ་	94
असहनाः	མ་བཟོད་	56
असि	འགྱུར་, དེ་ལ་	29,53
असित	དཀར་མིན་	114
असौ	གཾ་གླུ་	53
अस्थान	གནས་མིན་	53
अस्मदीय	བདག་གི་	74
अस्मात्	འདི་ལས, དེ་ནས་	14,101
अस्मिन्	འདི་ན་, བདག་གི་	75,106
अस्य	དེ་ཡི་	57

अस्या	དེ་ཉི་, དེ་ཡི་	77,34,
अस्त्रम्	མིག་ཆུ་, མཆི་མ་	41,103
अस्त्रे	མཆི་མ་རྣམས་	93
अस्त्रैः	མཆི་མ་མང་པོ་	107
अहनि	ཉིན་མོ་	87
अहनीय	ཉིན་མོ་	91
अहम्	བདག་	95,6
अहमिव	བདག་འདྲ་	8
अहरपि	གིན་པར་ཡང་ཉི་	110
आकाक्षन्ती	འདོད་པ་	89
आकाश	ནམ་མཁའ་	108
आकुल	བསྐོར་བའི་	25
आकैलासात्	གངས་ཅན་པར་ལ་	11
आक्षिपत्सु	འཕེན་པ་ན་	70
आखण्डल	མཆོད་སྦྱིན་བརྒྱ་པ་	15
आख्यं	ཞེས་གྲགས་	27
आख्याते	བཤད་ཚེ་	101
आख्येयम्	བརྗོད་པར་འོས་	104
आगण्ड	འགྲམ་པ་དག་ལས་	89
आगतम्	འོངས་པར་གྱུར་	100
आगार	གྲོང་ཁྱེར་	74
आघ्राय	མནམ་བྱ་	22

आलेख्या-नाम्	བགྲ་བའི་རི་མོ་རྣམས་	71
आलोके	མཐོང་ན, མཐོང་བར་གྱུར་	3,84
आवर्ज्य	འོག་ཏུ་བསྙ་	48
आवर्त	འཁོར་ལོ	30
आवर्तक	བསྐལ་བར་འཇུག་པའི་	6
आवलम्बा	འཆང་བཅན་	72
आवाम्	བདག་ཅག་གཉིས་	112
आविर्भूत	བསྟན་པ་	22
आशाबन्धः	ཕྲེང་བས་བཅིངས་	10
आशास्यम्	དབུགས་དབྱུང་བྱེད་	102
आशु	མྱུར་; ཤིན་ཏུ་མྱུར་བར་	115,
आश्रम	གནས་	102
आश्लिष्ट	གལ་བར་གྱུར་	2
आश्लेष	འཁྱུད་བྱ་	3
आश्वसत्यः	བསམ་པ་དགའ་བར་གྱུར་	8
आश्वास्य	དབུགས་དབྱུང་མཛོད་	115
आषाढ	ཆུ་སྟོད་ཟླ་བ་	2
आसन्न	ཉེ་བར་	87,92
आसन्ने	ཡོངས་ལ་, འོངས་ཚེ་	96, 25
आसाद्य	ལེགས་འོངས་ཚེ	23,36
आसार	ཆར་གྱིས་	17
आसारेण	བདུད་ཀྱིས་	18

उच्चैः	མཐོ་བའི, ཆེ་བའི་སྐྱེ་བོ་	38,17
उच्छिली-न्ध्राम्	གདུགས་དག་	11
उच्छून	ཆེ་བ་དག་ཏུ་གྱུར་	83
उच्छ्राय	ཤིན་ཏུ་མཐོ་བ་	60
उच्छवसित	དགའ་བདེ་, རླངས་པ་,	101,44,
	བསྐྱེད་བྱ་	60
उच्छवसित-शिथिलम्	འགྲོལ་	70
उच्छवा-सिना	དབུགས་དྲོན་	103
उज्जयिन्या	གྲོང་ཁྱེར་ཨུཛྫ་ཡ་ན་	29
उत्कण्ठ	དགའ་བས་ཕྲད་འདོད་གྱུར་,	104,
	མངོན་ཕྱོགས་	101
उत्कण्ठितेन	ཆེ་བར་ཕྲད་འདོད་ཉིད་ཀྱིས་	103
उत्कम्पात्	ཆེས་འདར་བས་	69
उत्काः	དགའ་བའི་ས་	11
उत्क्षेपात्	བསྐྱེད་པར་གྱུར་	49
उत्खात	བསྐུལ་བྱ་	45,54
उत्तमस्त्री	མཆོག་གི་དགའ་མ་	68
उत्तमानाम्	ཆེན་པོ་རྣམས་	55
उत्तराशाम्	བྱང་གི་ཕྱོགས་སུ་བགྲོད་	29
उत्तरेण	བྱང་གི་ཕྱོགས་ན་, བྱང་དུ་	74,16
उत्तीर्ण	བཀལ་ནས་	49
उत्थाप्य	སླང་ནས་ཀྱང་	99

उपल	རྡོ་	20
उपवन	ཛེ་བ་ཡི་ནགས་	25
उपसर	དེ་རྗེས་	32
उपसरण	འོངས་པ་	83
उपहार	མཆོད་	34
उपहृत	མཆོད་དོ་	57
उपान्त	ཉེ་བར་	76
उपेक्षेत	གཡོག་བཞིན་	8
उपेया	ཉེ་བར་འོངས་	92
उर्मि	རླབས་	52
उर्वीम्	ས་གཞི་	39
उर्व्या	ས་གཞི་	22
उल्का	མེ་ཡི་གདུགས་	55
उल्लङ्घित	བརྒལ་བར་མཛོད་	47
उष्णम्	ཚོ་བ་	12
उष्णैः	ཚོན་མོ་	88
उष्णोच्छवास	དབུགས་ཚོན་	103
ऊर्ध्वम्	སྟེང་དུ་	60
ऊर्ध्वम्=(विष्णु)	གང་ཞིག་ (གཙུག་ན་ཟླ་ཕྱེད་ འཛིན་པ་)	57
उरु	བརླ་	97
एकम्	གཅིག་ཏུ་བཀོད་པ་	48

एकान्ततो	མཐའ་གཅིག་པ་	111
एकस्थं	གཅིག་ཏུ་ཚོགས་པ་ལྡན་	105
एकवेणीं	ལན་བུ་རྣམས་ནི་གཅིག་གྱུར་	90
एतत्	དེ་འདྲ་, དེ་ནི་	102, 15
एत्य	ཞེས་ནི་བྱས་ནས་	12
एनम्	སླར་ཡང་	47
एभिः	དེ་རྣམས་ཀྱིས་ནི་, དེ་རྣམས་	70,109
एवं	དེ་ལྟར་	102
एव	བསྒྲོད་ཅིང་, ཉིད་	16,101
एष्यति	འདོད་	96
ऐरावत	ས་སྲུངས་བུ་	64
औत्सुक्यात्	མཚོག་ཏུ་དགའ་བས་	5
कः	གང་ཞིག་	8
ककुभ	ཀ་ཀུ་བྷ་	24
कच्चित्	ནམ་	84
कटाक्ष	ཟུར་མིག་	37
कठिन	(སྲོ་བོ་), རྩུབ་པ་	93,90
कणिका	ཐིགས་པ་	99
कण्ठ	མགྲིན་པ་	35,98
कण्ठलग्ना	མགྲིན་འཁྱུད་	113
कतिचित्	འགའ་ཡིས་	2
कतिपय	ཉུང་ཟད་	25

कमलवदन	ཆུ་སྐྱེས་གདོང་	41
कमलानि	པདྨ་རྣམས་	50
कर	ལག་པ་	70,43,97
करका	གྲོག་སེར་	56
करण	བྱེང་པ་	57
कररुधि	འོད་ཟེར་རབ་ཏུ་འགྲོ་བ་	41
करुणा	སྙིང་རྗེ་	94
करेण	ལག་པས་, ལག་པ་ཡིས་	90,93
करोति	འགྱུར་, བྱེད་པ་ཡོད་	95,46
कर्ण	རྣ་བ་	28
कर्णे	རྣ་བར་, རྣ་བ་ལ་	46,104
कर्णोत्पल	རྣ་བའི་ཨུཏ྄པལ་	28
कर्तुम्	བྱ་བར་, བྱ་བའི་ཆེད་དུ་	80,42,
कलत्रः	དགའ་མ་	40
कलभ	གླང་ཕྲུག་	80
कलामात्र	ཆ་གཅིག་	88
कल्पयामि	བདག་སེམས་སོ་	116
कल्पवृक्ष	དཔག་བསམ་ཤིང་	68,64
कल्पित	བཞིན་	4
कल्याणि	དགེ་ལྡན་མ་	111
कश्चित्	འགའ་ཞིག་	1
कषायः	བསྐ་བའི་རོ་ལྡན་	33

कामात्	ཆགས་པས་	70
कामार्ता	འདོད་པའི་དོན་དུ་	5
कामि	བདག་པོ་	73
कामिनी	འདོད་ལྡན་མ་	65,69
कामिनीनाम्	འདོད་ལྡན་མ་རྣམས་	69
कामी	འདོད་ལྡན་	2
काल	དུས་	36
कालक्षेप	ཡུན་རིང་བྲོགས་པར་	24
काले	དུས་སུ་, དུས་ལ་, དུས་ཉེ་	41,36,
काले, काले	དུས་དག་ཏུ་	12
किं	ཅི་	3,17, 14
किञ्चित्	ཅུང་ཟད་	16,43
किञ्चिदूनः	ལྷག་མར་ལུས་པ་ཉིད	101
कितव	གཡོ་མ་	113
किमपि	ཅི་ཞིག་ཡིན, ཅི་ཡང་	114,113
किल	ངེས་པར་	109
किसलय	འདབ་མ་	89
किसलयः	ཡལ་འདབ་, ལོ་མ་	77,11
किसलये	ཡལ་ག་རྣམས་	108
कीचकाः	སྨྱིག་སྦྲོམ་	58
कीर्तिम्	གྲགས་པ་	47
कुञ्ज	ནགས་ཀྱི་ཁང་པ་	20

कृत्य	བྱས་ནས	116
कृत्याः	བྱ་བ་བྱས་པ་ཉིད་	40
कृत्वा	བྱས་ནས་	51,117
कृषिफलम्	འབྲུ་རྣམས་འཕེལ་	16
कृष्ण	ནག་པོ་	51
कृष्णशार	དཀར་ནག་	49
केका	རྨ་བྱའི་སྒྲ་	24
केतक	ཀེ་ཏ་ཀའི་མེ་ཏོག་	3
केतकैः	ཀེ་ཏ་ཀའི་ཆུ་སྐྱེས་	25
केश	སྐྲ་, ལན་བུ་	52,105
केशान्	སྐྲ་རྣམས་	105
केसर	གེ་སར་, གེ་ས་ར་ཡི་ཤིང་ཆེན་	22,77
कैलाश	ཀཻ་ལ་ཤ་ཡི་རི་	60
को	ཇི་ལྟར་	43
कोविद	ཤེས་པ་ཡོད་	32
कौतूहला-नाम्	བལྟ་བར་འདོད་	49
कौरवम्	ཀུ་རུ་བ་	50
कौलीन	སྐྱེ་བོ་ངན་པ་	114
क्रमेण	རིམ་གྱིས་	111
क्रियेव	བྱ་བའི་དོན་ཉིད་	116
क्रीडा	རོལ་སྣོག, རོལ་རྩེད་	63,35
क्रीड़ा	མཛེས་པའི་, མཆོག་ཏུ་རོལ་	76,80,2

क्षुद्र	ངན་པའི་སྐྱེ་བོ་	17
क्षुद्रोऽपि	ངན་པའི་སྐྱེ་བོའང་	17
क्षेत्रम्	ཞིང་ལ་, ཞིང་	16,50
क्षेप	གཡོ་བ་	49
क्षोभ	གཡོ་ལྡན་	30
क्षोभात्	བསྐྱོད་ལས་	96
खं	མཁའ་ལ་	14,60
खचितं	འཕྲོས་	37
खण्डम्	དུམ་བུ་	32,15
खण्डितानाम्	བདག་པོ་སོང་བའི་	41
खद्योत	མེ་ཁྱེར་	80
खलु	ངེས་པར་	79,40,
खिन्न	དུབ་པའི་	40
खिन्नः	ཤིན་ཏུ་ངལ་བཞིན་, རབ་ཏུ་ངལ་	13
खे	མཁའ་ལ་	9
खेद	དུབ་བར་གྱུར་པའི་སྡུག་བསྔལ་	34
खेदात्	གདུངས་ལས་	91
गंगा	གཾ་གཱ་, གཾ་གཱའི་ཆུ་	45,65
गगन	མཁའ་	48
गगनगतयो	མཁའ་ལ་བགྲོད་པ་རྣམས་	48
गच्छेः	བགྲོད་པའི་	52
गच्छति	འགྲོ་	111

गन्धवत्याः	ཡིད་འོང་དྲི་ལྡན་	35
गमय	གནས་པར་མཛོད་	112
गम्भीर	ཟབ་པ་	66
गम्भीरध्वनि	ཟབ་པའི་དབྱངས་	68
गम्भीरायाः	ཟབ་མོ་དང་ལྡན་	42
गर्जित	སྙན་པའི་སྒྲ་སྒྲོག་	46
गर्जितम्	འབྲུག་སྒྲ་བསྒྲགས་པ	11
गर्जितानाम्	འབྲུག་དབྱངས་བསྒྲགས་	36
गर्जितैः	སྒྲ་ཆེན་བསྒྲགས་པས་	63
गर्भाधान	མངལ་ནི་རབ་ཏུ་འཛིན་	9
गलितम्	ལྷུང་བ་	46
गवाक्ष	(སྐར་མིག་)	99
गिरिम्	རི་པོར་	27
गीयते	གླུ་དབྱངས་སྒྲོག་	58
गुण	ཡོན་ཏན་, དོ་ཤལ་	48
गुरुणा	ཤིན་ཏུ་ལྕི་བའི་	1
गुरु	བླ་མ་	35
गुणवति	ཡོན་ཏན་ལྡན་མ་	109
गुरुतर	ཤིན་ཏུ་རིང་	87
गुरुभिः	མང་པོ་རྣམས་ཀྱིས་	91
गुरुषु	མང་མོ་	82
गुह्यकः	གསང་བ་པ་	5

गृह	ཁང་པ་, ཁང་བཟང་	25,63,74
गृहात्	ཁང་བཟང་ལས་	74
गेयम्	དབྱངས་སྙན་	85
गेहिन्या	དགའ་མ་	76
गोत्राङ्क	མིང་ནས་འབོད་བས་མཚན་	85
गोप	གླང་རྫི་	15
गौर	དཀར་ཞིང་མཛེས་	61
गौरः	དཀར་བའི་	97
गौरम्	དཀར་པའི་	54
गौरवाय	ལྕི་བ་ཉིད་	21
गौरी	གཽ་རི་	52
ग्रंथि	མདུད་པ་	98
ग्रथितम्	བསྒྲིགས་པའི་ཕྲེང་བ་ལྡན་པ་	65
ग्रहणम्	བཟུང་ནས་	23,52
ग्राम	གྲོང་	32,25
ग्रामवृद्धान्	གྲོང་གི་རྒན་མོས་	32
गात्रम्	ལུས་ནི་	94
गाढतप्तेन	ཤིན་ཏུ་གདུངས་བས་	103
गाढोत्कण्ठाम्	ཡིད་ལ་གཅགས་པ་མེད་པ་	82
गोढोपगूढम्	ཆེ་བར་འཁྱུད་པའི་	98
गाढोष्माभिः	གདུང་བ་མང་པོ་རྣམས་	100
गाण्डीवधन्वा	སྲིད་སྒྲུབ་	50

गाहमानः	བགྲོད་	50
ग्लानि	གདུང་བར་བྱེད་	72
घन	ཆེ་བའི་ཆུ་འཛིན་སྟུག་པོ་,	106,
	སྤྲིན་སྟུག་	21
घर्मलब्ध	ཚ་བས་གདུངས་པ་	63
घर्मान्ते	སོ་ག་རྫོགས་པའི་མཐའ་རུ་	106
घोषम्	དབྱངས་	66
च	འང་	111
चकित	སྐྲེངས་བྱེད་, གཡོ་བའི་,	29,81,
	འཇིགས་བཅས་	105
चकितम्	འཇིགས་ཤིང་སྐྲག་པ་	14
चक्र	འཁོར་ལོ་	111
चक्रवाकीम्	ངང་མོ་	82
चक्रे	སོང་ལ་	1
चक्षुः	མིག་ནི་	91
चटुल	གཡོ་བ་	110
चण्डि	གཡོན་མིག་ཅན་	105
चण्डीश्वर	དཔལ་མགྲིན་	35
चतुर	གཡོ་བ་	73
चतुरान्	དགའ་བས་	23
चटुल	གཡོ་ལྡན་	42
चन्द्रकान्ता	ཟླ་བ་ཆུ་ཤེལ་	72

छिन्न	ཆད་པར་གྱུར་,	69,
	ཆད་པ་	93
छेद	བཅད་པ་	61
जगत्	ཀུན་	92
जघन	མདུན་སྟོམ་	43
जन	སྐྱེ་བོ་	8
जनकतनया	སྐྱེད་བྱེད་བུ་མོ་	1
जनपद	གྲོང་ཁྱེར་	16
जनपदम्	ལྗོང་	50
जने	སྐྱེ་བོའི་	3
जन्मा	བྱུང་བའི་	55
जपापुष्प	དམར་པོའི་ཆུ་སྐྱེས་	38
जम्बूकुञ्ज	འཛམ་བུའི་ཤིང་	21
जम्बूवन	འཛམ་བུའི་ནགས་	25
जर्जरा	དུམ་བུ་དུམ་བུ་	71
जलकण	ཆུ་ཐིགས་	47
जलकणिका	ཆུ་ཡི་ཐིགས་པ་	99
जलकणैः	ཆུ་ཐིགས་རྣམས་ཀྱིས་	28
जलद	ཆུ་འཛིན་	18,13,11
जलधर	ཆུ་འཛིན་	36
जलमयम्	ཆུ་ཡི་རང་བཞིན་	94
जलमुचः	ཆུ་འཛིན་	71

जललव	ཆུ་ཐིགས་	72
जलौघ	ཆུ་ཆེན་	62
जह्नोः कन्या	ཛཧྣཱུའི་བུ་མོ་	52
जातं वंशे	རིགས་མཆོག་དང་ལྡན་	6
जानामि	བདག་གིས་ཤེས་	6
जाताम्	ཐོབ་	82
जानाम्	སྐྱེས་	28
जानीयाः	ཤེས་པར་མཛོད་ཅིག་	82
जाने	བདག་གིས་ཤེས་	95
जायाम्	མཛེས་མའི་	8
जाल	དྲ་བ་, དྲ་མིག་	71,91
जालकानि	དྲ་བ་མཛེས་པ་རྣམས་	28
जालकैः	མེ་ཏོག་ (རྣམས་ཀྱིས་)	99
जालमार्ग	དྲ་མིག་ནང་ནས་	91
जीमूतेन	ཆར་སྤྲིན་དག་གིས་	4
जीर्ण	རྙིང་པ་	31
जीवित	སྲོག་	4
जीवितम्	སྲོག་	82
जीवितं धारयेथाः	འགྲོ་བ་རྣམས་ཀྱིས་	115
ज्यम्	གཞུ་རྒྱུད་ཅན་	73
ज्योतिः	གཟི་ལྡན་, འོད་, རིན་ཆེན་	5,46,68
ज्ञात	ཤེས་ན་	43

तन्वीम्	ལུས་ཕྲ་མ་	92
तप	གདུང་བ་	110
तपानि	སྣང་བ་རྣམས་	106
तप्तम्	གདུངས་གྱུར་	103
तमः	མུན་པ་	39
तमेव	དེ་ཉིད་	76
तमोभिः	མུན་པ་ (རྣམས་)	39
तरु	ལྗོན་ཤིང་, ཤིང་, ཤིང་ཆེན་	1,3,108,
तर्कयामि	སེམས་པར་བྱེད་	95
तर्कयेः	བསམ་ན་	53
तव	ཁྱོད་ཀྱི་	102,109
त्वत्तः	ཁྱོད་ལས་	37
तस्मात्	དེ་ནས་, དེ་སླད་	52,42
तस्मिन्	དེ་ཡི་, དེར་, དེ་ལ་	41,2,20
तस्मिन्काले	དེ་ཡི་དུས་སུ་	98
तस्मिन्नपि	དེར་ཡང་	107
तस्मै	དེ་ལ་	4
तस्य	དེ་ཡི་, དེ་, དེ་ཡིས་	18,65,84
तस्याः	དེ་ཡི་, དགའ་མ་དེ་ཉེ་	43,53,21,
तां च	དེ་ཡང་	10
ताः	མཛེས་མ་དེ་རྣམས་	39
तामतीत	དེ་རྒལ་	31

ते	ཁྱོད་ཀྱིས་, ཁྱོད་,ཁྱོད་ཀྱི་	11,31,42
तेजः	ཉི་མ་, གཟི་ལྡན་	38,45
तेन	དེས་ན་	6
तेषाम्	དེ་ཡི་	26
तैः	དེ་རྣམས་	103
तैस्तैः	དེ་དང་དེ་རྣམས་ཀྱིས་	66
तोरण	རྟ་བབས་	74
तोय	ཆུ་	20,39,35
तोयम्	ཆུ་, ཆུ་ནི་	63,21
त्यज	དོར་ནས་	41
त्यजति	སྤངས་ནས་	31
त्याजितो	འདོར་བར་བྱས་པར་གྱུར་	97
त्रिदश	སྐབས་གསུམ་	60
त्रिनयन	མིག་གསུམ་པ་	115
त्रिपुर	གྲོང་ཁྱེར་གསུམ་	58
त्रिभुवन	སྲིད་པ་གསུམ་	35
त्रियामा	ཐུན་གསུམ་ཅན་མ་	110
त्र्यम्बक	མིག་གསུམ་པ་	60
त्वत्	ཁྱོད་ནི་, ཁྱོད་དང་, ཁྱོད་ཀྱིས་	13,11044
त्वन्मुख	ཁྱོད་ཀྱི་གདོང་	106
त्वमपि	ཁྱོད་ཀྱང་	18
त्वमसि	ཁྱོད་ནི་	7,113

त्वम्	ཁྱོད་ལའོ་	113
त्वयि	ཁྱོད་	8
त्वयि	ཁྱོད་ཉི་	6
त्वरयति	འཕྲོས་	100
त्वां	ཁྱོད་ལ་, ཁྱོད་ཉི་	9,6
त्वादृशा	ཁྱོད་འདྲ་	71
त्वमपि	ཁྱོད་ཀྱང་	94
त्वाम्	ཁྱོད་ཀྱིས་	17
दक्षिणेन	ལྷོ་ནས་	109
दग्ध	མེས་བསྲེགས་	22
दत्त	འབུལ་, འཛིན་བྱེད་	34,62
ददर्श	མཐོང་བར་གྱུར་	2
दधानः	འཛིན་བྱེད་	38
दध्यो	བྱུང་གྱུར་	3
दन्तिभिः	སོ་ལྡན་རྣམས་ཀྱིས་	44
दयिता	བརྩེ་ལྡན་མ་	4
दर्पण	མེ་ལོང་	60
दर्शय	བསྟན་པར་མཛོད་	39
दर्शित	མཐོང་	30
दल	འདབ་མ་	46
दवाग्निः	མེ་སྟག་	55
दशन	སོ་	61

दशपुर	ད་ཤ་ཞེས་བྱའི་གྲོང་ཁྱེར་	49
दशमुख	མགྲིན་བཅུ་	60
दशा	རྟག་ཏུ་	111
दशार्णा	གྲོང་ཁྱེར་ད་ཤ་ཞེས་པ་	25
दानात्	གནང་བར་མཛོད་	28
दानाद्	སྦྱིན་པར་བྱེད་པ་ཡིན་པ་	114
दाम	ལན་བུ་; ཕྲེང་ཐག་	90,29
दिङ्नागा-नाम्	ཕྱོགས་ཀྱི་གླང་པོ་རྣམས་	14
दिक्संसक्त	ཕྱོགས་ཀུན་	106
दिक्षु	བྱང་ཕྱོགས་གཞི་ལ་	26
दिव	སྐབས་གསུམ་པ་	32
दिवस	ཉིན་; ཉིན་ཞག་	78,82,86,
दिवसे	ཉིན་ལ་	2
दिवा	ཉིན་པར་	92
दीर्घ	རིང་; རིང་བ	110,37
दुकूलाम्	གོས་ལྷན་མ་	65
दुखम्	སྡུག་བསྔལ་	111
दुःखदुखेन	གདུང་བའི་སྡུག་བསྔལ་དག་	94
दुर्लभ	སྐལ་བ་དམན་པ	110
दूर	རིང་; རིང་ན་; ཐག་རིངས་	6,3,48
दूरवर्ती	རིང་ན་འདུག་པ་ཅན་	103
दूरात्	རིང་ནས་	74

	མཐོང་བར་འགྱུར་	20
द्रवम्	འཛག་གྱུར་	103
द्रुततर	མཆོག་ཏུ་མྱུར་བར་	20
द्रुतम्	མྱུར་དུ་	24
द्रुमाणाम्	ལྗོན་པ་རྣམས་	109
द्वन्द	ཁྲོ་ཤུག་	47
द्वार	སྒོ་	59
द्वारोपान्ते	སྒོའི་མཐའ་དང་ཉེ་བ་ན་	79
द्वितीय	གཉིས་པ་	82
द्विरद	གཉིས་འཐུང་	61
धनपति	གནོད་སྦྱིན་བདག་པོ་, ནོར་གྱི་ བདག་པོ་, གཏེར་གྱི་བདག་པོ་	73, 74,7
धनुः	གཞུ་ཡི་	15
धाम	གནས་	35
धार	གཟུང་	63
धारयन्ती	འཛིན་བྱེད་	94
धारा	ཆར་, གྲུ་ཆར་ཆེན་པོ་	106, 50
धीर	སྙན་པའི་	99
धीरता	བརྟན་པ་	116
धुन्वन्	བསྐྱོད་	64
धूत	གཡོ་བར་བྱེད་པ་ཡོད་	35
धूपैः	སྤོས་ཀྱིས་	34

धूम	དུ་བ་	5,71
धृतमिव	འཛིན་པ་བཞིན་	43
धैर्यात्	བརྟན་པ་	42
धौत	དཀར་བའི་, སྣང་བྱས་	7
ध्वनिः	སྒྲ་བརྙན་	58
ध्वनित	གླུ་དབྱངས་སྒྲོག་པར་བྱེད་	44
ध्वनिभिः	སྒྲ་དབྱངས་	100
न	མིན་	65
न अस्ति	ཡོད་མ་ཡིན་	105
नक्तम्	མཚན་མོ་	39
नखपद	སེན་རྗེས་	37
नखेन	སེན་མོས་	90
नगेन्द्रम्	རི་དབང་	64
न चिरेण	འཕྲལ་ལ་	18
न तथा पीडयेत्	དེ་ལྟར་ཤིན་ཏུ་གདུང་མིན་	87
नदति	སྒྲོག་པ་	9
नदी	ཆུ་ཀླུང་, ཆུ་བོ་	105,28
न दृष्ट्वान्	མི་མཐོང་མིན་	65
ननु	ངེས་པར་	58
न पुष्यति	ཉམས་པར་གྱུར་པ་ཉིད་	79
न प्रबुद्धा	རྒྱས་མིན་	91
न भवति	འབྱུང་མ་ཡིན་	17

नभसि	ནམ་མཁའ་དག་ལ་	11
नभस (श्रावण)	དབྱར་དུས་ཟླ་བ་གཉིས་པ་	4
न मन्दायन्ते	ཤིན་ཏུ་མགྱོགས་པར་	40
नमित	ཐུར་དུ་འཕྱང་བ་	74
न मोक्ष्यन्ती	གཏོར་མིན་	92
न मोघी	དོན་ཡོད་	42
नयन	མིག་, ཟུར་མིག་, འདྲེན་བྱེད་	9,38,61
नयनम्	འདྲེན་བྱེད་	96
नयनसलिल	འདྲེན་བྱེད་མཆི་མ་	89
नयनसलिलम्	མིག་གི་མཆི་མ་	41
नयनसलिलैः	མིག་ཆུས་	85
नयना	འདྲེན་བྱེད་	99
नयेथा	རང་ཉིད་, བསལ་བར་བྱས་	34
नरपति	མི་ཡི་བདག་པོ་	39
नर्तयेथाः	གར་དགབ་བྱེད་	46
नर्तित	རོལ་སྙེག་གར་བྱེད་	78
नलिन्या	པདྨོའི་ཡུམ་	41
नव	འཕྲུལ་ལ་, གསར་སྐྱེས་	94,45,28
न व्यपगत	འགྲོ་མི་འགྱུར་	75
न शक्ष्यति	མི་ནུས་	21
न सहते	(མི་བཟོད་)	107
न सुप्ताम्	ཟུམ་པ་མ་ཡིན་	91

नीड	ཚང་	25
नीता	སོང་, གསར་པ་དག་གིས་མཛེས་	88,
	ཁྲུས་	67
नीता	དེད་པ་	71
नीत्वा	ཁྲིན་ཁྲུས་ནས་	2
नीपं	ཆུ་སྐྱེས་མེ་ཏོག་	22
नीलकण्ठ	མགྲིན་སྔོན་	78
नीलम्	སྔོན་པོ་	43
नीवी	འོག་པག་	70
नुदति	བསྐྱོད་	9
नून	ངེས་པར་	19,9,83
नृत्त	གར་ཉི་, གར་	38,34
नेत्र	མིག་འབུར་, མིག་, འདྲེན་བྱེད་	83,49,71
नेष्यन्ति	འཁྱེར་བར་བྱེད་	63
नेमि	རྩིབས་	111
नैदाघम्	སོ་ཀ་	18
नौ	བདག་ཅག་གཉིས་	107
न्यस्त	བཀོད་	83,13
न्यासैः	བཀོད་པར་གྱུར་ཚེ་	37
पंक्तिम्	ཕྲེང་བ་	52
पङ्क	འདམ་	54
पक्व	སྨིན་པ་	81

पक्ष्म	རྫི་མ་	49
पण्यस्त्री	སྨད་ཚོང་མ་	27
पट	གསལ་བར་བྱེད་; གོས་	33,64
पटह	རྔ་ཆེན་	36
पटुकरणैः	མཁས་པའི་བྱེད་པ་རྣམས་	5
पञ्चवाण	མདའ་ལྔ་པ་	106
पञ्जर	གུར་	84
पतन्ति	ལྷུང་བར་གྱུར་	108
पतित	ལྷུང་བར་གྱུར་	107
पतितैः	ལྷུང་ཞིང་	69
पत्रच्छेद	རྣ་བའི་རྒྱན་	69
पत्नीम्	(བདག་མོ་) བདག་པོ་	10
पथ	ལམ་	39
पथि	ལམ་ལ་; ལམ་ནི་; ལམ་	30,14,
पथिक	ལམ་བགྲོད་	8
पदं	རྐང་; ཚིག་	13,104,
पद	གནས་པ་	57
पदसुख	རྐང་བའི་བདེ་བ་	62
पदैः	ཞབས་ཀྱིས་	12
पदवीम्	མཁས་ལམ་གཤེགས་པའི་དབང་ གིས་	8
पद्म	པདྨ་	79

परीयाः	བསྐོར་བ་མཛོད་	57
परुषम्	རྩུབ་པའི་	89
परुषैः	རྩུབ་པའི་	63
पर्ण	འདབ་མ་	31
पर्यङ्कं	མཐའ་ན་	93
पर्वत	རི་བོ་	24
पर्वते पर्वते	རི་བོ་རྣམས་ལ་	24
पवन	དྲི་བཞིན་	101,8,14
पवनः	དྲི་བཞིན་དག་	9
पशुपतिः	ཕྱུགས་བདག་	38
पशुपतेः	ཕྱུགས་བདག་	58
पश्चात्	ནུབ་ཏུ་, རྒྱབ་ནས་, ཕྱི་ནས་,	16,38,11
	ཕྱིས་ནས་	2,46
पश्य	བལྟ་བྱ་	87
पश्यन्	མཐོང་	34
पश्यन्तीनाम्	མ་མཐོང་མ་ཡིན་	108
पारावत	ཕུག་རོན་	40
पार्श्व	གཞོགས་	93,88
पाण्डुः	དཀར་པོའི་, དཀར་	25,19
पाण्डुच्छाया	བསྒྲིབས་དཀར་	31
याति	ལྷུང་བ་	10
पातैः	རབ་ཏུ་མང་པོ་ཕབ་པས་	50

पुष्करावर्तक	བསྐལ་པར་འདུག་པའི་ཆེ་བའི་ཆུ་ འཛིན་	6
पुष्करेः	ད་ཉམས་	68
पुष्प	ཆུ་སྐྱེས་, མེ་ཏོག་	28,45
पुष्पमेघी	སྤྲིན་གྱི་མེ་ཏོག་	45
पुष्पलावी	ཆུ་སྐྱེས་ཐོག་མ་	28
पुष्पैः कदम्बैः	ཀ་དམ་པ་ཡི་མེ་ཏོག་	27
पुण्यम्	བསོད་ནམས་	35
पुण्योदक	བསོད་ནམས་ཆུ་བོ་	1
पूर्णता	ཡོངས་སུ་གང་	21
पूर्यमाणाः	ཁེངས་པར་གྱུར་པའི་	58
पूर्व	དང་པོར་	91,102,
पूर्वोद्दिष्टाम्	སྔར་བསྟན་	32
पृच्छतः	དྲི་བ་	113
पृच्छति	འདྲི་	102
पृच्छन्ती	དྲི་བ་བྱེད་	84
पृथुम्	ཆེན་པོ་	48
पृषतैः	ཆུ་ཐིགས་དག་གིས་	64
पेयम्	''བདེ་སྐྱེས''	13
पेलवं	ཤིན་ཏུ་ཕྲ་བ་	94
पेशल	ཡིད་འོང་མཆོག་	76
पौर	གྲོང་གི་	29

प्रत्याश्वस्ता	དབུགས་དབྱུང་མཛོད་	99
प्रत्यासन्ने	འོངས་པར་གྱུར་ཆེ་	4
प्रत्यासन्नो	ཉེ་བ་ན་	77
प्रत्युक्त	ལན་གྱི་ཚིག་	116
प्रत्युद्यातः	ཡུན་རིང་གནས་པར་འདོད་	24
प्रत्यूषेषु	ཉེ་གཞོན་གྱིས་	33
प्रथम	དང་པོར་	22,80,17
प्रथयति	སྨྲ་རུ་འཇུག་པ་	27
प्रथित	ཞེས་པ་	26
प्रदिशसि	སྩྩིན་པར་མཛོད་	116
प्रधन	བཙོམ་	50
प्रबल	ཤེན་ཏུ་	83
प्रभवति	བྱུང་བ་, མཆོག་ཏུ་རྒྱས་པ་	15,11
प्रभवम्	ཡབ་གྱུར་	54
प्रभाणाम्	འོད་ཟེར་དང་ལྡན་པ་རྣམས་	49
प्रमत्तः	བག་མེད་	1
प्रमुख	མངོན་དུ་གྱུར་པ་	4
प्रयाणः	བགྲོད་པའི་	13
प्रवाह	(བརྒྱུགས་རྒྱུན་)	48
प्रवितत	བསྐྲིབས་པས་	106
प्रविष्टान्	ཞུགས་	91
प्रवृत्ता	ཞུགས་པའི་	109

प्रवृत्तिम्	ཚིག་	4
प्रवेशम्	འཆར་བ་	42
प्रशमन	ཞི་བར་བྱེད་	55
प्रशमित	བྲན་པར་བྱས་	17
प्रसन्ने	རབ་ཏུ་དང་བའི་	42
प्रसरम्	གཡོ་བ་	96
प्रसव	གེ་སར་	115
प्रसवरजसा पाण्डु	འཛུམ་ཞིང་དཀར་པའི་གེ་སར་	67
प्रसवि	གེ་སར་དང་ལྡན་	64
प्रसूत	རབ་ཏུ་འཁྲུངས་	68
प्रस्थ	གནས་པར་བྱ་	60
प्रस्थानम्	འགྲོ་བ་	43
प्रस्थित	ཞུགས་པའི་ཚེ་	29
प्रहतमुरजाः	རོལ་མོ་དབྱངས་སྙན་	66
प्रहित	གཡོ་བ་དག་གིས་མདའ་, ཕྱིར་	73,
	འོངས་	115
प्राची	ཤར་བ་	88
प्राणिनाम्	སྐྱེ་བོ་རྣམས་	102
प्राणिभिः	སྲོག་(ལྡན་)རྣམས་ཀྱིས་ནི་	5
प्रापणीया	ཐོབ་པར་བྱེད་	5
प्रापि	བཞིན་དུ་	46
प्राप्तये	ཐོབ་པར་	57

प्राप्ते	ཐོབ་	17
प्राप्य	ཐོབ་བྱ་ཡོད་, མཐོང་བྱས་ནས་,	74,
	ཐོབ་བྱས་ནས་	70,54
प्राप्य	ཐོབ་ནས་	37,32
प्रायः	ཕལ་ཆེར་, མང་ལས་	86,94,73
प्रायशो	ཕལ་ཆེར་	10
प्रार्थनम्	དོན་གཉེར་	110
प्रार्थना	འདོད་དོན་གཉེར་བར་བྱེད་,	33,117
प्रालेय	གངས་	59
प्रालेयाद्रे	གངས་ཀྱི་རི་	59
प्रावृषा	མཛེས་པའི་ཆར་སྤྲིན་	117
प्रासाद	ཁང་བཟང་	66
प्रिय	དགའ་མ་, དགའ་བྱེད་, མཛའ་	84,
	བོ་, དགའ་བས་	76,30,23
प्रियतम	བདག་པོ་མཆོག་	33,72
प्रियम्	དགའ་བ་	117
प्रियसखम्	དགའ་བའི་གྲོགས་བཟང་	12
प्रियायाः	དགའ་མ་	7
प्रियार्थ	དགའ་བའི་དོན་ལ་	24
प्रियेषु	མཛའ་བོ་རྣམས་ལ་	30,70
प्रीतः	དགའ་བཞིན་	4
प्रीति	མཛའ་བ་	4

फलद्योतिभिः	འབྲས་བུ་ཀྲུས་པ་	19
फलम्	འབྲས་, འབྲས་བུ་	26,36
फलाः	འབྲས་བུ་མང་པོ་	55
फेनैः	དབུ་བའི་	52
बद्ध	ཕྲེང་བ་བསྒྲིགས་པ་	75
बद्धा	བཅིངས་པ་, བཅིངས་པའི་	78,90
बधूभुक्त	ཆུང་མའི་	20
बन्ध	བཅིངས་པ་	70
बन्धु	རང་གི་གཉེན་, གཉེན་, གཉེན	51,34,
	འདུན་དག་	116,6
बर्ह	མཇུག་སྒྲོ་དོངས་, མཇུག་སྒྲོ་	46,105
बर्हेण	རྨ་བྱའི་སྒྲོ་	15
बलाकाः	ཆུ་སྐྱར་རྣམས་, ཆུ་སྐྱར་མཛེས་	23,
	མ་རྣམས་	9
बलि	སྔོ་བས་ལྡན་, གཏོར་མཾ་	59,36,84
बलिभुजाम्	གཏོར་ལེན་	25
बलिम्	གཏོར་མ་	57
बसतिम्	གནས་སུ་	39
बहु	མང་པོ་	111
बहुशो	མང་པོ་རུ་	108
बहुना	མང་པོ་	83
बाध	དུགས་	55

भव	ཁྱོད་ནི་	30
भवतः	ཁྱོད་ཀྱི, ཁྱེད་ནི་	53,29
भवम्	སྐྱེས་	47
भवति	འགྱུར་, འགྱུར་པ་ཉིད་	3,27,12
भवति हि	འགྱུར་པ་ཉིད་	92
भवतो	ཁྱོད་དང་, ཁྱོད་ནི་	12,11
भवनम्	གནས་	79
भवन्तम्	ཁྱོད་	9
भवन्ति	འགྱུར་	114
भवानी	རི་ཡི་སྲས་མོ་, ཨུ་མ་	38, 46
भवान्	ཁྱོད་ནི་	24
भविता	འགྱུར་	51
भवित्रीम्	འགྱུར་བ་	61
भवेत्	གྱུར་ཏོ་	109
भानुः	ཉིན་མོར་བྱེད་པ་	36
भानोः	ཉིན་མོར་བྱེད་པ་	41
भाययेस्ताः	འཇིགས་པར་བྱ་	63
भार	མང་པོ་	55
भारात्	སྦོམ་ཞིང་	81
भारेषु	ཚོགས་ལ་	105
भाव	མཐུ་	48
भावगम्य	ཡིད་ཀྱིས་རྟོག་བྱ་	84

भावात्	མཐུ་ལས་	48
भावी	འབྱུང་	58
भास	སྣང་བ་	80
भित्वा	བཅད་བྱས་ནས་	109
भिन्न	དུམ་བུར་བྱས་	83
भुज	ལག་པ་	38,60
भुजं	ལག་པས་	108
भुजम्	ལག་འགྲོ་, སྦྲུལ་	112,62
भुजलता	ལག་པའི་འཁྲི་ཤིང་	98
भुवः	ས་གཞིའི་མཛེས་མ་, ས་ལ་,	19,
	ས་གཞི་	48,66
भुवन	ས་གསུམ་	6
भुवि	ས་ཡི་གཞི་ལ་, ས་ལ་	47,86
भूः	འགྱུར་	39
भूतिम्	ས་དཀར་རྫོན་	20
भूदेव	དགེ་ཞིང་ཞེས་པར་གྱུར་ཅིག་	117
भूयः	སླར་ཡང་, ཡང་ནི་	113
भूयो भूयः	ཡང་ཡང་, ཡང་དང་ཡང་དུ་	85,93
भृगुपति	ཧྲྀ་གུའི་བདག་པོ་	59
भ्रंश	''ཀྲུ་བར་བྱེད''	2
भ्रंशिभिः	ལྷུང་བ་རྣམས་	31
भ्रातः	ཀྭ་ཡེ་གྲོགས་པོ་	95

भ्रातृजायाम्	བདག་གི་མཛེས་མ་	10
भ्रुकुटिरचना	ཁྲོ་གཉེར་རྣམས་	52
भ्रू	སྨིན་མ་	49, 96,16
भ्रूविलासान्	སྨིན་མའི་རོལ་སྟེག་	105
मघोनः	མཆོད་སྦྱིན་བརྒྱ་པ་	6
मणिभिः	རིན་ཆེན་ཕྲེང་བ་	78
मणिमय	ནོར་བུ་དང་ལྡན་; ནོར་བུའི་རང་	68,
	བཞིན་	66
मण्डप	ཁང་བཟང་	77
मण्डलेन	ཟླུམ་པོའི་	38
मत्	བདག་དང་; བདག་གི་	79,24,87,
मत्वा	ཤེས་བྱས་ནས་	73
मत्सादृश्यं	བདག་འདྲ་	84
मत्संयोगः	བདག་དང་ཕྲད་པ་	89
मथिताम्	ཉམས་པ་	82
मदकलम्	སྨྱོས་པའི་གདངས་སྙན་	33
मदिरा	ཆང་	77
मदीयैः	བདག་གི་	97
मदैः	སྨྱོས་པའི་	21
मद्	བདག་གི་	76
मद्गेहिन्या	བདག་གི་དགའ་མ་	76
मधु	ཆང་	68

मरुद्भिः	རླུང་གིས་	35
मलिनवसने	དྲི་མའི་གོས་	85
महतीम्	ཤིན་ཏུ་རིང་བ་ཉིད་	88
महत्का-मुकत्व	མཆོག་གི་གོ་འཕང་	26
महाकाल	ནག་པོ་ཆེན་པོ་	36
महिमा	གཟི་བརྗིད་	1
महीम्	ས་གཞིའི་ཆེད་དུ་	11
मां	བདག་ནི་	106
मा	མི་	117
मा गमः	བྲ་བ་མ་ཡིན་ཏེ་	111
माधवी	ཡལ་ག་	77
मानयिष्यन्ति	མཆོད་བྱེད་	23
मानस	ཡིད་ཀྱི་མཚོ་; མཚོ་	11,64
मानसम्	ཡིད་འོང་མཚོ་	75
मानयिष्यन्	མཆོད་པ་བྱེད་པར་འགྱུར་	47
मानिनी	ཁེངས་ལྡན་མ་	99
मा भू	མ་ཡིན་	114
माम	ཁོ་བོས་	108
मार्ग	ལམ་	75
मार्गः	ལམ་དུ་	69
मार्गम्	ལམ་ལ་; ལམ་ནི་	13,22
मालम्	གནམ་ཆུ་སྨུག་པ་	16

मुखानाम्	གདོང་	28
मुखानि	མགོ་བོ་	50
मुग्ध	རྨོངས་པར་འགྱུར་	14
मुञ्चतः	ཁམས་བདེ་མཛོད་	12
मुरज	རྔ་ཟླུམ་, རོལ་མོ་	58,66
मुहुर	ཡང་ཡང་	107
मुहूर्तं	ཡུད་ཙམ་	20
मूढ	རྨོངས་པ་	70
मूर्त्या	གཟུགས་འཛིན་	47
मूर्ध्ना	རི་རྩེར་	17
मूर्छना	དབྱངས་སྙན་དུམ་བུ་དུམ་བུར་ བཅད་	85
मूले	རྩ་བར་	78,88
मूष्टिः	ལག་པ་དག་གིས་	70
मृगाक्ष्या	རི་དྭགས་མིག་ཅན་	96
मृगाना	རི་དྭགས་	54
मे	བདག་གི་, བདག་དང་	74,13,7,
मेखलासु	རི་ངོས་རྣམས་ལ་	12
मेघ	ཆུ་འཛིན་	3
मेघाः	ཆར་སྤྲིན་	5
मेघम्	སྤྲིན་རྣམས་	2
मेचक	སྔོན་	61

यष्टि	སྡོང་བུ་	78
यस्मात्	(གང་ལས་)	26
यस्मिन्	གང་ཞིག་	57
यस्य	གང་གི་	74,46
यस्या	གཾ་གྲུ་	75
यस्याम्	གང་གི་	68
याः	གང་དེ་	51
याचित	ཞུ་བར་སེམས་	116
याच्ञा	མཆོད་སྦྱིན་	6
यापयन्ती	ལས་སྐྱེས་	88
यामाः	ཐུན་	110
याममात्र	ཐུན་ཚོད་བར་དུ་	98
यायाः	བགྲོད་པར་བྱ་	35
यावत	(ཇི་སྲིད་) དེ་ཧྲེད་རྫོགས་ནས་	107
यावत्	བར་དུ་	36
यियासोः	འགྲོ་སྙམ་ཡོད་ན་	24
युवति	ལང་ཚོ་མ་, ན་ཆུང་དག་	35,81
यूथिका	མེ་ཏོག་སེར་པོ་	28
येन	གང་གིས་	31,15
यो	གང་གི་	60
योषिताम्	བུད་མེད, བཙུན་མོ་རྣམས་	41,39
यौवनानि	ལང་ཚོ་མ་རྣམས་	27

रसाभ्यन्तर	རོ་མཆོག་དང་ལྡན་	30
राग	ཚོན་	34
रागैः	ཚོན་རྣམས་ཀྱིས་	107
राजधानी	རྒྱལ་བའི་ཁབ་ཏུ་	26
राजन्यानाम्	རྒྱལ་རིགས་མང་པོ་	50
राजराजस्य	ནོར་སྦྱིན་རྒྱལ་པོའི་	3
राजहंसाः	ངང་པའི་རྒྱལ་པོ་རྣམས་	11
रात्रौ	མཚན་མོ་	87
रात्रि	མཚན་མོ་	88
रात्रिम्	མཚན་མོ་	40
रात्रौ	མཚན་མོ་	92
रामगिरि	རཱ་མའི་རི་བོ་	1,102
राशी	ཕུང་པོ་ཉིད་	114
राशीभूत	གཅིག་ཏུ་སྤུངས་པར་གྱུར་	60
रिक्त	ལག་པ་ཕྲ་བར་གྱུར་, སྟོང་	2,21
रुचिना	འོད་ཀྱིས་	15
रुजा	ཉེངས་གྱུར་	28
रुणद्धि	འགོག་	10
रुदती	ངུ་བར་བྱས་	113
रुदित	མཆི་མ་བབས་	83
रुद्ध	འགོག་པ་, འགོག་བྱེད་,	४9,39,
रुद्धमार्ग	ལམ་བཀག་གྱུར་	103

लम्बम्	འཕྱང་བ་	89
लम्बी	འཕྱང་བ་	53
ललित	སྒེག་པའི་, རོལ་སྒེག་	66,34
लवम्	དལ་བུས་	22
लवैः	འབབ་པ་	93
लाङ्गली	སྨོབས་བཟང་	51
लावी	ཐོག་མ་	28
लिखन्ती	འདྲི་	84
लिखित	བྲིས་	79
लिह्	རེག་	66
लीला	རོལ་སྒེག་	37
लीलाकमलम्	པད་མཛེས་	67
लीलाम्	མཛེས་པའི་	61
लेखा	བྲིས་	46
लेशाः	དུམ་བུ་	108
लोचन	མིག་	104,51
लोचनाभ्याम्	མིག་དག་གིས་	104
लोचने	མིག་	112
लोचनैः	མིག་གིས་	29
लोचनैः	མིག་རྣམས་ཀྱིས་	16
लोध्र	ཚུ་སྐྱེས་	67
लोभात्	ཐོབ་ཕྱིར་	104

वनोपप्लवम्	ནགས་ནང་ཞིང་སྐམ་	17
वन्द्यैः	ཕྱག་བྱེད་	12
वपु	གཟུགས་	79
वपुः	ལུས་, སྐུ་	62,34,15
वप्र	རི་ཞོད་	2
वर	མཆོག་	7
वरमधिगुण	ཡོན་ཏན་མཆོག་དབང་	6
वरम्	མཆོག་	6
वर्ण	པགས་པ་	83
वर्णचौर	ཁ་དོག་བསྐུས་པར་གྱུར་	48
वर्णमात्रेण	ལུས་ཀྱི་ཁ་དོག་	51
वर्त्म	ལམ་	20,59,41
वर्धित	འཕེལ་	74
वर्ष	ལོ་ཡི་བར་	1
वर्षाग्रबिन्दून्	ཆར་ཐིགས་	37
वलयं	གདུ་བུ་	62,78,2
वलयि	ཚོན་རྩིས་	46
वलभौ	སྟེང་གི་ཕྱོགས་	40
वलिभिः	ལུས་མཛེས་	37
वल्मीक	གྲོག་མཁར་	15
वसन्तम्	གནས་	73
वसनम्	གོས་	43

वसतिः	གནས་སུ་	7
वसतिम्	གནས་	45
वसतिम्	གནས་པར་གྱིས་	1
वसुधा	ནོར་འཛིན་	44
वस्तुनि	དངོས་པོ་རྣམས་	114
वहति	ཤལ་	65
वा	འམ་	117,84
वाता	དྲི་བཞོན་རྣམས་	109
वातायन	དྲ་མིག་	87,92
वातैः	དྲི་བཞོན་གྱིས་	64
वानीर	ཤིང་ཆེན་	43
वान्त	སྐྱུག་བྲོ་	21
वापी	བཀོད་མ་བཟང་པོའི་ཆུ་	75
वामः	གཡོན་ནས་, གཡོན་པ་	9,97
वामपाद	གཡོན་པའི་རྐང་པ་	77
वायुः	རླུང་	44
वायौ	རླུང་གིས་	55
वारिधारा	ཆར་	55
वास	གནས་	78
वासः	གོས་	70
वासराणि	ཞག་	106
वासवीनाम्	རིན་ཆེན་མང་	45

वासस्	གོས་	61
वासितं	འགེངས་	21
वास्यति	བསྔོས་	44
वाहयेत्	བགྲོད་པར་བྱ་	40
विकार	རྣམ་འགྱུར་	16
विक्लवाः	སྐྲག་ཅིང་འཆི་	39
विक्षिपन्ती	སེལ་བར་བྱེད་པ་	89
विगणय	བགྲང་ཞིང་; གྲངས་ཀྱང་	111,106
विगमात्	བྱས་པའི་	57
विगलित	བྲལ་གྱུར་	90
विजयः	རྒྱལ་གྱུར་ལས་	58
वितत्य	ཁྱབ་པར་	60
विदिते	རིག་ཅིང་	6
विदित्वा	རིག་བྱས་ནས་	114
विदिशा	ཝི་དི་ཤ་	26
विद्युत्	གློག་	29,40,80
विद्युता	གློག་མ་	117
विद्युत्वन्तम्	གློག་འོད་ལྡན་བཞིན་	66
विद्युद्गर्भे	གློག་ནང་	99
विधि	ཤེས་པར་མཛོད་	100
विधिना	བསོད་ནམས་	103
विधिना	མཁེན་	31

वियोगेन	བྲལ་བར་གྱུར་བས་	79
विरचित	གནས་པའི་	62
विरचितपद	སྙན་པར་གྱུར་བའི་ཚིག་	85
विरचिता	ལེགས་བྲིས་	20
विरह	བྲལ་བར་, བྲལ་, བྲལ་བའི་, བྲལ་ལ་	31,88,90, 114
विरह	བྲལ་བ་, སྤོང་ལ་	8,1
विरहगुणितम्	ཡུན་རིང་བྲལ་བ་ལས་བྱུང་	112
विरहजम्	འབྲལ་ལས་བྱུང་བའི་	12
विरहतनु	བྲལ་བས་རྫུད་པ་	84
विरह	བྲལ་བས་	86
विलसत्	མཛེས་པ་ཅན་	49
विलसित	རོལ་བའི་	80
विलासम्	རྣམ་འགྱུར་	96
विवृत	ཕྱེ་ན་	43
विशति	འཇུག་པ་ཡིན་	103
विशद	དཀར་བ་, དཀར་པོ་	64,53
विशदानि	དཀར་པོ་རྣམས་ཀྱི་	42
विशालाम्	ཁང་བཟང་ཡངས་པ་	32
विशीर्णा	འོག་ཏུ་འབབ་ལྷུན་མ་	20
विशेष	ཁྱད་པར་	66
विशेषान्	ཁྱད་པར་	59

वीणि	ཕེ་ལྷང་	47
वीतनिद्राम्	གཉིད་བྲལ་	92
वृतयः	བསྐོར་བའི་	25
वृत्ति	གདུང་བ་, འཇུག་པ་	3,94
वृतेः	བསྐོར་བ་	77
वृद्धा	རྒན་མོ་	32
वृन्दम्	ཆེ་	65
वृन्दानि	ཚོགས་རྣམས་	100
वृष	ཁྱུ་མཆོག་	115,54
वृष्टि	ཆར་པ་	21
वृष्टिपात	ཆར་པ་དྲག་ཕབ་	56
वेणिमोक्ष	ལན་བུ་འགྲོལ་	100
वेणी	ལན་བུ་, ལུན་བུ་བཞིན་	19,31
वेत्रवत्याः	ཞི་ཏའི་མཚོ་	26
वेश	ཚུལ་གཟུང་	15
वेश्याः	ཚོགས་ཀྱི་མཛེས་མ་	37
वेष्टन	བསྐོར་བ་	76
वैडूर्य	རིན་ཆེན་	75
वैरिणा	ཆོམ་རྐུན་དག་གིས་	103
व्रज	དལ་གྱིས་གཤེགས་, བགྲོད་,	16,49,
	བགྲོད་བྱ་	28
व्रजेयुः	འོངས་	106

शब्द	སྒྲ་	104
शब्दायन्ते	སྒྲ་འབྱུང་	58
शमयितुम्	ཞི་བའི་ཆེད་དུ་	55
शमयेः	ཞི་བྱ་	18
शयन	ཉལ་ས་	92
शयनात्	གནས་ནས་	112
शयने	སྟན་མལ་གནས་ན་, མལ་གྱི་	113,93,
	སྟེང་དུ་, ཉལ་བར་གྱུར་	88
शय्योत्सङ्ग	མལ་སྟན་སྟེང་ན་	94
शर	སྨྱུག་མ་, མདའ་	47,50
शरच्चन्द्रिका	སྟོན་ཀའི་ཟླ་བ་	112
शरणं	སྐྱབས་ཉིད་	7
शरभा	རྐང་བརྒྱད་	56
शरवणभव	སྨྱུག་མའི་ཚལ་ནས་སྐྱེས་	47
शशिनि	རི་བོང་ཅན་	105
शशिरुचा	ཟླ་བའི་འོད་ཀྱི་ཟེར་	46
शश्वत	རྟག་ཏུ་	57
शाखम्	ཡལ་ག་	43
शान्त	ཞི་བ་	38
शान्तिनेयम्	སེལ་ལ་	41
शाप	ཧྲེ་བོ་ཁྲོས་པའི་བཀའ་ལུང་	112
शापस्य	བཀའ་ལུང་	90

शुक्ला-पाङ्गैः	གཙུག་ཕུད་ཅན་གྱིས་	24
शुचं	གདུང་བ་	87
शुचा	གདུང་	90
शुद्ध	དཀར་བ་ཉིད་, དག་	89
शुभ्रां त्रिनयन	བཞོན་མ་དཀར་པོ་	54
शूलिनः	རྩེ་གསུམ་ཅན་	36
शृंग	རྩེ་མོ་	14,60
शृङ्गे	རྩེ་ལ་	54
शृणु	ཉན་པར་མཛོད་	13
शेष	ལྷག་མ་	19
शेषम्	ལྷག་མའི་	40
शेषान्	ལྷག་མ་རྣམས་, ལྷག་མ་	86,88
शेषैः	ལྷག་མ་རྣམས་ཀྱིས་	32
शैल	རི་བོ་	80
शैलम्	རི་བོ་	12
शैलात्	རི་ལས་	115
शैलराज	རི་རྒྱལ་	52
शोकाम्	གདུངས་པར་གྱུར་	115
शोभाम्	མཛེས་	54
शोभी	མཛེས་པ་	59
श्यामः	ཁྲིག་ལེ་སྔོན་པོ་, སྔོ་བསངས་, ལྗང་སྔོན་	19,59, 25

श्लाघमानः	བསྔེན་ནི་བྱེད་བཞིན་པས་	18
षट्पद	རྐང་དྲུག	73
संकल्पैः	ཡིད་ལ་སེམས་ཞིང་	103
संक्षिप्येत	སྡུད་པ་	110
संगम	ལྷན་ཅིག་འགྲོགས་པ་,	107,
	འགྲོགས་པ་	53
संगमात्	ཕྲད་པ་	101
संगीत	འདུས་དབྱངས་	58
संगीताय	གླུ་དབྱངས་	66
संघट्ट	ཀུན་ཏུ་འཐབ་	55
संतप्तानां	ཤིན་ཏུ་གདུངས་གྱུར་	7
संदर्शनेषु	མཐོང་བར་གྱུར་པ་ན་	108
संदेशं	འཕྲིན་	13,7
संदेशार्थाः	ལེགས་བཤད་ཚེད་དུ་	5
संदेशाम्	འཕྲིན་ལྡན་	100
संदेशैः	འཕྲིན་རྣམས་	87
संधे	ཅུང་ཟད་	60
संध्या	ཐུན་མཚམས་	36
संनद्धे	འོངས་ཆེན་	8
संनिकृष्टम्	ཉེ་བར་གནས་	75
संनिपात	ཚོར་ཚོགས་པ་	5
संन्यस्त	ཡང་དག་བཞག་	94

सखीनाम्	གྲོགས་མ་	104
सखे	ཀྱ་ཨེ་གྲོགས་པོ་, གྲོགས་པོ་,	24,43,
	ཀྱ་ཨེ་གྲོགས་བཟང་	63
सख्यः	གྲོགས་མོ་རྣམས་	92
सख्याः	གྲོགས་སུ་གྱུར་མ་	77
सख्यास्तव	ཁྱོད་ཀྱི་གྲོགས་མོ་	95
सगन्धः	སྤོས་པའི་	9
सगर	དུག་ཅན་	52
सचित्रा	བཀྲ་པར་ལྡན་	66
सजल	བྲན་མ་, ཆུ་དང་བཅས་	64,24
सततगतिना	རྟག་འགྲོས་	71
सताम्	སྐྱེ་བོ་རྣམས་	116
सदृशं	བཞིན་	10
सद्भाव	ཕན་པའི་དངོས་པོ་	18
सद्यः	འཕྲལ་ལ་, འཕྲལ་དུ་, མྱུར་	98,10,16,
सनाथ	མདོག་དང་མཚུངས་	99
सन्	ཀྱི་	28
सन्निपत्य	མངོན་ཞུགས་ནས་	30
सन्निवृत्तम्	ལྡོག་པ་ན་	91
सन्निषण्णा	བསྙན་	88
सन्यस्त	བཀོད་པར་གྱུར་	61
सपदि	འཕྲལ་ལ་	53

सस्वरम्	འཕྲུལ་ལ་	113
सह	བཅས་	77
सहचर	རྒྱལ་པོ་མཆོག་	102
सहचरी	དགའ་མ་	23
सहचरे	ལྷན་ཅིག་སྤྱོད་	82
सहस्व	ལྷན་ཅིག་དག་དུ་	98
सहाया	གྲོགས་སུ་འགྱུར་;ཡང་དག་གནས་	11,68
सांध्यं	ཐུན་མཚམས་	38
सा	དེ་ནི་	94,84
साक्षात्	མངོན་སུམ་དུ་	73
सादर	གུས་པ་དང་བཅས་	34
सादृश्यम्	མཚུངས་པ་	105
साधु	ལེགས་པར་མཛོད་	17
साधो	ལེགས་པར་	79
साध्वी	ལེགས་པ་	87
सानु	རི་སྐྱེང་	2
सानुमान्	ངོས་ལྡན་	18,17
सानो	ངོས་ལ་	80
सान्तर्हासम्	ནང་ནས་རྒོད་པ་དང་བཅས་	113
साभ्र	སྤྲིན་དང་བཅས་	91
सारयन्ती	སེལ་བར་བྱེད་, སྐྱུར་བྱེད་མ་	93.90
सारयित्वा	ཕྱེ་བྱས་ནས་	85

सुचरितफले	ལེགས་བཤད་འབྲས་བུར་	32
सुतरा	ཤིན་ཏུ་	111
सुप्त	ཉལ་ས་	40
सुप्ते	ཉལ་བར་གྱུར་ལ་	92
सुभग	ཀུ་ཡེ་, སྐལ་པ་བཟང་པོ་	31,42,78
सुभगम्	བསྐལ་བཟང་, སྐལ་བཟང་	9,44,30,95,
सुर	ལྷ་	63
सुरगज	ལྷའི་གླང་པོ་	53
सुरत	ཆགས་གཞིར་	33
सुरत-जनिताम्	མཆོག་ཏུ་དགའ་བ་བསྐྱེད་པ་ཉིད་	72
सुरभयो	དྲི་བཟང་དང་ལྡན་	109
सुरभि	དགའ་བ་ཡི་; འདོད་འཇོ་	16, 47
सुरभिणः	དྲི་བཟང་ཅན་	106
सुरभित	དྲི་བཟང་འཛིན་	54
सुरिभतनया	འདོད་འཇོའི་བུ་མོ་	47
सुरभिम्	དྲི་བཟང་	22
सुरभिषु	དྲི་བཟང་ལྡན་པ་	34
सुरभौ	དྲི་ལྡན་	24
सुरयुवतयो	ལྷའི་མཛེས་མ་རྣམས་	63
सुलभ	རྙེད་པ་	102
सुहृद	སྙིང་གྲོགས་	101

स्तन	ནུ་	19
स्तन-परिचित	ནུ་རྒྱས་	69
स्तनाभ्याम्	འོ་མ་འཛིན་པ་དག་	81
स्तनित	འབྲུག་དབྱངས, སྙན་པར་སྒྲོག་	99,39,30
स्तनित	སྙན་པའི་སྒྲ་བསྒྲགས་, ལྷུང་ལྷུང་ སྐད་སྙན་	23,26
स्तनित-विमुखो	སྒྲ་སྒྲོགས་མིན་པར་	93
स्तम्भ	སྡོང་པོ་	97
स्तम्भित	སྤང་བྱ	62
स्तबक	མེ་ཏོག་ཆུན་འཕྱུང་	74
स्तोकनम्रा	བར་དོག་མཆོག་ཏུ་མཛེས་	81
स्त्री	བུད་མེད་	33
स्त्रीणाम्	བུད་མེད་རྣམས་	72
स्त्रीणाम्	དགའ་མ་རྣམས་	30
स्थः	གནས་, གནས་ནས་	102,87,92
स्थल	ས་ལ་གནས་པའི་, ས་	91,106
स्थलानि	གཞི་ལ་	68
स्थली	ས་ལ་གནས་པའི་	108
स्थां	གནས་	84
स्थानात्	གནས་	14
स्थातव्यम्	གནས་པར་མཛོད་	36
स्थापित	སྒྱུར་བར་བྱེད་	86

स्थायि	གནས་ནས་	25
स्थित	གནས་	7
स्थितः	གནས་པ་	60
स्थित्वा	གནས་བྱས་ནས་, གནས་ཏེ་	20,3
स्थिर	བརྟན་པ་	57
स्थूल	ཆེ་བའི་	48
स्थूलहस्त	ལག་པ་ཆེ་བ་	14
स्थूला	བརྒྱུས་པ་བཞིན་	108
स्नान	ཁྲུས་, ཁྲུས་བྱ་	35,1
स्नपयतु	ཁྲུས་ནི་བྱེད་པར་འགྱུར་	45
स्नानात्	ཁྲུས་ཀྱིས་	89
स्निग्ध	སྙུམ་པའི་, རྣམ་མཛེས་,	61,19,
	སྣན་པའི་, མཛེས་པའི་	66,75
स्निग्धः	རབ་བཟང་	1
स्निग्धा	མཛའ་བའི་	92
स्निग्धया	འོད་ཀྱིས་	39
स्नेह	མཛའ་བ་, མཛའ་བོ་	12,114
स्नेहम्	མཛའ་བ་	95
स्नेहशून्यम्	ཉེས་པར་བྱེད་པ་	96
स्पन्दि	གཡོ་བར་བྱེད་	96
स्पर्श	རེག་པའི་, རེག་པར་	90,104
स्पर्शम्	རེག་པར་བྱ་བ་མཛོད་	62

स्पृष्टम्	རེག་པ་	109
स्पृष्टा	རེག་པ་	71
स्फटिक	རབ་དཀར་ཤེལ་; ཤེལ་	78,53,64
स्फुट	བསལ་	72
स्फुटित	རྒྱུས་	33
स्फुरित	གཡོ་བ་, གཡོ་བཞིན་,	29,76,
	ཁྱབ་པར་བྱེད་	15
स्मरसि	དྲན་	34
स्मरामि	བདག་ནི་ཤིན་ཏུ་དྲན་པར་འགྱུར་	76
स्यन्दिनः	འབབ་པ་	72
स्यात्	བྱེད་པར་འགྱུར་, འགྱུར་,	41,
	འགྱུར་པ་ཡིན་	81,110
स्यात्	བསྒྲུགས་པར་གྱུར་	58
स्यूता	(བཙེམས་) ཁྱབ་པ་''	75
स्रस्त	གཡོ་ལྡན་	65
स्रोत	ཆུ་བོ་, ཆུ་གཏེར་, སྣ་ཡིས་	53,44
स्वकुशल-मयीम्	རང་ཉིད་བདེའམ་	4
स्व	རང་གི་, རང་ཉིད་	99,1
स्वङ्गम्	ཡན་ལག་	105
स्वर्ग	མཐོ་རིས་	52
स्वल्पीभूत	ཉུང་ཤས་	32
स्वाङ्ग	རང་གི་ཡན་ལག་	56

स्वागतम्	ལེགས་པར་འོངས་སམ་	4
स्वागती-कृत्य	ལེགས་པར་འོངས་སམ་བྱས་ནས་	24
स्वादु	རོ་ཞིམ་	26
स्वप्न	རྨི་ལམ་	98,108
स्वप्नज	(རྨི) ལས་བྱུང་	89
स्वप्ने	རྨི་ལམ་དུ་	113
स्वयम्	རང་གིས་	85
स्वर्गिणाम्	མཐོ་རིས་	32
स्वाम्	རང་གིས་	79
स्वित्	ཐེ་ཚོམ་དུ་གྱུར་	14
स्वेद	རྔུལ་ཐིགས་	28
हंस	ངང་པ་	59
हंसा	ངང་པ་རྣམས་, ངང་པའི་ཚོགས་	25,75
हंत	ཨེ་མ་	105
हर	འཕྲོག་བྱེད་, མཛད་དུ་གསོལ་,	46,7,
	འཕྲོག་པ་	7,38
हरति	ཕྲོགས་	14
हरिणी	རི་དྭགས་མོ་, རི་དྭགས་	105,81
	མིག་ཅན་	
हरित	ལྗང་, འཕྲོག་བྱེད་	22,23
हर्तुं	རབ་ཏུ་སེལ་བར་བྱེད་པར་	41
हर्म्य	ཡང་ཐོག་	68

हर्म्या	ཁང་བཟང་	7
हर्म्येषु	ཁང་པ་རྣམས་ན་	34
हलभृत	སྟོབས་བཟང་	61
हस्त	ལག་པ་, ལག་	97,37,74,
हस्तन्यस्त	ལག་པར་བཀོད་ལ་	83
हस्ता	ལག་པ་ཅན་	37
हार	དོ་ཤལ་	93,69
हारियष्यन्	འཁྱེར་ནས་	4
हालाम्	ཆང་	51
हास	རྒོད་པ་, བཞད་ལྡན་	113,56
हि	གང་ཕྱིར་, ནི་, ཉིད་	21,116,84
हित्वा	དོར་ནས་, སྤང་བྱས་ནས་	90,62,51
हिमांशु	ཚེས་གཅིག་ཟླ་བ་	88
हतम्	ཕྲོགས་	32
हत्वा	འཕྲོག་པར་བྱས་ནས་	43
हृदयम्	སྙིང་གི་དགའ་བ་	10
हृदय	ཐུགས་འཛིན་	79
हृदयनिहतः	སྙིང་ལ་སེམས་པའི་	86
हृदया	སྙིང་གི་	101
हेतुः	དོན་དུ་, ཆེད་དུ་	45,27
हेतोः	ཆེད་, ཆེད་དུ་, སྟོབས་ཀྱིས་	80,108,3
हेम	གསེར་	64

तिब्बती-संस्कृत सन्दर्भ सूची

བཀའ་ལུང་	शापस्य	90
བཀའ་ལུང་དག་གིས་	शापेन	1
བཀུར་སྟི་བསྙེན་བཀུར་བྱེད་	अर्हसि	42
བཀོད་	न्यस्त	13,83
བཀོར་པར་གྱུར་	सन्यस्ते	61
བཀོད་པར་གྱུར་ཚེ་	न्यासैः	37
བཀོད་མ་བཟང་པོའི་ཆུ་	वापी	75
བཀྲ་བར་ལྡན་	सचित्राः	66
བཀྲ་བའི་ཕ་ལམ་གཉིས་སྐྱེས་	शिखरिदशना	81
བཀྲ་བའི་རི་མོ་རྣམས་	आलेख्यानाम्	71
རྐང་	पदम्	13
རྐང་བཀོད་	चरणन्यासन्	57
རྐང་བརྒྱད་	शरभा	56
རྐང་དྲུག་	षट्पद	73
རྐང་པ་	पादः, पाद	59,34,37
རྐང་པ་བསྐྱོད་ཚེ་	अतिक्रम्य	59
རྐང་བའི་བདེ་བ་	पदसुख	62
སྐེད་རྒྱན་	काञ्ची	30
སྐེད་རྒྱན་སྐ་རགས་སིལ་སིལ་ཅན་	कांचीगुणयाः	30
སྐད་ཅིག་	क्षण	110,88,28
སྐད་ཅིག་ཀྱང་	कथमपि	92

སྐྱེ་མཆེད་	स्कन्दम्	45
སྐྱེ་བོ་	जन	8
སྐྱེ་བོ་ཀུན་	पुंसां	12
སྐྱེ་བོ་ངན་པ་	कौलीन	114
སྐྱེ་བོ་རྣམས་	परिजन, सताम्, प्राणिनाम्	92,116,102
སྐྱེ་བོའི་	जने	8
སྐྱེངས་ཆེད་	चकित	29
སྐྱེད་བྱེད་བུ་མོ་	जनकतनया	1
སྐྱེད་མོས་ཚལ་	उद्यान	74
སྐྱེད་ཚལ་	उद्यान	7,35
སྐྱེས་	भवम्	47
སྐྱེས་པ་	मध्ये, जानाम्	81,28
སྐྱེས་པའི་	रुह	31
སྐྱོན་བྱུང་	दोषमुत्पाद्य	71
སྐྲ་	केश	105,52
སྐྲག་ཅིང་འཆི་	विक्लवाः	39
སྐྲ་ལྡན་མ་རྣམས་	सीमन्तिनीनाम्	101
སྐྲ་རྣམས་	केशान्	105
སྐྲ་ཡི་ལན་བུ་	अलकम्	89
བསྐ་བའི་རོ་ལྡན་	कषायः	33
བསྐལ་པར་འཇུག་པའི་ཆེ་བའི་ཆུ་འཛིན་	पुष्करावर्तक	6

ཁང་བཟང་ཡངས་པ་	विशालाम्	32
ཁང་བཟང་ལས་	गृहात्	74
ཁམས་	धातु	107
ཁམས་བདེ་མཛོད་	मुञ्चतः	12
ཁེངས་ལྡན་མ་	मानिनी	99
ཁེངས་པར་གྱུར་པའི་	पूर्यमाणाः	58
ཁོ་བོས་	माम	108
ཁྱད་པར་	विशेष, विशेषान्	66,59
ཁྱབ་བདག་	भर्तु	35
ཁྱབ་པ་	स्यूता	75
ཁྱབ་པར་	वितत्य	60
ཁྱབ་པར་བྱེད་	स्फुरित	15
ཁྱིམ་	भवन	34
ཁྱུ་མཆོག་	वृषः, वृष	54,115
ཁྱེད་ནི་	भवतः	29
ཁྱེར་འོངས་	उपनत, प्रहित	101,115
ཁྱོ་ལྡན་	अविधवा	100
ཁྱོ་ཤུག་	द्वन्द	47
ཁྱོ་ཤུག་དག་	मिथुन	19
ཁྱོད་	भवन्तम्, ते, त्वम	9, 31,8
ཁྱོད་ཀྱང་	त्वमपि, त्वापि	18,94
ཁྱོད་ཀྱི་	भवतः	53

མཁའ་ལ་བགྲོད་པ་རྣམས་	गगनगतयो	48
མཁས་དང་མི་མཁས་	प्रकृतिकृपणाः	5
མཁས་པའི་བྱེད་པ་རྣམས་	पटुकरणैः	5
མཁས་ལམ་	पदवीम्	8
འཁོར་གྱི་ཚོགས་ཀྱིས་	गणैः	34
འཁོར་དུ་	गण	57
འཁོར་བ་	उपनतम्	111
འཁོར་ལོ་	आवर्त, चक्र	30,111
མཁྱེན་	विधिना	31
འཁྱམས་ཤིང་བྲལ་བ་	विश्लषित	7
འཁྱུད་པ་	आलिंगय	12
འཁྱུད་པ་རྣམས་ནི་བྱེད་	आलिङ्गितानि	23
འཁྱུད་བྱ་	आश्लेष	3
འཁྱེར་ནས་	हारयिष्यन्	4
འཁྱེར་བར་བྱེད་	नव्यन्ति	63
འཁྱོག་པོའི་	वक्रः	29
འཁྱོག་པོར་འགྲོ་ཞིང་	भङ्गीभक्तया	62
འཁྲི་ཤིང་	श्यामा	105
འཁྲུལ་འཁོར་	यंत्र	63
གཾ་གཱ་	तस्या, गंगा, असौ, यस्या	54,45,53,75
གཾ་གའི་ཆུ་	गङ्गा	65

གེ་སར་	प्रसव, केसर	115,22
གེ་སར་ལྡན་	प्रसवि	64
གེ་སར་གསལ་བར་རྒྱས་	सूचिभिन्न	25
གོས་	वसनम्, वास, पट, वास्	43,70,64
གོས་ལྡན་མ་	दुकूला	65
གཽ་རི་	गौरी	52
གྱུར་པ་ཡིན་	स्यात्	110
གྱུར་ཏོ་	भवेत	109
གྱེན་དུ་འཕར་	उद्वर्तन	42
གྱེན་ཕྱོགས་	उन्मुखीभिः	14
གྲགས་པ་	कीर्तिम्	47
གྲངས་ཀྱི་	गणनया	86
གྲངས་ཀྱང་	विगणय	106
གྲངས་བཞིན་	गणनातत्परां	10
གྲིབ་མ་	छाया, छायया	1,53
གྲིབ་བསིལ་	छाया	28
གྲིབ་བསིལ་བྱ་	छायया	50
གྲིབ་འོད་	छाया	64
གྲུ་ཆར་རྒྱས་བྱ་	आरुह्य	16
གྲུ་ཆར་ཆེན་པོ་	धारा	50
གྲུབ་པ་ཉིད་	सिद्ध	73
གྲུབ་པ་རྣམས་	सिद्धाः	23

དགའ་བས་	चतुरान्, प्रीतिम् प्रीत्या	23,64,34
དགའ་བས་སྤུ་ལོང་རྒྱས་	पुलकितम्	27
དགའ་བས་ཕྲད་འདོད་གྱུར་	उत्कण्ठ	104
དགའ་བྱེད་	रमयन्, प्रिय	113,76
དགའ་མ་	प्रणयिनि, प्रियाया, प्रिय, सहचरी, अङ्गनानाम्, कलत्र	3,7,4. 23, 92,40
དགའ་མ་དེ་ནི་	तस्याः	83
དགའ་མ་རྣམས་	अङ्गनानाम्, स्त्रीणाम्, रतैर्या	29,30,88
དགའ་མ་སྣར་མ་	रेवती	51
དགའ་མ་ལུས་ཕྲ་	तन्वी	81
དགའ་ཞིང་ཆགས་པའི་	प्रीतिस्निग्धैः	16
དགའ་བཞིན་བརྗོད་	व्याजहारः	4
དགའ་བྱེད་བཞིན་	प्रीतः	4
དགུན་སྨད་	शिशिर	82
དགེ་	कुशलम्	102
དགེ་ལྡན་མ་	कल्याणि	111
དགེ་བའི་	कुशलैः	115
དགེ་ཞིང་ཤེས་པར་གྱུར་ཅིག་	भूदेव	117
བགྲང་ཞིང་	विगणय	111
བགྲོད་	व्रज, गाहमानः, प्रोषिताना	62,49,29
བགྲོད་པ་	अवतीर्णाम्	52
བགྲོད་པ་ན་	तीर्णः	20

བགྲོད་པ་རྣམས་ཀྱི་	गतयो	48
བགྲོད་པའི་	गच्छः, प्रयाणः	52, 13
བགྲོད་པར་བྱ་	यायाः, वाहयेत, गच्छेः	35,40,21
བགྲོད་བྱ་	व्रज	28
མགོ་བོ་	मुखानि	50
མགྲིན་	कण्ठः	35
མགྲིན་འཁྱུད་	कण्ठलग्ना	113
མགྲིན་སྔོན་	नीलकण्ठ	78
མགྲིན་བཅུ་	दशमुख	60
མགྲིན་པ་	कण्ठ	3,98
འགའ་ཞིག་	कश्चित, कस्याचित्	1,40
འགའ་ཞིག་དང་ཡང་	कामपि	113
འགའ་ཡང་	क्वचितपि	105
འགའ་ཡིས་	कतिचित्	2
འགེངས་	वासितम्	21
འགོག་	रुणद्धि	10
འགོག་ཅིང་	रुद्ध	96
འགོག་པ་	रुद्ध	89
འགོག་བྱེད་	रुद्ध	39
འགྱུར་	भविता, भवति, भवन्ति, भवति, स्यात्, भू, असि, करोति	57,70,114, 21,3,12,81,39,29,95
འགྱུར་བ་ཉིད་	भवति हि, भवति	92,94

འགྱུར་བ་	भवित्रीम्	61
འགྱུར་ཞེས་	भवतो	116
འགྲམ་པ་	गण्ड	90,28
འགྲམ་པ་དག་ལ་གནས་པ་ལས་	गण्डाभोगात्	90
འགྲམ་པ་དག་ལས་	आगण्ड	89
འགྲམ་པ་ལ་	कपोलाद्	93
འགྲམ་པའི་	वक्त्रः	105
འགྲོ་	गच्छति	111
འགྲོ་སྙམ་ཡོད་ན་	यियासोः	24
འགྲོ་རྣམས་ཀྱིས་	जीवितं धारयेथाः	115
འགྲོ་བ་	प्रस्थानम्	43
འགྲོ་བར་འགྱུར་	गन्तुम्	24
འགྲོ་བས་	चारेण	62
འགྲོ་མི་འགྱུར་	न वयपगत	75
འགྲོ་ཚེ་	गते	61
འགྲོགས་པ་	संगम	53
འགྲོལ་	उच्छ्वसित-शिथिलम्	70
འགྲོལ་བར་བྱ་	उद्वेष्टनीयाम्	90
རྒན་མོ་	वृद्धा	32
རྒལ་	अतीत, वहति	31,65
རྒོད་པ་	हास	113
རྒོད་པ་བཞིན་	विहस्येव	52

རྒྱན་རྣམས་	आभरणम्	94
རྒྱབ་ཏུ་ཕྱུས་ནས་	उद्गृहीत	8
རྒྱབ་ནས་	पश्चात्	38
རྒྱལ་གྱུར་	विजयः	58
རྒྱལ་པོ་མཆོག་	सहचर	102
རྒྱལ་པའི་ཁབ་ཏུ་	राजधानी	26
རྒྱལ་པོའི་ཕོ་བྲང་	सौध	29
རྒྱལ་རིགས་	क्षत्र	50
རྒྱལ་རིགས་མང་པོ་	राजन्यानाम्	50
རྒྱས་	विस्तार, स्फुटित,आधात	19,33,3
རྒྱས་མིན་	न प्रबुद्धा	91
རྒྱུ་བར་བྱེད་	भ्रंश	2
རྒྱུ་བྱེད་	चारिन	65
རྒྱུ་མཚན་	अपेक्षया	17
རྒྱུགས་	प्रवाह	48
རྒྱུད་མངས་	तन्त्री	85
སྒེག་པའི་	ललित	66
སྒོ་	द्वार	59
སྒོ་ཡི་མཐའ་དང་ཉེ་བ་དག་ན་	द्वारोपान्ते	79
སྒོ་ཡི་ནང་དུ་	देहलीम्	86
སྒྲ་	शब्द	104
སྒྲ་སྒྲོགས་མིན་པར་	स्तनितविमुखो	98

ངང་པ་	हंस	59
ངང་པ་རྣམས	हंसा	25
ངང་པའི་རྒྱལ་པོ་རྣམས་	राजहंसाः	11
ངང་པའི་ཚོགས་པ་	हंसा	75
ངང་མོ་	चक्रवाकीम्	82
ངན་པའི་སྐྱེ་བོ་	क्षुद्र	17
ངན་པའི་སྐྱེ་བོའང་	क्षुद्रोऽपि	17
ངལ་བ་	क्लान्त, श्रम	28,54
ངལ་བར་	क्लेशिना	89
ངལ་བའི་	क्लान्त	37
ངལ་ཆེ་	क्लान्त	18
ངལ་གསོ་	विश्राम	27
ངལ་གསོའི་ཆེད་དུ་	विश्रामहेतु	27
ངལ་གསོས་	विश्रान्त	28
ངུ་བར་བྱས་	रुदती	113
ངེས་	नूनम्	89
ངེས་པ་	नूनन्	19
ངེས་པར་	किल, नूनम्, अवश्यम्, ननु, खलु	109,79,48, 83,9,63,58
ངེས་པར་བལྟ་བཞིན་	निर्दिशान्तो	23
ངོ་ཚ་	ह्री	70
ངོ་ཚས	शङ्का	71

རྔ་ཡབ་འཛིན་པས་	चामरैः	37
རྔུབ་	पीयमानः	44
རྔུལ་ཐིགས་	स्वेद	28
སྔར་བསྟན་	पूर्वोद्दिष्टाम्	32
སྔོ་བསངས་	श्यामः	59
སྔོན་	मेचक	61
སྔོན་	पुरा	113
སྔོན་འགྲོ་	आपृच्छ	12
སྔོ་པོ་	नीलम्	43
ཅི་	किं	14,17,13
ཅི་ཞིག་ཡིན་	किमपि	114
ཅི་ཡང་	कथमपि, किमपि	108,3,113
ཅིང་	अपि	89
ཅུང་ཟད་	किंचित्, संधे, कथमचित्, कतिपय, कथम्, मन्द	43,16,60,8 5,25,89,
ཅུང་ཟད་ཅུང་ཟད་	मन्दमन्दा	110
ཅུང་ཟད་གནས་པ་	व्यवसित	116
ཅེའོ་	इति	109
ཅེས་	इति	5
ཅེས་པ་	इति	101
གཅིག་	एक	92,88
གཅིག་ཏུ་	एकम्	48

གཅིག་ཏུ་ཚོགས་པ་དང་ལྡན	ऐकस्थम्	105
གཅིག་ཏུ་སྤུངས་པར་གྱུར་	राशीभूत	60
གཅིག་པུ་	एक	10
གཅིག་པུར་	एकाम्	82
གཅིག་ལ་	एक	77
བཅད་པ་	च्छेद	61
བཅད་བྱས་ནས་	भित्त्वा	109
བཅས་	सह	77
བཅིངས་པ་	अवलेपन, बद्धा, बन्र्ध	14,78,70
བཅིངས་པའི་	बद्धा	90
བཅོམ་	प्रधन	50
ལྕང་ལོ་ཅན་	अलका	7
ལྕང་ལོ་ལྡན་མ་	अलकां	65
ལྕི་བ་ཉིད་	गौरवाय	21
ཆ་གཅིག	कलामात्र	88
ཆགས་པས་	कामात्	70
ཆགས་གཟེར་	सुरत	33
ཆང་	मदिरा, मधु, हालाम्	77,68,51
ཆད་པ་	छिन्न	93
ཆད་པར་གྱུར་	छिन्न	69
ཆར་	वाराधारा, उत्सर्ग, धारा	55,39,106
ཆར་གྱིས་	आसार	17

ཆར་ཐིགས་	वर्षाग्रबिन्दून	37
ཆར་པ་དྲག་ཕབ་	वृष्टिपात	56
ཆར་སྤྲིན་	मेघः, अभ्र	5,65
ཆར་སྤྲིན་དག་གིས་	जीमूतेन	4
ཆར་པ་	वृष्टि	21
ཆུ་	रयं, अम्भः, अपां, वय, सलिल, जल, तोय, तोयम्	21,53,51,1 3,43,65,45
ཆུ་སྐྱར་རྣམས་	वालाकाः	23
ཆུ་སྐྱར་མཛེས་མ་རྣམས་	बलाकाः	9
ཆུ་སྐྱེས་	कुसुम, कमल, पुष्प, लोध्र, कुवलय,अम्भोज	10,34,33,28, 27,67,96
ཆུ་སྐྱེས་འཐོག་མ་	पुष्पलावी	28
ཆུ་སྐྱེས་གདོང་གི་	कमलवदनाम्	41
ཆུ་སྐྱེས་མེ་ཏོག་	नीपं	22
ཆུ་ཀླུང་	नदी	105
ཆུ་ངོགས་	तीर	28
ཆུ་ཆེན་	जलोघ	62
ཆུ་གཏེར་	स्रोत, सलिल	5
ཆུ་སྟོད་ཟླ་བ་	अपाढ़	2
ཆུ་ཐིགས་	जललव, जलकण, सलिलकणिका	72,47, 71
ཆུ་ཐིགས་ཀྱིས་བྲན་	शिप्रा	33
ཆུ་ཐིགས་དག་གིས་	पृषतैः	64
ཆུ་ཐིགས་རྣམས་ཀྱིས་	जलकणैः	28

ཆེ་བའི་ཁ་ཞེང་དང་ལྡན་མཐའ་ན་	तीरोपान्त	26
ཆེ་བའི་ཆུ་	श्रोतसां	13
ཆེ་བའི་ཆུ་འཛིན་	पुष्कर	6
་སྟུག་པོ་	घन	106
ཆེ་བའི་སྡུག་བསྔལ་རྣམས་ཀྱིས་	व्यथाभि	110
ཆེ་བར་འཁྱུད་པའི	गाढोपगूढम्	98
ཆེ་བར་ཕྲད་འདོད་ཉིད་ཀྱིས་	उत्कण्ठितेन	103
ཆེ་ཞིང་མཐོ་	प्रोढ	78
ཆེད་	हेतोः	80
ཆེད་དུ་	हेतु, हेतोः, मोक्षः, अर्थी	27,108,63
ཆེན་པོ་	पृथुम्	48
ཆེན་པོ་རྣམས་	उत्तमानाम्	55
ཆེར་འགྱུར་	उपचित	34
ཆེར་སྒྲོག་	उद्गातु	85
ཆེས་ཆེར་ཁྲོས་པ་	क्रोध	7
ཆེས་འདར་བས་	उत्कम्पात्	69
ཆོམ་རྐུན་དག་གིས་	वैरिणां	103
མཆི་མ་	अश्रु, अस्र, बाष्पः, सलिल	108,103,3
མཆི་མ་རྣམས་	अस्रे, अश्रुभिः	93,88
མཆི་མ་བབས་	रुदित	83
མཆི་མ་མང་པོ་	अस्रैः	107
མཆི་མ་འཛག་པས་	सास्रेण	103

མཆོད་པ་བྱེད་པར་འགྱུར་	मानयिष्यन्	47
མཆོད་པའི་ཆེད་དུ་	अर्घाय	4
མཆོད་པར་འགྱུར་	संपत्स्यन्ते	25
མཆོད་བྱེད་	मानयिष्यन्ति	23
མཆོད་སྦྱིན་	याच्ञा	6
མཆོད་སྦྱིན་བརྒྱ་པ་	मघोनः, आखण्डल	6,15
འཆང་བ་	आलम्बन	4
འཆང་བ་ཅན་	अवलम्बा	72
འཆར་བ་	प्रवेशम्	42
འཆི་མེད་	अमर	19
འཆོང་བར་བྱེད་	लंघयिष्यन्ति	56
ཇི་ལྟར་	को	43
ཇི་ལྟར་ཡིན་	कथम्	106,110
མཇུག་སྒྲོ་	बर्ह	105
མཇུག་སྒྲོ་དོངས་	बर्ह	46
འཇིགས་བཅས་	चकितं	105
འཇིགས་པ་	भयात्	73
འཇིགས་པར་བྱ་	भाययेस्ता	63
འཇིགས་པས་	भयात्	47
འཇིགས་ཤིང་སྐྲག་པ་	चकित	14
འཇུག་པ་	वृत्तिः	94
འཇུག་པ་ཡིན་	विशति	103

འདུག་ཚེ་	पतिताम्	80
རྗེ་བོ་	भर्तुः	84,1
རྗེ་བོ་ཁྲོས་པའི་བཀའ་ལུང་	शाप	112
རྗེ་ཡི་	भर्तुः	100
རྗེས་མཐུན་	अनुकूल	33
རྗེས་འབྲང་	अनुचर	3
རྗེས་ལ་	मौलेः	57
རྗེས་སུ་འགྲོ་	अनुग	49
རྗེས་སུ་འགྲོ་ཚེ་	अनुसरेः	59
རྗེས་སུ་མཐུན་	अनुकूल	9
རྗེས་སུ་བྱེད་པ་	अनुकृति	71
རྗེས་སུ་བརྩེ་བའི་	अनुक्रोश	117
རྗོད་པར་བྱེད་	व्यञ्जयन्ती	31
ལྗང་	हरित	22
ལྗང་སྔོན་	श्याम	25
ལྗོང་	जनपदम्	50
ལྗོན་པ་རྣམས་	द्रुमाणाम्	109
ལྗོན་ཤིང་	तरु	1
བརྗེད་པར་གྱུར་	विस्मृत	96
བརྗོད་པ་	कथितम्, आह, वाचालं, वक्तुं, उक्तम्	113,95,99, 95
བརྗོད་པར་འོས་	आख्येम्	104
ཉ་	शफर, मीन	42,96

ཉ་ཡིས་	मीन	96
ཉན་འདོད་	श्रोष्यति	101
ཉན་པར་མཛོད་	शृणु	13
ཉམས་	व्यस्त, विपदा	106,102
ཉམས་པ་	मथिताम्	82
ཉམས་པར་གྱུར་པ་ཉིད་	न पुष्यति	79
ཉམས་པར་བྱས་གྱུར་	अस्तगमित	1
ཉལ་	सुप्त	40
ཉལ་བར་གྱུར་	शयने, आश्लिष्ट	88,2
ཉལ་བར་གྱུར་ལ་	सुप्ते	92
ཉལ་ས་	शयन	92
ཉི་	तेजः	38
ཉི་མ་	सूर्य	106
ཉི་མ་ནུབ་པར་གྱུར་པས་	सूर्यापाये	79
ཉི་གཞོན་གྱིས་	प्रत्यूषेष	33
ཉིད་	हि, एव	55,54
ཉིད་ཀྱིས་	आत्मनः	102
ཉིན་	दिवस	78
ཉིན་ནས་བརྩམས་ཏེ་	अवधेः	86
ཉིན་པར་	दिवा	92
ཉིན་པར་ཡང་ནི་	अहरपि	110
ཉིན་མོ་	अहनि, अहनीव	87,91

རྙིང་པ་	जीर्ण	31
རྙིངས་གྱུར་	रुजा	28
སྙན་པར་གྱུར་བའི་ཚིག་	विरचितपद	85
སྙན་པར་སྒྲོག་	स्तनित	30
སྙན་པར་སྒྲོག་ཅིང་དགའ་བར་བྱེད་	चाटुकारः	33
སྙན་པའི་	धीर, मधुरम्, स्निग्ध, मन्द्रास्निग्धैः	99,9,66, 100
སྙན་པའི་སྒྲ་	निह्लादः	58
སྙན་པའི་སྒྲ་སྒྲོག་	गर्जित	46
སྙན་པའི་སྒྲ་བསྒྲགས་	स्तनित	23
སྙན་པའི་ཚིག་གིས་སྨྲ་	मधुरवचना	84
སྙན་པའི་ཡིད་འོང་	मधुर	58
སྙམ་པ་	आस्वादयन्ती	86
སྙིང་གི་	हृदया	101
སྙིང་གི་དགའ་བ་	हृदयम्	10
སྙིང་གྲོགས་	सुहृद	101
སྙིང་གྲོགས་དག་	हुहृदाम्	40
སྙིང་རྗེ་	करुणा	94
སྙིང་ལ་སེམས་པའི་	हृदयनिहतः	86
སྙེག་པར་བྱེད་པ་	गच्छन्तीनाम्	39
བསྙེན་ནེ་བྱེད་བཞིན་པས་	श्लाघामान्	18
ཏེང་ཏའི་རོ་	तिक्त	21

གཏམ་	कथा, कथयत	32,13
གཏམ་གྱི་ཆེད་དུ་	कथयितुम्	104
གཏུང་བར་བྱ་	उपभुज्य	13
གཏེར་གྱི་བདག་པོ་	धनपति	7
གཏོང་བར་བྱེད་	च्युत	98
གཏོང་མིན་	न मोक्ष्यन्ति	92
གཏོར་བ་	प्रत्यादेशात्	96
གཏོར་བར་གྱུར་	प्रेरणा	70
གཏོར་མ་	बलि	57,84,36
གཏོར་ལེན་	बलिभुजाम्	25
རྟ་བབས་	तोरण	74
རྟག་འགྲོས་	सततगतिना	71
རྟག་ཏུ་	दशा, शश्वत	111,57
རྟོག་ཅིང་	परिणत	2
ལྟ་བར་བྱེད་	दृष्ट, प्रक्षितानि	38, 42
ལྟ་བུའི་	निभां	80
ལྟ་བུར་དཀར་བའི་	उदग्र	115
ལྟ་བྱེད་	वीक्ष्यमाणः	34
ལྟ་ཆེ་	प्रख्या	92
ལྟར་	अभिन्न	64
ལྟེ་བ་	नाभि	81

ལྟེ་བ་དང་ལྡན་པ་	नाभैः	30
ལྟོ་འཕྱང་	लम्बमानस्य	43
སྟན་མལ་གནས་ན་	शयने	113
སྟན་མེད་ས་ལ་ཉལ་	अवनिशयन्	87
སྟེང་གི་ཁྲུ་ཕུབས་	वलभौ	40
སྟེང་དུ་	उपरि,ऊर्ध्वम्, उपरि	111,60,49
སྟེང་དུ་འགྲོ་བ་རྣམས་	आरोहणषु	62
སྟེང་ནི་	उपरि	96
སྟེང་འོག་མཆུ་	अधरोष्ठम्	83
སྟོང་ན་	रिक्त	21
སྟོན་ཀའི་ཟླ་བ་	शरच्चन्द्रिका	112
སྟོན་པར་བྱེད་པར་འགྱུར་	सूचयिष्यन्ति	22
སྟོབས་ཀྱིས་	हेतोः	3
སྟོབས་ལྡན་	बलि	59
སྟོབས་བཟང་	हलभृत, लाङ्गली	61,51
བརྟན་པ་	धीरता, धैर्यात्,स्थिर	116,42,57
བརྟེན་པར་མིན་པ་	अशरणम्	110
བལྟ་	पीयमान, सिष	16,51
བལྟ་བར་འདོད་	कौतूहालानाम्	49
བལྟ་བར་བྱ་	लक्षयेथा	79
བལྟ་བར་བྱེད་བཞིན་	वीक्षमाणा	23
བལྟ་བྱ་	पश्य, प्रेक्षणीयाम्	87,61,76

ཐོག་མ་	लावी	28
ཐོག་མར་	आधम्	30
ཐོག་སེར་	करका	56
ཐོན་	उत्सर्ग	20
ཐོན་པ་	उद्गार	71
ཐོབ་	लब्ध, निर्वेक्ष्यावः	98,112
ཐོབ་	जाताम्	82
ཐོབ་གྱུར་	लाभात्	104
ཐོབ་འགྱུར་	लब्धा	26
ཐོབ་ནས་	प्राप्य	32,37
ཐོབ་པ་	लब्ध	108
ཐོབ་པ་ཉིད་	लब्ध	6
ཐོབ་པར་	प्राप्तये	57
ཐོབ་པར་འགྱུར་	आपतस्यते, लप्स्यते	15,42
ཐོབ་པར་བྱེད་	प्रापणीया	5
ཐོབ་པས་	लप्स्यसे	36
ཐོབ་བྱ་ཡོད་	प्राप्य	74
ཐོབ་བྱས་ནས་	प्राप्य, श्रुत्वा	54,11
མཐིང་ནག་	श्याम	15
མཐའ་གཅིག་ལྷན་	अत्यन्त	111
མཐའ་གཅིག་པ་	एकान्ततो	111
མཐའ་དག་མིན་	असकल	83

མཐའ་ན་	पर्यङ्क	93
མཐུ་	भाव	48
མཐུ་ལས་	भावात्	48
མཐོ་	तुङ्गम्	66
མཐོ་བའི་	उच्चेः, उच्चैः	65,38
མཐོ་རིས་	स्वर्गिणाम्, स्वर्ग	32,52
མཐོ་རིས་བདག་པོའི་གཞུ་	अमरधनु	74
མཐོང་	दृष्टिपातम्, दृष्टः, दर्शित,पश्यन्	105,113
མཐོང་ན་	आलोके	3
མཐོང་ནས་	दृष्ट्वा	22
མཐོང་བ་	दृष्टे, अवकाशाम्, उन्मुखी	57,89,101
མཐོང་བར་གྱུར་	आलोके, ददर्श, प्रेक्ष्य	84,2,76
མཐོང་བར་གྱུར་པ་ན་	संदर्शनेषु	108
མཐོང་བར་འགྱུར་	प्रेक्षिष्यन्ते	48
མཐོང་བར་བྱས་ནས་	दृष्ट्वा	79
མཐོང་བྱ་མིན་	अदृष्टः	104
མཐོང་བྱས་ནས་	प्राप्य	70
མཐོང་ཚེ་	इष्टे	114
མཐོང་ཚེ་	दृष्टे	40
འཐབ་པའི་	तालैः	78
འཐུང་	आददानः	64
འཐུང་འགྱུར་	पास्यसि	26

འཐུངས་	आदातुं, तासाम्	48,51
འཐུངས་ནས་	आदायम्	21
འཐོན་པར་བྱེད་	निष्पतन्ति	71
འཐོན་པས་	उद्गीर्णैः	34
ད་ལྟ་	अधुना	79
ད་ཤ་ཞེས་བྱའི་གྲོང་ཁྱེར་	दशपुर	49
དག་	शुद्ध	89
དང་པོ་ཉིད་དུ་	आद्येव	81
དང་པོ་ཉིད་ནས་	आद्ये	90
དང་པོར་	प्रथम, पूर्व	22,80,17,
དམ་དུ་	संभ्रम	23
དམ་དུ་འཁྲུད་པ་	निर्दश्यालेष	108
དལ་	परिमित्	82
དལ་གྱིས་འགྲོ་མཁས་	अलसगमना	81
དལ་གྱིས་དལ་གྱིས་འགྲོ་	संसर्पन्त्य	30
དལ་གྱིས་གཤེགས་	व्रज	16
དལ་འགྲོ་	विहरत	62
དལ་བུ་དལ་བུས་	नीचैः, मन्दं मन्दम्	44,9
དལ་བུ་རྣམས་ཀྱིས་	शतकैः	68
དལ་བུས་	लवम्	22
དུ་བ་	धूम	5,71

	शङ्के, जानामि	87,96,6
བདག་ཅག་གཉིས་	नौ, आवाम्	107,112
བདག་ཉིད་	आत्मानम्, आत्मा, कृतात्मा	111,42,45
བདག་དང་	मत्, मया, मयि, मे,	79,88,82
བདག་དང་ཕྲད་པ་	मत्संयोगः	89
བདག་འདྲ་	अहमिव, मत्सादृश्यम्	8,84
བདག་ནི་	मा	106
བདག་ནི་ཤིན་ཏུ་དྲན་པར་འགྱུར་	स्मरामि	76
བདག་པོ་	"पत्नीम्", प्रणयि, कामि,कान्त	10,65,73,
བདག་པོ་མཆོག་	प्रियतम	33,72
བདག་པོ་སོང་བའི་	खण्डितानाम्	41
བདག་པོར་	प्रणयिनी	98
བདག་ལ་	मे, मयि	107,95,98
བདག་སེམས་སོ་	कल्पयामि	116
བདུགས་པའི་དྲི་བཟང་	संस्कार	34
བདུད་ཀྱིས་	आसारेण	18
བདུད་རྩི་	अमृत	91
བདེ་སྐྱེས་	पेयम्	13
བདེ་ལྡན་	सुखिनः	3
བདེ་བ་	सुखम्	111
བདེ་བའི་	सुखा	98
བདེ་བའི་ཆེད་དུ་	सखयितुम्	87

འདུས་དབྱངས་	संगीत	58
འདོད་	काम, इच्छा	64,38
འདོད་འགྱུར་	कांक्षति	77
འདོད་ཅེང་	अभिलाषी	77
འདོད་འཇོ་	सुरभि	47
འདོད་འཇོའི་ངོ་བོ་ཉིད་	कामरूपम्	6
འདོད་འཇོའི་བུ་མོ་	सुरभितनया	47
འདོད་དོན་གཉེར་བར་བྱེད་	प्रार्थना	33
འདོད་ལྡན་	कामी	2
འདོད་ལྡན་མ་	कामिनी	69,65
འདོད་ལྡན་མ་རྣམས་	कामिनीम्	69
འདོད་པ་	इच्छामि, आकांक्षन्ती, कामा	107,80,6
འདོད་པའི་	इच्छा, इष्टान्	88,117
འདོད་པའི་དོན་དུ་	कामार्ता	5
འདོད་པའི་ཡོངས་སྤྱོད་	आत्माभिलाषम्	112
འདོད་པར་གྱུར་པ་རྣམས་	इत्सित	116
འདོད་པས་གཟིར་བ་	उत्सुकानि	100
འདོད་བཞིན་རྒྱུ་བྱེད་	कामचारिन	65
འདོར་བའི་	विहातुम्	43
འདོར་བར་བྱས་པར་གྱུར་	त्याजितो	97
འདྲི་	लिखन्ती, पृच्छति	84,102
འདྲི་ལྡོག་བྱེད་	निहितम्	94

འདྲེན་	नयना	99
འདྲེན་བྱེད་	नेत्र, नयन, नयनम्, प्रेक्षणा	71,24,36
འདྲེན་བྱེད་མཆི་མ་	नयनसलिल	89
རྡོ་	उपल	20
རྡོ་ཡི་ཐེམ་སྐས་	सोपान	52
རྡོ་ཡི་བྲག་ཕུག་རྣམས་ཀྱིས་	शिलावेश्मभिः	27
རྡོ་ཡི་གཙུག་ལག་ཁང་	कन्दर	58
རྡོ་ལ་	दृषदि	57
རྡོ་ལེབ་	शिलम्	54
རྡོ་ལེབ་གཞི་ལ་	शिलायाम्	107
ལྡོག་པ་ན་	सन्निवृत्तम्	91
སྡིག་པ་རྣམས་	पापाः	57
སྡུག་བསྔལ་	आपन्नार्ति, दुःखम्	55, 111
སྡུད་པ་	संक्षिप्येत	110
སྡོང་པོ་	स्तम्भ	97
སྡོང་བུ་	यष्टि	78
བརྡུང་ས་པ་	आहत	68
བརྡོད་ནས་	वक्ष्यति	18
ན་ཆུང་	वधू	16
ན་ཆུང་དག་	युवति	81
ནག་པོ་	कृष्ण	51
ནག་པོ་ཆེན་པོ	महाकाल	36

ནགས་	वन, कानन	38,17,44
ནགས་ཀྱི་	कानन	19
ནགས་ཀྱི་ཁང་པ་	कुञ्ज	20
ནགས་ཀྱི་གླང་པོ་	वनगज	21
ནགས་ནང་ཤིང་སྐམ་	वनोपप्लवम्	17
ནང་	अन्तर	80
ནང་གི་སྙིང་པོ་དང་ལྡན་	अन्तःसार	21
ནང་གི་བདག་ཉིད་	अन्तरात्मा	94
ནང་གི་བསམ་པ་	अन्तः, मन्यभाव, आत्मना	51,95,111
ནང་དུ་	उत्सङ्ग, अन्तर	29,3
ནང་ན་	अन्तः	62
ནང་ནས་རྒོད་པ་དང་བཅས་	सान्तर्हासम्	113
ནམ་	कच्चित	84
ནམ་མཁའ་	आकाश	108
ནམ་མཁའ་དག་ལ་	नभसि	11
ནམ་ཡང་	क्षणमपि	117
ནི་	हि	84
ནི་ཙ	नीचैराख्य	27
ནི་ཙུ་ལ་	निचुल	14
ནུ་	स्तन	19,69
ནུ་རྒྱས་	स्तनपरिचितः	69
ནུབ་ཏུ་	पश्चात्	16

གནས་པར་གྱུར་	संस्थे	3
གནས་པར་བྱ་	प्रस्थ	60
གནས་པར་བྱས་ཚེ་	कृतवसतयो	75
གནས་པར་མཛོད་	स्थातव्यम्, गमय, अन्वास्येनाम्	36,112, 98
གནས་པས་	आसीनानाम्	54
གནས་བྱ་སྟེ་	वक्ष्यति	17
གནས་བྱས་ནས་	स्थित्वा, नीत्वा	20
གནས་མ་ཡིན་	अस्थान	53
གནས་ཚེ་	आरुढे	19
གནས་སུ་	वसतिः, बसतिम्	7,39
གནས་སུ་བསྒྲོད་	आसाद्य	36
གནོད་སྦྱིན་	यक्षः	1
ནོར་སྦྱིན་བདག་པོ་	धनपति	73
གནོད་སྦྱིན་རྣམས་	यक्षाः	68
གནོད་སྦྱིན་བུད་མེད་རྣམས་	यक्षाङ्गनानाम्	70
མནམ་བྱ་	आध्राय	22
རྣ་བ་	श्रोत्र, कर्ण, श्रवण	13,28,104
རྣ་བ་ལ་	कर्णे	104
རྣ་བའི་ཨུཏྤལ་	कर्णोत्पल	28
རྣ་བའི་རྒྱན་	पत्रच्छेद	69
རྣ་བའི་ཡུལ་	श्रवणविषयम्	104
རྣ་བར་	कर्णे	46

པདྨ་ཀྲུས་པ་	कमलमुकुल	75
པདྨ་ཅན་	पद्मिनी	82
པདྨ་དག་	कमलम्	79
པདྨ་རྣམས་	कमलानि	50
པདྨའི་རྩ་བ་	बिस	11
པདྨོའི་ཡུམ་	नलिन्याः	41
པེ་ཚང་	वीणि	47
དཔག་བསམ་ཤིང་	कल्पवृक्ष	64,68
དཔལ་	श्री	96,67
དཔལ་གྱི་མཛེས་པ་	श्रीमुषाम्	49
དཔལ་མགྲིན་	चण्डीश्वर	35
དཔལ་དང་ལྡན་	श्रीः	117
དཔལ་དང་ཕུན་	श्रीविशालाम्	32
དཔུང་པ་	प्रकोष्ठः	2
ལྤགས་	अजिन	38
སྤང་	स्तम्भित	62
སྤང་བྱས་ནས་	हित्वा	51
སྤངས་ནས་	त्यजति	31
སྤངས་པ་	मुक्त	43
སྤངས་པར་གྱུར་	वियुक्त	102
སྤངས་ཤིང་	विप्रयुक्तः	2
སྤུ་	बाल	55

ཕྱི་བྱས་ནས་	सायित्वा	85
ཕྱི་རོལ་	बाह्य	7
ཕྱི་བྱས་ནས་	नीत्वा	2
ཕྱིར་	इति	16
ཕྱིར་ཕྱོགས་	विमुखः	17,51,29
ཕྱིར་ཕྱོགས་མིན་པར་	विमखो मास्म	29
ཕྱིས་ནས་	पश्चात्	46
ཕྱུགས་བདག་	पशुपति, पशुपतेः	38, 58
ཕྱེ་མ་	चूर्ण	70
ཕྱེད་	मध्य	78
ཕྱེད་ལྷན་	अर्धरूढ	22
ཕྱོགས་ཀུན་	दिक्संसक्त	106
ཕྱོགས་ཀུན་ཁྱབ་པར་	छन्नोपान्तः	19
ཕྱོགས་ཀྱི་གླང་པོ་རྣམས་	दिङ्नागानां	14
ཕྱོགས་བཅུ་	प्रतिदिशम्	60
ཕྲ་	क्षामा	81
ཕྲ་གྱུར་	तनुता	103
ཕྲ་བའི་ལུས་	प्रतनुम्	106
ཕྲ་མོ་	तनुम्	48
ཕྲ་མོ་རྣམས་ལ་	प्रतनुषु	105
ཕྲད་འདོད་མཚོག་ཏུ་གྱུར་	अविरतोत्कण्ठम्	103
ཕྲད་པ་	संगमात्	101

བར་དུ་	यावत्	36
བར་དོག་མཚོག་ཏུ་མཛེས་	स्तोकनम्रा	81
བེ་ཏྲའི་མཚོ་	वेत्रवत्याः	26
བི་དི་ཤ་	विदिश	26
བིམྦ་	बिम्ब	81
བུ་	तनय	74,52,101
བུ་ག་	रन्ध्र	44
བུ་མོ་	तनया	47
བུད་མེད་	वनिता, योषिता, स्त्री	34,41,33
བུད་མེད་རྣམས་	स्त्रीणाम्, अङ्गनानाम्	72,86
བུད་མེད་རྣམས་ཀྱིས་	अङ्गनाभिः	14
བྱ་བ་དང་བཅས་	सव्यापाराम्	87
བྱ་བ་བྱས་པ་ཉིད་	कृत्याः	40
བྱ་བ་མ་ཡིན་ཏེ་	मा गमः	111
བྱ་བའི་ཆེད་དུ་	कर्तुम्	107,42
བྱ་བའི་.....ཉིད་	क्रियेव	116
བྱ་བར་	कर्तुम्	80
བྱ་བར་འོས་	अर्हसि	55
བྱ་བར་མཛད་	कुर्वन्	64
བྱ་མེད་	निर्विनोदाम्	87
བྱང་གི་ཕྱོགས་ན་	उत्तरेण	74
བྱང་གི་ཕྱོགས་སུ་བསྒྲོད་	उत्तराशां	29

བྱང་དུ་གདོང་ཕྱོགས་མཛོད་	उदंमुखः	14
བྱང་དུ་	उत्तरेण	16
བྱང་ཕྱོགས་གཞི་ལ་	दिक्षु	26
བྱམས་པར་གྱུར་	सौहार्दाद्	117
བྱས་	कृता, कृतम्	85,110
བྱས་ནས་	आबद्ध, कृत्वा, कृत्य	9,51,117
བྱས་པ་	कृत्त	61
བྱས་པའི་	विगमात्	57
བྱུགས་པས་	मधुनो	96
བྱུང་གྱུར་	दध्यो	3
བྱུང་བ་	प्रभवति	15
བྱུང་བའི་	जन्मा	55
བྱུང་བས་	उपचितैः	107
བྱུང་ཞིང་ལྷུང་བ་	परिणताम्	47
བྱེད་པ་	करण, सुलभ, व्याकुला	57,102,84
བྱེད་པ་བཞིན་	"अकरोत्", कुर्वन्	52,36
བྱེད་པ་ཡོད་	करोति	46
བྱེད་པར་འགྱུར་	स्यात्	41
བྱེད་པོ་ཚངས་པས་	धातुः	81
བྲན་པ་	सजल, सिञ्न्न	64
བྲན་པར་བྱས་	प्रशमित	17
བྲལ་	विरह	88

བྲལ་གྱུར་	विगलित	90
བྲལ་བ་	विरह	8,88
བྲལ་བའི་	वियोग, विरह	110,90
བྲལ་བར་	विरह	31
བྲལ་བར་གྱུར་བས་	वियोगेन	79
བྲལ་བལ་	विरहेः	86
བྲལ་བས་ཧྟུད་པ་	विरहतनु	84
བྲལ་ལ་	विरह	114
བྲལ་ལས་	विप्रयोगः, विप्रयोगे	87,10
བྲིས་	लेखा, लिखित	46,79
བྲོ་གར་	आस्वादः	43
བྷྲྀ་གུའི་བདག་པོ་	भृगुपति	59
བླ་མ་	गुरु	35
བླངས་པ་	उत्खात्	54
བློན་པོ་མཆོག་	प्रतिपुरुषं	6
བློས་	बुद्धया	117
དབང་གྱུར་	अधिकार	1
དབང་པོའི་གཞུ་	इन्द्रचापम्	66
དབུ་བའི་	फेनैः	52
དབུགས་ཀྱི་རླུང་གིས་	निःश्वासेन	89
དབུགས་དྲོན་ཤུགས་རིངས་	उच्छ्वासिना	103
དབུགས་དབྱུང་བྱེད་	आशास्यम्	102

འབྲས་བུ་ངེས་པར་གྲུབ་པ་	अमोघ	73
འབྲས་བུ་འཚང་ཞིང་རོལ་རྩེད་བྱེད་	परिणमयिता	44
འབྲས་བུ་དམ་པ་	फलति	18
འབྲས་བུ་མང་པོ་	फलाः	55
འབྲས་མེད་	निष्फल, विफल, मोघा	56,70,6
འབྲུ་རྣམས་འཕེལ་	कृषिफलम्	16
འབྲུག་སྒྲ་བསྒྲགས་པ་	गर्जित	11
འབྲུག་དབྱངས་	स्तनित	39,99
འབྲུག་དབྱངས་བསྒྲགས་པ་	गर्जितानाम्	36
འབྲོག་དགོན་རྣམས་སུ་	अरण्येषु	22
འབྲོང་གི་དགའ་མ་	चमरी	55
འབྲོས་	त्वरयति	100
སྦོམ་ཞིང་	भारात्	81
སྦྱིན་པར་བྱེད་པ་ཡིན་པ་	दानाद	114
སྦྱིན་པར་མཛོད་	प्रदिशसि	116
སྦྲང་རྩི་བྱེད་	मधुकर	49,37
སྦྲང་རྩིའི་བུ་	शर्ङ्गिगण	48
མ་མཐོང་མ་ཡིན་	पश्यन्तीनाम्	108
མ་ཆོངས་	अलंघयम्	56
མ་བྱེད་	मा स्य	39
མ་ཚང་མེད་པ་	अविकलम्	36
མ་བཟོད་	असहनाः	56

མི་བཟད་	विषमाम्	90
མིག་	लोचने, लोचन दृष्टिः नेत्र, नयन	112,104, 107,80,49
མིག་གི་མཆི་མ་	नयनसलिलम्	41
མིག་གིས་	लोचनैः	29
མིག་ཆུ་	अस्त्रं	41
མིག་ཆུས་	नयनसलिलैः	85
མིག་དག་གིས་	लोचनाभ्याम्	104
མིག་ནི་	चक्षुः	91
མིག་རྣམས་	दृष्टीः	48
མིག་རྣམས་ཀྱིས་	लोचनैः	16
མིག་འབུར་	नेत्र	83
མིག་མཛེས་གཡོ་བ་	प्रेक्षिते	105
མིག་སྨན་	अञ्जन	61,96
མིག་ཟུར་	अपाङ्ग	96,46
མིག་གསུམ་པ་	त्र्यम्बक, त्रिनयन	60,115
མིག་ནས་འབོད་པསམཚན་	गोत्राङ्क	85
མིན་	न	65
མུ་ཏིག་	मुक्ता	108
མུ་ཏིག་དོ་ཤལ་	मुक्तागुणम्	48
མུ་ཏིག་དྲ་བ་	मुक्ताजाल	65,69
མུ་ཏིག་རྣམས་	मुक्ता	97

སྨྱོས་པའི་གདངས་སྙན་	मदकलम्	33
སྨྱོས་པར་བྱེད་	अभिमत	51
དམག་ཚོགས་	चमूनाम्	45
དམན་པ་འཛིན་པ་	दैन्यम्	83
དམན་མིན་	नाधमे	6
དམའ་	निम्न	81
དམར་པོ	रक्तम्, रक्त	38,77
དམར་པོའི་ཆུ་སྐྱེས	जपापुष्प	38
རྨ་བྱའི་སྒྲ་	केका	24
རྨ་བྱའི་སྒྲོ་	बर्हेण	15
རྨི་ལམ་	स्वप्न	108,98
རྨི་ལམ་དུ་	स्वप्ने	113
རྨོངས་པ་	मूढ	70
རྨོངས་པར་འགྱུར	मुग्ध	14
སྨད་ཚོང་མ་	पण्यस्त्री	27
སྨིན་པ་	पक्व, परिणत	81,19
སྨིན་མ་	भ्रू	96,16,49
སྨིན་མ་འཁྱོགས་པོ་	सभ्रूभङ्ग	73
སྨིན་མ་གཡོ་	सभ्रूभंगम्	26
སྨིན་མའི་རོལ་སྟེག་	भ्रूविलासान्	105
སྨོས་ཀྱི་རོལ་	सीरोत्कषण	16
སྨྱུག་སྦོམ་	कीचकाः	58

རྩེ་ལ་	शृंगे	54
རྩེ་ལས་	अग्रात्	15
རྩེ་གསུམ་ཅན་	शूलिन	36
རྩོམ་པ་	आरम्भ, आरम्भम्	38,86
རྩོམ་པའི་	आरम्भैः, आरम्भ	25,56
རྩོམ་པར་བྱེད་པ་	आरम्भः	73
བརྩེ་ལྡན་མ་	दयिता	4
ཚ་བས་གདུངས་པ་	धर्मलब्ध	63
ཚང་	नीड	25
ཚང་ར་	नितम्ब	43
ཚངས་པ་འཇུག་པ་	ब्रह्मावर्त	50
ཚལ་	वण	47
ཚིག་	प्रवृत्तिम्, पद, उदन्तः, वचन	4,85,104
ཚིག་ནི་	वचनम्	4
ཚིམ་བྱེད་	आमोक्ष्यन्ते	37
ཚུལ་གཟུང་	वेश	15
ཚེས་གཅིག་ཟླ་བ་	हिमांशु	88
ཚོགས་	गण, अनुचित	35,117
ཚོགས་ཀྱི་མཛེས་མ་	वेश्याः	37
ཚོགས་རྣམས་	वृन्दानि	100
ཚོགས་པ་	संपर्क, समस्तः	44,58
ཚོགས་འཛིན་	संभृत	117

མཛའ་བོ་	प्रिय, स्नेह	30,114
མཛའ་བོ་རྣམས་ལ་	प्रियेषु	70,30
མཛའ་	उपपद्य	31
མཛད་དུ་གསོལ་	हर	7
མཛེས་	शोभां	54
མཛེས་ལྡན་	कान्तिमत्	32
མཛེས་པ་	अभिख्याम्, अभिरामा, शोभी,कान्तः, चारुणा,	79,53.59,77, 74,83,15
མཛེས་པ་ཅན་	विलसत्, परिचितं	49,49
མཛེས་པ་དམན་པ་ཉིད་	क्षामच्छायम्	79
མཛེས་པའི་	लीलाम्, रचनानि, स्निग्ध, क्रीडा	61,68,75, 80,76
མཛེས་པའི་ཆར་སྤྲིན་	प्रावृषा	117
མཛེས་པའི་རི་བོ་	क्रीडा शैल	76
མཛེས་པར་གྱུར་	प्रेक्षणीय	2
མཛེས་པར་བྱས་	रचित	76
མཛེས་མ་རྣམས་	वनिता	8
མཛེས་མའི་	कान्तया, जायां	74,8
མཛེས་འོད་	छायां	105
མཛོད་	कुर्वीथा	56
འཛག་གྱུར་	द्रवम्	103
འཛག་པ་ཉིད་དུ་འགྱུར་པ་	मोचयिष्यति	94
འཛགས་པའི་	श्रुति	109

ཟུམ་པར་བྱས་ནས་	मीलयित्वा	112
ཟུར་མིག་	नयन, कटाक्ष, अपाङ्ग	73,37,29
གཟི་བརྗིད་	महिमा	1
གཟི་ལྡན་	ज्योतिः, तेज	5,45
གཟུགས་	वपु	79
གཟུགས་བརྙན་	छाया	42
གཟུགས་འཛིན་	मूर्त्या	47
གཟུགས་གཞན་	अन्यरूपान्	82
གཟུང་	धार	63
གཟུང་ནུས་	निहितात्	100
བཟང་པོ་	कुशलिनम्	114
བཟུང་ནས་	ग्रहण, ग्रहणम्	23,52
ཟླ་བ་	मास, मासान्	86,2,112
ཟླ་བ་ཆུ་ཤེལ་	चन्द्रकान्ता	72
ཟླ་བའི་རྐང་པའི་འོད་ཟེར་	पादानिन्दोः	91
ཟླ་བའི་འོད་	इन्दोः, चन्द्रपाद, चन्द्रिका	83,72,7
ཟླ་བའི་འོད་ཀྱི་ཟེར་	शशिरुचा	46
ཟླ་ཕྱེད་	इन्दु, अर्धेन्दु	52,57
ཟླུམ་པོའི་	मण्डलेन	38
འང་	च	14
འམ་	वा	84,117
འོ་མ་	क्षीर	109

འོ་མ་འཛིན་པ་	स्तनभ्याम्	81
འོག་ཏུ་	नीचेः, अधः	111,50
འོག་ཏུ་བལྟ་	आवर्ज्य	48
འོག་ཏུ་འབབ་ལྡན་མ་	निशीर्णा	20
འོག་པག་	नीवी	70
འོག་པགས་དག་ལས་	रशनाः	37
འོངས་	व्रजेयुः, निपतनि	106,84
འོངས་གྱུར་	अत्यति, उपगत	36,53
འོངས་ཐོབ་ལས་	संपर्कात्	27
འོངས་པ་	उपसरण	83
འོངས་པ་རྣམས་སུ་	गच्छल्सु	82
འོངས་པར་གྱུར་	गतानाम्, आगतम्	32,100
འོངས་པར་གྱུར་ཚེ་	प्रत्यासन्ने	4
འོངས་ཚེ་	अवनते आसन्ने	48,25
འོངས་ཚེ་ན་	आयत्तम्, संनद्धे	16,8
འོད་	ज्योतिः	46
འོད་ཀྱིས་	स्निग्धया, रुचिना	39,15
འོད་ཀྱིས་ཁྱབ་	छाया	68
འོད་ལྡན་	सवितुर, छाया	69,25
འོད་འཕྲོ་བ་	वंशप्रकाशैः	78
འོད་ཟེར་	अर्चिः	70
འོད་ཟེར་དང་ལྡན་རྣམས་	प्रमाणाम्	49

ཡུན་རིང་དག་ཏུ་	चिरम्	3
ཡུན་རིང་གནས་པར་འདོད་	प्रत्युद्यातः	24
ཡུན་རིང་བྲལ་བ་ལས་བྱུང་	विरहगुणितम्	112
ཡུན་རིང་མིན་	अचिरात्	95
ཡུན་རིང་འོངས་ལས་	चिरविलसतात्	40
ཡུལ་	समर, देशान्, विषयम्	51,117
ཡུལ་དུ་	विषयम्	36
ཡུལ་ལ་	विषये	81
ཡོངས་ལ་	आसन्ने	96
ཡོངས་སུ་བསྐྱུང་	संपात	80
ཡོངས་སུ་གང་	पूर्णता	21
ཡོངས་སུ་བགྲང་	परिगणनया	23
ཡོངས་སུ་ངལ་ཆེ་	श्रमपरिगतं	17
ཡོངས་སུ་དོར་བར་གྱིས་	परिहरन	14
ཡོངས་སུ་མི་ཤེས་	अपरिगणयन्	5
ཡོངས་སུ་སྨིན་པ་	परिणत	25
ཡོངས་སུ་གསལ་	परिचयात्	9
ཡོད་མ་ཡིན་	न अस्ति	105
ཡོན་ཏན་	गुण	6
ཡོན་ཏན་མཆོག་དབང་	वरमधिगुण	6
ཡོན་ཏན་ལྡན་མ་	गुणवति	109
གཡོ་	तुलयितुम्, अवधू	21,37

རླབས་ཕྲེང་	वीचि, वीचिषु	30,105
རླུང་	वायु	44
རླུང་གིས་	मरुद्भि, वायौ, अनिलेन	35,55,99
བརླ་	उरुः	97
བརླན་	सिक्त	106
བརླན་པ་	आर्द्र	94
བརླན་པ་ཉིད་	अर्द्रः	18
བརླན་པའི་	आर्द्रा	85
ལག་	हस्त	67
ལག་འགྲོ་	भुजग	112
ལག་པ་	कर, हस्त, भुज, स्कन्ध	97,70,97
ལག་པ་ཅན་	हस्ताः	37
ལག་པ་ཆེ་བ་	स्थूलहस्त	14
ལག་པ་དག་གིས་	मूष्टिः	70
ལག་པ་ཕྲ་བར་གྱུར་	रिक्त	2
ལག་པ་ཡིས་	करेण	93
ལག་པའི་འཁྲི་ཤིང་	भुजलता	98
ལག་པར་བཀོད་ལ་	हस्तन्यस्त	83
ལག་པས་	करेण, भुजं	90,108
ལང་ལིང་	स्खलित	30
ལང་ཚོ་མ་	युवति	35
ལང་ཚོ་མ་རྣམས་	यौवनानि	27

སེམས་མེད་	अचेतन	5
སེམས་བཞིན་	चेतसीव	42
སེམས་ལ་	चेतः	3
སེལ་བར་བྱེད་	सारयन्ती, विक्षिपन्ती	93,89
སེལ་ལ་	शान्तिं नेयम्, अपनयन	41,28
སོ་	दशनः	61
སོ་ཀ་	नैदाघम्	18
སོ་ཀ་རྫོགས་པའི་མཐའ་རུ་	घर्मान्ते	106
སོ་གཉིས་	गज	20
སོ་ལྡན་རྣམས་ཀྱིས་	दन्तिभिः	44
སོང་	नीता	88
སོང་སྟེ་	गत्वा	60
སོང་ནས	गत्वा	26
སོང་བས་	गत्वा	113
སོང་ལ་	चक्रे	1
གསང་བ་པ་	गुह्यकः	5
གསང་བའི་བདག་པོ་	यक्षेः	7
གསལ་	वक्तम्	57
གསལ་བར་བྱེད་	सूच्यते, पट	69,33
གསལ་བ་	व्यक्ति	83
གསལ་བྱས་	व्यक्ति	12
གསར་སྐྱེས་	नव	28

སླར་ཡང་	एनं, भूयः, पुनः, पुनरपि	47,16,65
སླར་ཡང་འཕྲིན་རྣམས་	प्रत्यादेशान्न	116
སླར་ལྡོག་བྱ་	निवृत्तः	115
སླེབ་ནས་	वक्ष्यसि	54
བསླུ་བའི་ཚེད་དུ་	नियमन	59
བསླུས་པ་	वंचित	29
བསྲུང་བ་	रक्षा	45
ལྷ་	देवम्, सुर	47,73,63
ལྷ་རྣམས་	देवतानाम्	108
ལྷ་མོ་	अङ्गनानाम्	10
ལྷ་ཡི་གླང་པོ་	सुरगज	53
ལྷག་པར་གདུངས་	आधिक्षामा	88
ལྷག་མ་	शेष, शेषां	19,88
ལྷག་མ་རྣམས་	शेषान्	86
ལྷག་མ་རྣམས་ཀྱིས་	शेषैः	32
ལྷག་མའི་	शेषम्	40
ལྷག་མར་ལུས་པ་ཉིད་	किंचिदूनः	101
ལྷན་ཅིག་འགྲོགས་པ་	संगम	107
ལྷན་ཅིག་དག་ཏུ་	सहस्व	98
ལྷན་ཅིག་གནས་	सार्धम्	88
ལྷན་ཅིག་སྤྱོད་	सहचरे	82
ལྷའི་མཛེས་མ་རྣམས་	सुरयुवतयो	63